Winter Roses

Winter Roses

A Story Of Lost Love And Lost War

A NOVELLA BY JOHN BINGHAM

Copyright 2015 John Bingham
All rights to usage are reserved. No part of this novella may be reproduced in any form, except in brief quotations from articles or reviews, without the author's written permission.
ISBN: 1519113439
ISBN 13: 9781519113436
Library of Congress Control Number: 2015918781
CreateSpace Independent Publishing Platform
North Charleston, South Carolina

"Winter Roses" is dedicated to my loving and patient wife of 53 years, Ann, for her many relevant suggestions to improve the manuscript, and our children, Phil, Greg and Jean, for their continuing encouragement; editors Del and Chuck for their sharp eyes and good counsel; the Ravens, whose daily heroism embodied the American ideal in comrades-in-arms, first in war and then as brothers in peace; Lao pilot Kham P. Manivanh for his help in locating Scar's surviving family; and to the memory of the Hmong Army's late Lt. General Joua Bee Cheng; his wife, Palee, along with Cha and his brothers and sisters; Linda Chang; Major Yee Chang and his son Fu.

Ann and I are honored to play a part in the Hmong and Laotian peoples' assimilation into America by sharing with others the story of their courage and sacrifices in the face of impossible odds, while saving the lives of countless American soldiers.

Our Hmong and Laotian Americans stand tall in the long line of immigrants who have come to America and helped to make it a better place.

The book is historical fiction—historical in that the content covers events told to me by the people who either experienced them or observed them, and fictional because I was often not privy to their dialog, the events' specific locations and settings, actions taken by the participants, and descriptions of the consequences. Therefore, I created both dialog and narrative for the events described herein.

As for sources, I depended upon my memory of stories told to Ann and me by Marie, Frank, their children, Mark and Mike; by the pilots who knew and flew with Frank as Forward Air Controllers (FACs) in the Vietnam War and then by his fellow elite Raven FACs during our covert war in Laos. Wikipedia also played a helpful role, primarily by confirming and clarifying needed supplementary information.

The Ravens will know Frank's true identity and mine because several of them flew with him, and they know his story as well as mine. His children will also recognize themselves in this book. Revealing my identity along with their own as well as Frank's and Marie's would be their decision. In good faith, I chose to use pseudonyms in the hope that they would help protect those who may still suffer from the emotional scarring of long-ago, darker days.

Ann and I reviewed the files of the Traverse City *Record-Eagle,* including Frank and Elizabeth's wedding date, the birthdates of their two children, Frank's service dates in the Korean War and Elizabeth and Frank's obits. We also offer our thanks and appreciation to Michigan State University Archivist Jennie Russell for information on Frank and Elizabeth's years and studies at MSU; Peg Siciliano, archivist, The History Center of Traverse City, to review Frank and Elizabeth's high school yearbooks; Anne Swaney and Jan Geht, Archivists, Northwestern Michigan College, for information on whether Mai Tran, Vietnamese spy for the U.S. and Frank's mistress, ever made it to the United States; Toni M., Grand Traverse Bay, for her assistance and shared memory of Frank and Elizabeth; the Mason County Clerk's office in Ludington, MI, for confirmation of the Delaney family's move back to Traverse City; Hmong-Americans Cha and Palee Cheng for their late father and husband's story, Lt. General Joua Bee; Linda Cheng for her mother's story; Hmong-Americans Fu Chang and his father, Yee Chang, for their stories; Wa Ger's son, Cher, for his detailed account of Frank's death in the skies above Laos as told to him by his father; Laotian-American Kham P. Manivanh, for sharing his story of war, capture and escape, and for helping me find Wa Ger's surviving relatives; and attorney-at-law Howard Hertz, principal, HertzSchramPC, for his expert counsel and sharp eye.

Table of Contents

	Prologue: A Wolf Lake Encounter	1
	Foreword	5
Chapter 1	Requiem I	7
Chapter 2	Escape From Brutality	25
Chapter 3	Marie Meets Frank	42
Chapter 4	Run-up to marriage	54
Chapter 5	Benning's School For Boys	74
Chapter 6	Another AFB, Another Wedding	84
Chapter 7	With Tigers And A Battleship	111
Chapter 8	Save A Fighter Pilot's Ass	123
Chapter 9	Back to Battle, Back to Home	147
Chapter 10	Save A Mistress Or A Marriage	162
Chapter 11	Barflies	172
Chapter 12	The Fog Lifts	217
Chapter 13	Detox And Sobriety	232
Chapter 14	Ravens At War	238
Chapter 15	Requiem Revisited	247
Chapter 16	Post Mortem	256
Chapter 17	Death In The Sky	264
Chapter 18	Aftermath	270
Chapter 19	Comrades-In-Arms	276
	The Children's War	276
	Requiem III	278
	Yee Chang, S-2	287

The Girl of The Nine Glowing Embers	298
Master of the White Mountains	329
And One For Marie	334
About the author	337
Glossary	339

Special thanks to special Raven friends: Mike, who helped me understand the Ravens' war in Laos, along with his good guitar, fine writing, and mastery of both glass art and contemporary sculpture; Growth and Chad for reaching out to me at a moment when I needed it most; Craig for his help in walking me through his steps in publishing his fine memoir; Ed for his encouragement; and Jim and Larry, the first responders in my search for information about the Ravens' covert war in Laos and Frank's role in it. I am also grateful to Vietnam War FACs David and Jonathan for inviting me to join them on a Memorial Day at the Mall to pay tribute to our fallen warriors through USAF period songs with guitar accompaniment.

Cover design by David Jankowski

Prologue: A Wolf Lake Encounter

Ann and I had spent a week in August of 1971, vacationing at the family cottage. It overlooked Wolf Lake, a small, crystalline gem spring-fed by the frigid Lake Superior watershed in the eastern part of Michigan's Upper Peninsula. On the last night of our vacation, we had a picnic on the beach complete with a big bonfire to warm the children after they'd splashed and shivered in the Superior-cold water. They'd dive off the springboard at the end of the dock and come up shrieking from the cold, then swim back to shore where we'd wrap them in huge bath towels. After a few dives they were more than ready for their dinner of hot dogs on a stick, roasted over the fire and served with a side of potato chips.

While the children were eating, a loon that had been fishing at the north end of the lake began its takeoff --not an easy task for a bird with a full load of fish in its belly for its young nesting on one of the nearby smaller ponds. The children cheered as the bird wing-slapped its way across the water, finally lifting off to begin circling around the lake's natural bowl. If it had tried a straight-line takeoff and flight over the old-growth white pines that towered above the lake, it would have smacked headlong into them.

John Bingham

Faster and faster it flew, gaining altitude with every lap until it had enough momentum to slingshot over the trees. As it crossed over them, it called to its mate with a clear, wild gabble of success; the loon family would not go hungry that night.

After the children finished, Ann made s'mores for them while I waded out with my fly rod and caught and cleaned four nice, pan-sized rainbow trout for dinner. We fried them in butter in a cast-iron skillet nested in a bed of coals: kings and queens would envy that meal. We even had s'mores for our dessert, which the children appreciated because they knew we'd make s'more for them.

By then dusk had arrived and the evening's feature entertainment would soon begin. I spread a tarp, inflated two oversized air mattresses and zipped together our XXL double sleeping bags. Ann went up to the cottage with the children so they could brush their teeth, change into their pajamas and bring down five pillows. Ann had also changed into her PJs, so I went up and put on mine. We crawled into the bags to watch the Perseids meteor showers streak across the Milky Way, and tried to identify the major constellations.

Framed by the forest and with no ambient light sources, the stars looked as if they were huge, glowing balls of phosphor imprinted on the inky blackness of the heavens.

The storm of shooting stars was soon eclipsed by a front-row view of the northern lights: sheets of green, yellow and white fire rippling from horizon to horizon, exchanging colors every few seconds. The children had never before seen a light show as spectacular as this and watched with eyes and mouths open wide. It was an evening they would never forget.

One by one, the kids dozed off while Ann and I watched the show until we also fell asleep, snuggling together for warmth as the fire died and the night grew colder.

Everyone slept well until our youngest, Jean, needed to make a potty trip. I took the flashlight so we wouldn't trip over a root or stump on our way up the

Winter Roses

hill. She ran to the cabin and hopped on the potty just in time. I waited outside to enjoy a few fast puffs on a cigarette. She came out and caught me at it, and again pleaded with me to quit. Her argument was powerful and to the point; she didn't want cigarettes to kill me. I knew that I had to quit; just the thought of leaving her and the rest of our beautiful family behind too soon and forever made me shudder. Besides, I was growing sick of sneaking smokes whenever and wherever I thought I could, like a teenager at an open window puffing and coughing, and frantically trying to fan away the smoke to avoid getting caught.

After she told me that I smelled awful, like cigarette smoke, I told her a quick story about a make-believe comical lumberjack named Pierre who had trouble finding a date for the Lumberjack Ball and wound up with a black bear for his partner. For the bear's dress, Pierre draped her with a bright-red curtain from the cottage. The couple danced so well and made so many friends that they won the title of King and Queen of the Ball even though the bear's breath was far worse than Pierre's, who also smoked cigarettes.

Jean giggled and told me that the bear's breath must have been really bad to be worse than Pierre's cigarette breath.

We found our sleeping-bag nest and settled in after waking everyone else by climbing back into the crowded-but-cozy double bags. Older son Phil did not appreciate her sandy foot on his face and he told her to watch where she was stepping. Sweet little Jean gave him a big hug and he couldn't help but laugh. Greg the Grouch groaned and told them to pipe down so he could get some sleep.

I woke up early the next morning and discovered that a cold mist had settled over the lake, blanketing it so thickly that I couldn't even see beyond 30 feet or so. Suddenly, I heard the damnedest noise—very loud and strung-out grating, hoarse cackles that one could easily imagine came from a dinosaur in rut. It was close by and seemed to be coming from the lake. By this time, Ann was also awake and whispered, "What on earth is making that noise?" I whispered back that I didn't know, but it was something I'd never heard before.

John Bingham

The mist lifted a little and we discovered the mysterious creature that had made such an infernal noise. It was a huge raven, standing on the edge of the dock not 20 feet away and glaring at us with baleful, black eyes. After a series of calls that sounded something like "grrrrick, grrrrraaaack, grrrruuuuck, " it lifted its wings and flapped off into the mist.

It was the largest raven by far of any I'd ever seen. At the time, I wondered if it might be a premonition of some bad event to come but quickly dismissed the thought. I didn't believe in premonitions. Maybe in my youth I'd simply absorbed too much of Edgar Allen Poe's "The Raven."

Two months later my best buddy was shot down and killed, and I thought then that the raven had spoken. The memory of that creature haunts me to this day.

In Harmony Church, Georgia, the field office and HQ for Ft. Benning's Ranger cadre, an ageless poem hung on the wall as a required read for prospective Rangers and other Army trainees who sought and qualified for specialized Ranger skills:

> *"At the end of the fight is a tombstone white*
> *with the name of the late deceased--*
> *and the epitaph drear: a fool lies here*
> *who tried to hustle the East."*
> -RUDYARD KIPLING

Foreword

*M*y wife Ann's sister, Marie, loves Frank and he loves her. They marry and strive to meld their two families into one. Their honeymoon promises happiness, but their few short years together become an emotional roller coaster run off-track by war, infidelity, violent death, trauma, and alcoholism. His first combat tour as a FAC (Forward Air Controller) in Vietnam begins to unravel the family's tenuous bonds, already frayed by his first wife's horrific suicide and Marie's divorce from a brutal wife-beater. His affair with a young Vietnamese woman-- who served as his squadron's interpreter and sometime spy--pours gasoline on Marie's smoldering alcoholic fires. Her "social drinking" turns into raging alcoholism complete with blackouts, lost weekends, and endless family squabbles.

Frank escapes the domestic madness by volunteering for a very different madness-- a second combat tour, this time to fly and fight as an elite Raven FAC in the green hell of the covert war in Laos.

Marie continues to self-medicate with alcohol but vows to quit drinking before Frank returns home. The children assume her responsibilities as best they can while trying to keep up with their schoolwork and maintain their own high school relationships—all the while coping with their teenagers' imbalanced hormones.

For this family's wounds, there is little time for closure; war waits for no one. But there is always hope, even for a future built upon a too-short past that was at best rocky and at

John Bingham

worst disastrous. While compartmentalizing can buy time for the inevitable reckoning of anger, anxiety, panic, and a deep, abiding fear that follows in the footsteps of stark, bad memories, happiness can still be the absence of pain and sorrow.

One

Requiem I

In the fall of 1949, Frank enlisted in the Air Force after he graduated from high school, leaving behind his sweetheart Elizabeth, who had enrolled at Michigan State University. A measure of his love for her can be found in their high school yearbook; her nickname was "Lizzy" and under Frank's photo there's a sentence that reads, "Izzy ever without Lizzy?"

After completing his basic training at Lackland AFB in Texas, he moved on to advanced training in small-unit supply and logistics. He studied hard, learned fast and made corporal three days before he was sent to Korea.

Only their parents knew they were engaged and would likely be married when he returned. It would not be a big wedding, which neither Elizabeth nor Frank wanted.

While his job did not have the glamour, excitement and danger of the pilots who flew fighters, fighter-bombers and reconnaissance aircraft, he took it seriously because he knew that no mission could be completed without his skill and resourcefulness in obtaining the materials, parts, support equipment, and ordnance that kept the base's aircraft operational and mission-ready.

John Bingham

A fast promotion to sergeant was his reward and he decided when he got his stripes that he would make the Air Force his career, but not as a ground-pounder. He would become a pilot and used what free time he had to plan his strategy to become one. He also vowed that if he was fortunate enough and smart enough to become a pilot and later, one with command responsibilities, he would never forget the importance of good supply to a unit's morale and performance where it counted—in delivering the right goods to keep the pilots, crews and their planes combat-ready at all times.

If doing his job right meant taking on officers who were ripping off the Air Force and selling taxpayer goods on the black market-- or those who couldn't bring themselves to acknowledge any deficiency in their faked, chrome-plated effectiveness reports—so be it. He knew he had the persistence and savvy to get what he needed and he wasn't afraid to take on anyone who stood in his way. And his superiors knew it, because he was honest in all of his dealings with them.

He in turn learned to be doubly careful when dealing with them. He spent a lot of time on the rifle and pistol range and wanted everyone to know that he'd earned his expert marksman qualification. *Maybe I'm being paranoid, he thought. But some of these bastards would kill to protect their "business interests" and I'll be ready if one of them thinks I'm a threat and comes after me.*

A skill he quickly learned was the art of scrounging. While some of his peers might have considered scrounging as stealing, the fact was that shipments were often screwed up—some items missing, some stolen by the omnipresent REMFs (Rear Echelon Mother Fuckers), deliveries made to the wrong units, partial deliveries with incorrect or substituted back-ordered goods that were useless, even jeeps, trucks, weapons of all sorts and mismatched ammunition.

Recognizing that going strictly by the book was an impossible task, Frank decided it was time to get smart about his supply management.

Winter Roses

I'm going to start the biggest "Swap Club" in the whole damned Air Force and I'll even cook the books if necessary to make sure that anything that shows up on base or disappears from base will be strictly a matter of official record. To the Inspector General, we'll be clean and proper, a role model for others. I'll focus my skills on building relationships with my supply peers from other units—including the Army ground-pounders if necessary-- who have to be experiencing similar problems and are also bartering to get what they need. To get started, all I need to sweeten my deals is plenty of cartons of cigarettes and a few cases of good Scotch along with blended whiskies.

Frank implemented his plan immediately with the tacit approval of his base's CO, who had arranged a back-door connection for the cigarettes and whiskey to get started.

He commandeered a Jeep and driver, and together they began a tour of troops and officers to share his plan to get what they needed to stay well and fight the damned war. They heartily agreed, but drew the line at "midnight requisitions," i.e., the armed services' favorite euphemism for outright theft. Leaving behind a carton of the smokes and a fifth of good whiskey was successful as his good-faith way of sealing the deal with his new partners.

The tactic paid off immediately when an Army supply sergeant reached him on the field telephone and told him he'd just received a mess of insulated mechanics' coveralls that he didn't need and wondered if Frank could use them. Frank replied that he certainly could, because the mechanics had been freezing their asses off while they serviced the aircraft in the unheated Quonset-style hangers.

He had nothing to trade in kind at the moment but promised his new buddy that he'd be the first to learn of anything that arrived unordered. His word—along with the cigarettes and liquor--was good enough, and the sergeant was kind enough to loan him a small utility trailer to haul the coveralls back to base.

Other swap-out deals he made during the remainder of his tour involved a wide range of assorted useful and useless goods, some actually intended for his base's use and some misdirected to Christ-only-knew-where. He said later that you couldn't imagine the things that passed in and out of his hands. Here were just a few examples:

- Uncountable condoms, also good for rainproofing matches and keeping rain out of rifle barrels
- Lingerie
- Dr. Grabow briar pipes with filters but no tobacco
- Men's satin pajamas with matching robes
- Women's satin pajamas with matching robes
- Cigars by the thousands, ranging from White Owls to good Cuban leaf
- Saki, assorted Korean beers, Soju liquor, Cheongju rice wine and even bootleg white lightning, the latter usually arriving in five-gallon jerry cans
- Captured Chinese- and Russian-made infantry weapons, which were souvenirs worth a lot of money to the REMF crowd; that, or the REMFs just stole them if they were tagged for shipment home
- Pigs, chickens, goats, ducks, and geese from appreciative ROK natives who received help from the camp medics and often, spare warm GI-issue clothing. He quickly passed along the livestock to the camp cooks for much-needed variety from C and D rations
- Earthen pots of kimchee for the few Americans who enjoyed eating fire
- Four cartons of boxer shorts with red hearts and a ruler imprinted on the fly
- Amateur magician kits
- Boxes of 8 x 10 glossy pin-up photos (Betty Grable and Rita Hayworth were still the favorites among the WWII vets who were called up for Korean duty)
- Uncountable decks of playing cards
- Exquisite, hand-carved ivory miniatures of Buddha, much in demand by pilots as good-luck talismen
- Medical supplies and equipment of all kinds, which he quickly forwarded to the base's M.A.S.H. unit

into flight school in San Antonio. Elizabeth went back to her family home near Traverse City.

She joined him at San Antonio's Randolph AFB, where she pinned on his wings and gave him a big hug and a kiss, drawing whistles and cheers from his fellow flight students.

His first assignment was at Offutt AFB in Nebraska, where he would serve as co-pilot on the country's first strategic nuclear bomber, the B-47. Offutt was headquarters for the Strategic Air Command (SAC). While he longed to become a fighter pilot, he rationalized his new position as "better to be flying something than nothing." He was also pleased to learn that the B-47 was a hot aircraft with plenty of speed and good maneuverability for the aircraft's size.

A drawback was rotating three-month TDY assignments at the huge NATO AFB in Zaragoza, Spain. The B-47 did not have transoceanic range, so the airplanes were disassembled stateside and sent over in cargo ships. Later, when SAC was able to bring more pilots and navigators into the B-47 fold, the three-month stays were cut to three weeks—much to the happiness of the pilots, their wives and their families.

The Delaney family grew quickly; Frank, Jr., was born in 1953 and Jennifer followed in 1954. Frank was fortunate to be home with Elizabeth for the children's births.

The children were bright, personable and active, and got along well with their peers. They were also curious and mischievous at times; Elizabeth thought perhaps too much so while Frank believed the mischief was normal for healthy children. Their playmates often came to visit, play games and stay for dinner; as they grew older, sleepovers became a major source of entertainment. When

John Bingham

Jennifer's' friends were there, Frank, Jr., took this as his opportunity to torment them with non-stop teasing, including chasing them with garter snakes he'd caught in his mother's vegetable garden. The boyish prank crossed the line for Elizabeth, especially after he'd slipped the critter into Jennifer's bed when she had overnight company.

Their screams reverberated throughout the house and Frank, Jr. drew a week's grounding for that trick. Still, he thought it was well worth the punishment. Soon after, Jennifer retaliated with the help of her friends. They chased him down the street late one afternoon after school and caught him, then tied him to a telephone pole by tying an old piece of rope around his midsection. The girls knew their wraps wouldn't hold for long so they tickled him for only a few moments and then ran away as fast as they could. He shouted for help, loud enough for his mother to hear him a half a block away when she was pinning clothes on the clothesline.

She came running to the front of the house, frantic with fear that he'd been playing and was seriously hurt. She looked down the block and spotted him leaning against the pole and still yelling for help. She ran to him, immediately discovered the source of his anguish and quickly unraveled his bonds while he swore vengeance.

Elizabeth reminded him of that horrible snake that he'd sneaked into his sister's bed and that, as far as she was concerned, justice had been served and if he knew what was good for him, he'd better forget any notion of getting even.

Chastened, Frank, Jr. meekly agreed and was glad to forget it, anyway. The strength of those girls holding him while they tied him to the pole had surprised him and it made a lasting impression.

He and Jennifer declared a lasting peace and played together often with each other and their mutual friends. This gave Jennifer access to Frank, Jr.'s friends while several of her friends appealed to him.

Winter Roses

They grew together, went to school together and played together. Sometimes they worried about their dad. They knew he was a pilot who flew a big airplane, but he never told them where he was going, why and what he did there.

One day when Frank was on a mission, they learned about a plane that crashed near the base and burned. Everyone inside was killed, and they thought that the same thing might happen to him. Elizabeth tried to reassure them that this would not happen because their daddy was a very safe pilot who always inspected his plane carefully before every flight and that he had a very good ground crew that made sure that his plane was always in good condition and safe to fly. When Frank returned, he read the crash's investigation report and learned that the cause of the crash was pilot error. Armed with that information, he was able to tell them that the pilot was young and inexperienced, and that he had much more experience along with a very good crew who helped him make sure that no mistakes would be made.

Frank, Jr. asked him about the possibility of war with the Russians and Frank couldn't dance around the question. He told the children that the reason why he and thousands of other men and women were in the Air Force was to help prevent a war with Russia or any other country that wanted to go to war with America. "It's working," he said. "Sometimes they make threats about going to war with us, but they know how powerful our armed forces are and I believe that they wouldn't dare attack us because they know we would destroy them."

Jennifer said how scared she was when a siren started and she had to crawl under her desk and put her arms over her head and neck.

Frank, Jr. said that this frightened him, too. Frank replied that it was just practice to make sure they're ready in case we are attacked, and that it would help keep them safe. "But," he added, "We most likely would know in advance that the enemy is planning to attack, and you and your mother would be taken to a safe place, one the enemy would not attack."

They accepted their parents' reassurances and went on with their lives. Like millions of other American children—and their parents—they carried with them the nagging fear of nuclear war.

It was always there and was fed by the knowledge that their chances of survival in all-out nuclear war would be nonexistent.

It wasn't until American and Russian nuclear-weapon stockpiles--along with the capability to deliver the weapons via ICBMs, nuclear-powered submarines, bombers, fighter-bombers, even Army artillery and heavy-mortar shells--reached such levels of overkill that MAD (Mutually Assured Destruction) became macabre reassurance that nuclear war was an impossibility for all but madmen.

Change came quickly for the family. Frank came home one evening after he'd been gone for over three weeks on an extended mission. Elizabeth hated these long missions because she never knew when he would have to leave, where he was going, what he did there, and how long he'd have to stay there.

He announced that he would be leaving a week later for Homestead AFB in Dade County, Florida, near Miami. He told them that the weather was warm all year-round there and that they'd be able to enjoy outdoor activities of all sorts. He had been promoted to first lieutenant and would move up from his B-47's co-pilot/navigator's position to pilot and aircraft commander.

He would catch a military aircraft flight to Homestead. With the help of a base sergeant who coordinated personnel moves, Elizabeth could take more time to arrange the logistics of the move. She would then drive the family's Chevrolet station wagon to Homestead.

Winter Roses

The rainy season arrived early that year in southern Florida, and Frank, Jr., thought that "icky-sticky" was a good description of the near-daily rainfalls followed by the re-emergence of a smoldering, subtropical sun.

For an active eight-year-old from a northern climate, the heat and humidity were especially uncomfortable and this afternoon was no exception. Going to Jimmy's house after school for ice cream would be a treat and the thought of real air conditioning waiting in their homes made the bicycle dash to Jimmy's and back again almost bearable.

He jumped off the school bus before it had come to a complete stop, which guaranteed a growl from the driver and a warning to stop that or he'd tell the principal who'd tell his parents and he'd be grounded again.

"Aw jeez, Mr. Infante," he said. "I'm sorry. I got excited because it's Friday and besides, the door opened while the bus was still moving a little bit, and I thought that meant I could jump out. I knew I wouldn't get hurt. Jeez, I jump off fences and the neighbor's garage roof without getting hurt. Can I please have another chance? I promise I'll never do it again. I really do promise not to and you'll see that I really mean it this time."

"OK, I'll let it go this time, and I promise that I won't tell anyone that you jump off fences and garages if you don't tell anyone that my bus door opens before the bus stops. It's broken and I'll have it fixed on Monday. Do we have a deal?"

"Thanks, Mr. Infante. You bet we have a deal."

Mr. Infante couldn't help but nod his head in agreement and hide a smile. He liked the boy because he reminded him of his own youth…carefree, enthusiastic, likable and with just a tad of insolence, a kid who tested you every chance he got and you'd both be smarter for it.

The kid's brass made Mr. Infante laugh as he ground the bus into first gear and drove off, shaking his head and thinking that the kid was going to go far with his gift for quick-on-your-feet bullshit.

Frank, Jr. put his lunchbox on the kitchen counter and called out, "I'm home, Mom!"

Strange, no answer. Maybe she's upstairs in the bathroom or bedroom. "I'm getting my bike and going over to Jimmy's house!" *Still no answer.* He went to the garage to retrieve his bike. *Jimmy and I will be back in a few minutes anyway for cookies.*

When he reached the far corner of the garage, he heard a deep sigh. He turned to see his mother standing with her back towards him. He saw that she was holding his dad's service revolver in her hand. As she raised the gun to her temple with one swift, fluid motion, he stared open-mouthed, not wanting to believe what he was seeing but knowing it was for real. Just as she pulled the trigger, he shouted, "No, mom!" but then he realized it was too late, his words had been drowned in a sharp blast that rang in his ears.

A now-blurred vision had seared its way forever into his psyche, one of blood, bone splinters and brain tissue splattering the wall as she sagged to her knees and then fell over sideways.

He heard the front door slam. Seven-year-old Jennifer was home from school and he shouted to her to come into the garage. She found him crying as he knelt over their mother and dropped down beside him to see the beautiful, blonde hair that she loved to brush now matted with blood. She cried out, "Mommy, what's wrong?" There was no answer, so she bent down, shook her mother's arm and screamed, "Please please please, mommy, wake up!"

Winter Roses

Frank, Jr. thought that his sister shouldn't see any more of this and dragged her outside while she tugged against him, arguing that she wanted to stay with her mommy. He looked across the street and saw Jimmy and his mother standing on their porch steps. "Mom's hurt bad," he shouted. "Can you help us?"

Jimmy's mother had heard the gun's report, wondered what it was and came out on the porch to see if someone had lit a firecracker—a big firecracker. When she saw the children burst out of the garage's side door crying out that their mother was hurt, she grabbed Jimmy by the arm and dashed across the street. Seeing the fear frozen in their eyes, she knelt and gathered them into her arms. "Was that a firecracker or a gunshot I heard? Were you playing with your daddy's gun?" They were too shocked to answer and Jennifer buried her face in her dress to hide from her terror and reject the horrible thing she'd seen. Frank, Jr. stammered that something was wrong with their mother and asked if she could help her. She tried to comfort them with assurances that everything would be all right and daddy would be coming soon to make things better.

Holding hands, they walked to the garage's open side door.

She told the children to stay outside while she went in to see what might be wrong. She took a long look at Elizabeth lying on the floor. "Elizabeth," she said, "Are you sick or hurt? Can I help you?" No answer.

She stepped forward, leaned over for a closer look and saw the blood-soaked hair surrounding a swollen, misshapen face that was no longer recognizable, and threw up.

Trying hard to calm her shakiness, she came back out and told them their mom needed to go to the hospital. They walked back across the street and went inside her house. She tried to give them cookies and milk to help quiet their fears, but Frank, Jr. and Jennifer refused. Their stomachs were still churning from the terrible sight of their mother lying face down on the garage floor and not moving. When she called the ambulance service, she asked the driver not to frighten the children any further by blaring the siren and flashing emergency lights as he drove up to the house

---

Frank was on alert when the base commander came in, took him aside and said that Elizabeth had been in an accident and couldn't be seen until the hospital called to tell them they were ready for visitors. "Ready for 'visitors,' sir?" he asked. "Do you mean that I can't see my own wife when she needs me?" Now he was shouting. "What the hell is going on? Sir, I've got to see her and the children, and now!"

He bolted for the door and almost made it when his CO tackled him and tried to pin him down while shouting to his pilots and navigators—who were standing back and watching the fiasco unfold--to get off their asses and help him. His bellow jolted them to their senses and they rushed over to pull the struggling pair apart before either or both got hurt. The CO calmed Frank down by reminding him that the hospital doctors were well trained and qualified to handle emergencies. After escorting him to his chair, his navigator stayed by his side in case he made another run at the door.

The phone rang and the CO quickly answered. "OK. We'll be there in a few minutes. Are the children in the visitors lounge? Is a base or hospital escort there to reassure them? Good. Good. We'll meet you there. Thanks, doctor."

The CO drove with the navigator in the front seat. Frank tried to get straight answers to his questions, but his CO dodged them with feigned ignorance and assurances that the doctor would be able to answer them. Knowing his boss was blowing smoke to buy time, Frank realized that something terrible indeed had happened to Elizabeth and that he'd better be ready to face the worst possible news.

Winter Roses

They walked into the hospital and the CO asked the lady at the front desk to advise the doctor that he was with Lieutenant Delaney in the lobby.

Frank went into Elizabeth's room while his base commander and navigator stayed behind with the children. When he saw her gray, grotesquely swollen face with a thick bandage wrapped around her head, he knew immediately she was gone. The doctor told him that she had died from a gunshot wound and the bullet had caused massive brain trauma, too much for the hospital staff to save her. He added that she died instantly and without suffering.

Anticipating Frank's next question, he continued. "It looks like the wound was self-inflicted. When the medical examiner rules tomorrow on the cause, we'll know for sure. We'll keep her here tonight, so you can stay with her as long as you'd like. I'm very sorry for you and your family.

Frank thanked him and said that he had more questions. The doctor replied that he'd try his best to answer them. He subconsciously covered her head with the bed sheet.

"Could it have been an accidental shooting? Maybe the children were playing with my service revolver and Elizabeth got shot by mistake?"

"That's possible, but again, the medical examiner will tell us that tomorrow."

"Where did it happen?"

"Your neighbor across the street said she thought it was in your garage."

"Are the children OK?"

"Physically, they're fine. Emotionally, they're a wreck. They need you."

"I'll spend a few minutes alone with Elizabeth. Could you go out to the waiting room and tell them that I'll be there shortly?"

When the doctor left, Frank turned to Elizabeth's bedside, pulled back the sheet, took a deep breath and leaned over and kissed her. He carefully wiped his tears away from her face with his polka-dotted silk flight scarf that she'd given him when he won his wings. At first he thought it was ridiculous but he'd worn it anyway, ignoring the good-natured kidding from his crew. It became his talisman when he was on alert and in the air.

"Sweet Jesus," he whispered to himself. "The memories are starting already."

He kissed her now-cold lips once more, told her he loved her and always would. He lowered his head and his shoulders shook in quiet sobs as the thought of life without her stabbed him in the heart and in his gut.

"Dear God, Liz, why? I loved you and our children loved you. Was your life as a pilot's wife too much to bear? Were you too lonely when I was gone? I know I was often on training missions all over the world and I couldn't tell you where I was and when I would be home. Was that the problem? Jesus Christ, what does anything matter now? You're gone and that's it.

"I'll raise the children, starting right now. They're waiting for me and I'll pass along your love for them. No one will ever replace you in their lives or mine. But we'll make it through this and we'll try to make you proud of us. God, we'll miss you. We can't tell you how much we'll miss you. But we can tell you that you'll be in our hearts every moment of every waking day; for me, Jennifer and Frank, Jr. there'll only be one Elizabeth, always. We love you and we hope and pray that you've found peace in your escape from whatever was torturing you."

Taking a deep breath, he said the first of his goodbyes and walked out to the waiting room.

Winter Roses

He hugged the children before telling them that their mother had died and that they wouldn't see her anymore. He realized that they had no real-world concept of death or infinity, but told them regardless that their mother was now in heaven and that she loved them very, very much. They cried harder than he could imagine any child could cry and he fought hard to hold back his own tears. He had to be stronger for them now than he'd ever been.

No one knew the reason why Elizabeth had ended her young life. There was no note of farewell and all she left behind were questions that could not be answered. She was buried in her family's plot, in a small cemetery in the northwest corner of Lower Michigan's peninsula.

Stately pines stand over the graves like sentinels and when their branches moan and sigh in concert with the never-ending Lake Michigan winds, a visitor can easily imagine that they are grieving, too.

Frank was ordered to take a 30-day furlough after unsuccessfully arguing that two weeks would have been enough to recover from the shock and make arrangements for the children's care while he was on duty. He used the time to request and receive a transfer to Kincheloe AFB base in Michigan's eastern Upper Peninsula, about a hour-and-a-half's drive from his in-laws' farm. The transfer allowed him to fulfill his service obligations while the children's grandparents cared for them during weekdays and Frank's alert weekends.

He visited them every chance he could and often took them on trips to the Upper Peninsula's scenic forests, rivers and lakes, and told them Longfellow's tales of the land of Hiawatha, Lake Superior (Gitche Gumee to Longfellow and Gitche Gamee to the Ojibway Indians) and Gitche Manitou, the great spirit and creator of all things to the Ojibway.

The children especially loved picnicking and swimming in Gitche Gumee. Frank told them tales from the epic poem, which both thrilled and frightened them. When they learned that angry Nahma, the giant sturgeon that lived in Lake Superior, had swallowed Hiawatha and his canoe as punishment for trying to catch him, they were afraid to swim without their dad close beside them. For Frank, this was a form of torture: even in the hottest of summer months the frigid Lake Superior waterline on his body felt like a hot wire wrapped around him. Below that everything went numb in minutes. The children laughed when their dad would yell, "I'm freezing!" This was their signal to start a good water fight and at least the exertion helped to warm him.

Another special trip was taking the ferry to Mackinac Island. The island was big medicine in helping to ease their sorrow. Frank would hire a horse-drawn carriage to take them around the island and then buy them lunch—which also meant a dessert of Mackinac fudge that was so sweet it made him gag. No matter, the children loved the stuff. After that came a tour of the restored Fort Mackinac complete with soldiers in period uniform staging demonstrations of their close-order drill, firing their rifles and a brass cannon with a roar that made them jump no matter how tightly they blocked their ears.

The children became more attached than ever to their dad, who tried his hardest to be the best father he possibly could be considering the demands of piloting a strategic bomber during the Cold War. With every visit and outing, he recognized more clearly that they needed a mother—and that he needed a wife.

Two

Escape From Brutality

Walt had almost dozed off in his recliner when he got the call, but he answered it anyway since he thought it might be a customer who needed help. He was always there for them and they knew it; his attention to their concerns and his patience were a legend in little Sault Ste. Marie. They were also a big reason why the Montgomery Ward store he managed was now consistently profitable. Equally important, they set a good example for his employees to do the same, and many of them bought into it because they knew they'd be rewarded not only with raises but with plenty of sincere compliments and thanks for their outstanding customer service.

"Hello, Mr. Golling?"

"Yes," Walt replied. "How can I help you?"

"Mr. Golling, my name is Jim Lawrence and I live here in Nehigh, Nebraska. You don't know me but I know your daughter, Marie. She lives just down the street and shops for her groceries at my store.

John Bingham

"Lately, I've been worried about her because she's been coming into the store with bruises on her face. When I ask her what happened, there's always some made-up reason like slamming into an open pantry door without looking where she's going, or tripping and falling over one of the kid's toys—even falling off a skittish horse. Now I'm not stupid. Someone who barely has enough money to buy a box of cereal, a pound of bologna, some hot dogs and a couple of loaves of bread doesn't have enough money to go horseback riding, let alone pay a babysitter while she rides. You should also know that she lives just down the block from me and I hardly ever see her out with the boys anymore.

"Now she's not only coming in beaten up, but she's skinny as a rail and looks like one of those Nazi death camp survivors. The boys are also thin and pale and frankly, Mr. Golling, I think they're all malnourished.

"I extend her credit so she can buy more nutritious food, but I don't make much money and I can't keep it up without getting paid because it shorts my family.

"So I thought I'd call you and let you know of her situation. Frankly, I think her husband is running around and drinking his paychecks while he's off base. I've known that kid since he was a boy. He was a spoiled brat then and he's a spoiled brat now. He was a hellrake and a bully in high school, but the girls fell for him because he was big and strong for his age and played football. Now he's in the Air Force and is making what he thinks is enough money to play around and support a family, which he doesn't seem to be doing. In fact, I think the situation is a lot worse than that. From the looks of her face, I think that he's beating her up every time he comes home. I hate to tell you all of this, but I had to call you and let you know what I believe is going on before it's too late."

Walt thanked Jim and told him he'd be there in two days to get Marie and the boys and bring them back to the family's home in the Sault. He asked him to tell Marie that he was coming to get them and to arrange their pick-up in his store to minimize the chance of a confrontation with her husband should he show up. He also asked Jim to tally how much Marie owed so he could pay him back.

Marie would hide the clothes they needed for the trip in the carriage she kept in the downstairs entryway. When Walt explained to his wife, Louise, what was happening and told her that he'd be leaving in the morning to get them, she immediately said that she'd go with him. But he discouraged that, telling her that there might be a problem if her husband showed up and tried to stop Marie from leaving.

That very night, Marie's husband came home and beat her. Sticking to his MO, he first raped her. Next came the face-slapping that got progressively harder, ending with a punch, all the while raving in a loud, hoarse voice that she was no goddamned good in bed and no goddamned good anywhere else and that he was sorry he'd ever married a slut like her. Their two boys in the next room heard all of this, but stayed quiet with their arms around each other, shaking in fear. The first time they had cried out in terror, he rushed into their room and spanked them so hard with his belt that he raised bloody welts all over their buttocks.

Marie had never wanted to tell her parents about the big mistake she'd made by marrying this monster, but was now relieved that Jim had told her father about his cruelty to her and their little boys. She was especially relieved when Jim told her that her dad was already on the way to bring her, Mark and Mike to the Sault. He would arrive the next morning, which was Sunday. With luck, her husband would come home drunk and pass out, too drunk to even think about sexual abuse. Finally, she and the boys would be able to begin a new life far, far away.

The escape went flawlessly. Just as she thought, he had closed the bar. This time, he'd caught a ride home with a woman who appeared to be as drunk as he was. She watched from her bedroom window while he undressed the woman as she giggled and protested. Then she couldn't stand to watch any more. She went to bed and pretended to be asleep when he staggered in and passed out on the couch. He was snoring early the next morning as she crept out of the bedroom with the boys.

Seeing the slob lying there with his zipper down and beer belly bulging out from under a stained Air Force sweatshirt made her stomach churn and she fought hard to keep from throwing up by realizing it could wake him.

Let a sleeping dog lie, she thought. *If I had a hatchet right now I'd split your skull to your spine, you rotten son of a bitch. Rather than risk losing the children and going to prison, I'll forgo that satisfaction and hope that you'll be caught someday, prosecuted and sent to jail for a long, long time.*

On the way home, she stared at the endless Nebraska and Kansas cornfields racing by the window and reflected on the wild side of her teenage years. *Perhaps this stemmed from the family's bouncing around the Midwest, never able to establish lasting roots and friendships during her dad's early years as a Montgomery Ward store manager. He was a specialist in turning around struggling stores in such small towns as Waterloo and Sheldon, Iowa; Deadwood, South Dakota; and Alliance and North Platte, Nebraska.*

In North Platte, he and the family had finally felt they'd be there long enough to build a new home, which Marie especially liked. After dark and when everyone had gone to bed, she'd shinny down a tree to join her waiting friends below for a party.

They'd often drive to Kansas where they bought their beer from storeowners who didn't regularly check buyers' IDs. If they did, Marie and her friends had fake IDs. The storeowners also knew that selling to Nebraskan underage drinkers wasn't as risky as selling to their hometown teenagers. In minutes, they'd be back over the border and Nebraska's problem, not theirs.

Winter Roses

The favorite party place was a remote levy on the North Platte River. A driftwood campfire took the chill out of the night air. Drinking the beer led to chug-a-lug contests, singing, telling jokes, bad-mouthing teachers, and necking. Sneaking away for more amorous adventures usually ended before anything got started in a blizzard of hoots from their classmates.

Not all of the beer and liquor they bought was for their own consumption. There was always a teenagers' market for alcoholic beverages, and entrepreneurial Marie and her pals capitalized on it. On their forays to Kansas, they made sure they returned with a full trunk and a good selection to sell to their peers for twice what they paid for it. This profitable enterprise always ensured enough money for future parties.

Jesus, I was wild. But I was lucky, too. I can't believe I'd ride in the rumble seat of that bastard's hot rod while he played "chicken" with other classmates. I can't believe the children and I survived his constant beatings and bullying. I can hardly believe that we escaped without injury, maybe even death if he knew we were leaving him. God only knows what he's capable of. Thank God we'll never know!

During the trip to her new home, Marie felt as if she was even breathing better without the constant fear of her husband's sadistic ravages. Now she couldn't wait to begin planning her divorce. She appreciated her dad's restraint in not getting on her with "I told you so." He knew very well that she needed time to heal, and an argument over what she should or shouldn't have done would just add to her hurt.

When Walt pulled into the driveway, her mother, kid sister Ann, younger brother Ron, Wolfie the dog and Ichabod the duck were waiting for them. Her mother cried when she saw Marie's swollen and bruised face and Marie sobbed for joy that she was back in her family's care and home. She vowed that she'd never again be blinded by the likes of her husband. Her memories of fatuous cheering while he ran for touchdowns had vanished with every passing mile on her trip to her new home and she reveled in her newly discovered recognition of her family's importance in her life. *What I ever saw in that pervert is beyond me. But he's gone from my life for good and he'll never again hurt me or my children. He can practice his bullying and sadism on someone else.*

Her mother took care of Mark and Mike while Marie began her job search and grew her list of contacts in little Sault Ste. Marie. She was bright, personable and attractive, and was soon able to parley those attributes into a job as a media sales representative for a Canadian TV station just across the St. Mary's River in Sault Ste. Marie, Ontario.

Besides selling airtime to Michigan businesses that wanted to attract Canadian customers, she wrote commercials for them even though she'd never had any training in the art. She also wrote press releases without any formal journalism training, along with local-interest news stories destined for viewers on both sides of the border, which made her even more valuable to the station.

She won a nice promotion when her station manager made her the sports editor. Her primary responsibility was covering the Sault (pronounced "Soo") Greyhounds hockey team, which competed in the Northern Ontario Hockey Senior-A league. She traveled on the bus with the team, and took a lot of good-natured razzing from the players: first, because she was a woman and second, because she didn't know anything about the game. Several players helped her learn the game's basics en route to the out-of-town games, and her good looks helped make sure that she got plenty of attention.

The team's best player—a muscular six-footer by the name of Gino Marchietti--asked her out and she agreed. He was older than most of the players, just as she was. She didn't know much about him, other than that he was a Sault Ste. Marie, Ontario, all-around sports superstar. Not only did he excel in hockey, he was the best softball pitcher and hitter in Ontario. He was even the curling champion of the town's recreational league. She often saw him in the

Winter Roses

Sault Ste. Marie, Michigan, nightclubs with other women and thought that she would be careful not to faun over him as they did.

They decided to go to a movie on the Michigan side, get a couple of drinks and call it a night. He'd leave in time to catch the last ferry home. This was her first date since her dad had rescued her and she was on guard for anything that might happen.

He scored points with her dad, who loved to go to the Greyhounds-Indians (the Sault, Michigan team) games because they were great league rivals and the games were always exciting.

Gino scored more points by promising him two free tickets right behind the Greyhounds' bench. They'd play the Indians the next day on the American side of the river. He said that he'd leave the tickets at the window for them and that he'd be happy to give Marie an interview right after the game to cover his star performance. Marie and her dad laughed, but Gino said, "I'm serious!" He then laughed and said, "I'm kidding, of course."

Her dad laughed with him. "Of course," he added. "Who else is as confident as the great Marchietti?" "That'sa right, Walt. Who else? Wanna know who else? Nobody else, that'sa who". He pretended to hit her dad on the chin with his fist and added, "That's what I'm gonna do to any Indian who comes near me tomorrow, you wait and see!"

Marie couldn't believe her date's braggadocio. She knew he was full of himself, but she rationalized it by thinking that all good athletes must have swollen heads. *It was certainly true of my wife-beating ex-husband, who was the football, basketball and baseball star that all the girls chased. Unlucky me, I won.*

"I hate to break up a good conversation, but we'd better get going before we miss the movie."

Gino agreed and he put on his coat. Before they reached the door, he stopped and thanked her dad for his hospitality.

"I enjoyed talking with you and thanks again for the beer. After the game tomorrow and Marie's interview, let's go over to Herb's Black Cat and I'll buy you a beer.

"And don't hesitate to root for the Indians tomorrow even though we'll beat them. I don't want you to be disappointed, so I'm telling you that now so you can be ready."

"Hell, Gino, I won't be disappointed. It's only a game, right?"

He caught Gino by surprise with that one.

Gino frowned for a second and replied, "Yeah, sure, Walt. Maybe it's only a game, but I make a good living by playing hockey. It's a great way to earn a living."

Marie held her breath, waiting for her dad's reply.
"No offense intended. It's only a game, but it's also a game I love to watch and now Marie is making part of her living as the Greyhounds' sports reporter. I'll look forward to seeing you play tomorrow and taking you up on that beer. Enjoy the movie, you two!"

Marie breathed again and smiled when Gino reached over to shake Walt's hand. "Buonacotte, amico! See you tomorrow!"

"Si, amico. Buonacotte!"

In the car, Gino told Marie how much he liked her dad.

"He's a straight shooter, like me, eh? I like a man who tells you what he believes even though you might disagree with him. Like I said, hockey may be a game, but it's my living and that's something that deserves respect. Do you think that your dad respects me and my hockey?"

"He sure does,' responded Marie. "He only wishes that you played for the Indians instead of the Greyhounds."

He laughed and said, "Your dad's a smart man, sweetie."

"Sweetie? What makes you think I'm a 'sweetie?' "

"I've been around, you know. I can tell a sweetie when I see one."

Marie laughed. "OK. Just don't call me 'sweetie pie.' "

During the film, Gino's hand reached over and held her hand. They held hands until the film was almost over, when his hand drifted down to her leg. She pulled her leg away abruptly and whispered loudly, "Don't try that again, buster. If you do, I'll break your fingers and you won't be playing hockey tomorrow."

"Hey, girl, ease up, eh? Most girls like that."

"I'm not a girl and I don't like it. I know jiu-jitsu and I'm not kidding about breaking your fingers. You'll know in a hurry how far you can go with me, so I'm warning you now to go easy."

"OK, OK, I'll behave...sweetie."

"OK, OK, you'd better behave...sweetie." She took his hand in hers this time, and firmly placed it on the armrest. He got the message quickly and resisted the temptation to go any further, at least until later.

After the film was over, he suggested that they walk around the corner to a small bar that had a great jazz jukebox. It wasn't crowded; the cold night had obviously kept many of the patrons at home. They both ordered Old Fashioneds. He went to the jukebox and then remembered that American jukeboxes don't accept Canadian coins. The bartender wouldn't take them because of the unfavorable exchange rate, so Mary gave him two American quarters with a request for the Freshmen, Brubeck and anything by Coltrane.

They spent the time talking about jazz greats and enjoying a second Old Fashioned. Gino got frisky again and tried to play footsie under the table but she withdrew her foot the second his shoeless foot touched hers. *He must still think that I'm as easy as his other American and Canadian bimbos, but he's badly mistaken. If he keeps trying, he'll regret it. I'll make sure he never forgets me, for all the wrong reasons.*

Two drinks were enough, and Gino suggested that they leave and go for a ride. He said there was a nearby hill that gave a great view of the two cities at night, and that they should drive up there to see it. She agreed, saying that she was still new to Sault Ste. Marie on either side of the river and would like to see both cities all lit up.

Gino drove up a winding road to the hilltop, stopped, and shut off the engine and headlamps. Marie asked if he knew the name of the hill and he replied that they were parked atop a huge gravel pit.

"Just look over the mounds of gravel and earth to see the cities. You can see the fire and sparks fly in the Algoma steel works to the left, and there's the city park over to the right. We should go for a walk there one of these nights, eh?"

He pointed out the scenic spots of the two cities and told her to look at the lights reflecting on the river. She saw blues, reds, pinks, and whites dancing and changing colors like a gigantic kaleidoscope, moving in every direction across waters chopped up by the ferry and the huge lake freighters, and thought that they were indeed beautiful. He put his arm around her and pulled her close to him. "It isn't too bad being Gino's sweetie, isn't it?" he asked.

"Not too bad at all, providing Gino minds his manners and keeps his right hand exactly where it is right now."

He pulled her a little closer and she planted her hand firmly on his lower chest to act as a brake in case of any further advances. He must have thought that she wanted to feel his well-muscled torso and took her advance as a signal for his own. In one fast move, he had her right breast cupped in his right hand and his left hand on her knee, creeping slowly up her skirt.

"That's enough, Gino. Stop it and don't touch me any more. We're calling it a night." She tried to pull his hands off and found that she didn't have the strength. She couldn't budge them.

"Aw, c'mon, sweetie," he said. "I know you're a lonesome woman who hasn't had a man in a long time and you won't find a better man than Gino. Trust me and try me, you'll love it and want more, eh? And Gino can give you more—more than anyone else in the two cities." As he talked, his hand traveled faster up her skirt. "Feel me," he said. "I'll undo my belt buckle and unzip my pants. Then you can find out just how big and hard a real man can get, eh?"

With his canned, let's-have-sex spiel over, she reached over and clamped her hands on his breast hand, pried up his first two fingers and bent them back with all her strength. He howled in pain and tried to pull away. She yanked his fingers back even harder and he yelped again, this time begging her to stop.

"Promise you'll keep your dirty hands off me?"

"I promise."

"You'd better." She let go and he massaged the blood back into his fingers.

"Nobody ever treated Gino like that before."

"Well, Gino never met me before. Are you cooled off now?"

"Not really. Some women like a good fight before sex and I think you're one of them, eh?" He moved quickly across the seat and reached for her again.

"That's it, buster. We're done for the night, but not before I leave you with a souvenir for your efforts." She raised her right hand, clenched it into a tight fist and punched him as hard as she could right on his nose. She heard the cartilage crackle and watched as the blood streamed from his flared nostrils, mixing with involuntary tears that blurred his vision. Her fist was cocked and ready for a second blow, but the first was quite enough.

"Jesus Christ, woman, are you crazy? Nobody punches Gino! You bitch, I'll get even with you and you can count on that, eh?" He fumbled for his handkerchief, tore it apart, stuffed the pieces into his nose and leaned back on the seat to try and stop the bleeding.

He looked over and saw the passenger-side door wide open. Marie was nowhere in sight.

"Goddammit, where the fuck did she go?" He reached over and slammed the door shut, then slid back to start the engine, reaching for the car keys while still trying to stop the bleeding. They weren't there.

He rolled down his window, leaned out and shouted as loud as he could. "You stole my keys, you bitch! Get them back to me and I promise I won't touch you. I gotta catch the last ferry and you steal my keys. Gimme my keys and I'll bring you home, eh? We'll forget all of this and pretend nothing happened, OK?"

Winter Roses

"Not OK! I don't have your keys! They're closer to you than you think! And I'll freeze in hell before I'll get in a car with you again!"

He looked and felt all over the car seat for the keys, then slid his free hand between the cushions to see if they had fallen into the cracks. *They aren't there.* He then got out of the car and tried to find the keys on the floor or under the seats with only the dim overhead dome light to help spot them. *Still no luck.*

Getting frantic because he had less than a half hour to catch the last ferry home, he raked his fingers over the mats and tore a fingernail on his right hand-- which was his best shooting hand even though he was ambidextrous.

Trying under the rear floor mats paid off. There they were, tucked under the right rear mat. He jumped into the front seat, started the car and floored it, spinning around and throwing gouts of gravel behind him. He wondered why there was a cold draft coming through the car as he started up the gravel-and-dirt road to the asphalt roadway that would take him back to town. "Aw, shit!" he exclaimed. "The right rear door's still open!"

He stopped, jumped out, ran around the car to shut the door and came face-to-face with a smiling Michigan State trooper.

"Hello, Gino. I've been waiting for you. The nice young lady sitting in my car told me you weren't nice to her.

"Hell, no, officer, she hasn't been nice to me. Look at my nose, eh? She broke it with a sucker punch."

"What did you do to deserve that, Gino?"

"Nothing that any single man my age wouldn't do. Look, officer, I have to make the last ferry back to Canada in a few minutes. Can we speed this up?"

"Is that true?"

"Relax, Gino, there's no hurry. Did you know that you were trespassing on private property?"

"No way. I've been coming up here for the past three years."

"No doubt. But there was a bad accident two weeks ago. A drunk driver ran off the edge of the pit, rolled over and over and was killed when he fell out and hit a rock. We posted the sign to stay off the property right after that and you must have missed it. We've been keeping an eye on it ever since and I'm glad we were. Otherwise, I wouldn't have been here to find Marie walking back to the road. It's not nice to let a lady walk such a long way home by herself at night."

"Yeah, but she's no lady, eh? The little bitch damned near snapped off my fingers besides breaking my nose."

"Well, she told me her side of the story. You sure didn't treat her like a lady. All she did was defend herself. What do you think would happen if she decided to press charges against you for attempted rape?"

"Haw. That's a laugh. I'd tell the jury and the judge that she beat the living shit out of me and that I never touched her."

"Never?"

"OK, OK. I touched her first."

"You mean you grabbed her and groped her first, right?"

"OK. I got carried away. I thought I treated her better than that. If it makes her feel any better, I'll apologize to her. But she damned well better apologize to me, eh."

Winter Roses

The trooper said that his proposal seemed fair to him. The two of them walked to the trooper's car. Gino peered in and asked her to roll down the window, which she did after the trooper nodded his head in approval.

"Marie Sweetie Pie, I'm sorry for what I did and I hope you accept my apology. I'll never do that again."

"You bet you won't. From now on, our relationship is strictly all business. I'll interview you and that's it. Do you understand?"

"Yeah, I understand." He turned to the trooper and said, "I only have 10 minutes to make the last ferry. Would you call your HQ and get someone over to the dock to hold the ferry for a few minutes until I get there? They know who I am."

The trooper smiled and said, "I'll bet they do. You can leave now. But don't get stopped for speeding. I won't issue a ticket for trespassing this time, but make sure you don't ever come back up here. Have I made myself clear and do you agree to that?"

"I sure do, officer. Thanks."

Before he left, he turned around, made sure the trooper wasn't looking and gave Marie the finger. She just sat there and shook her head in disgust.

He made his ferry with moments to spare.

She and her dad went to the game and she went up to the news box instead of sitting with him behind the players' bench. He offered her seat to a little boy who was with his parents a few rows up and they approved. The boy was so happy to be so close to the action that he wanted to get even closer. He stood up on his seat with his face and hands pressed to the Plexiglas. The Greyhounds coach gave him a puck, a well-used stick and an autographed jersey, and the boy was beside himself with delight.

The jersey just cleared the floor, and Walt told him to stand up on the bench and wave to the players who were still skating their warm-ups.

Gino saw Walt and the boy, skated over and told Walt to lift him to the top of the Plexiglas screen so he could take him on a spin around the rink. He sat the boy atop his shoulder and the crowd cheered as the pair skated around the rink with the boy smiling and waving. Even Marie cheered and waved, and gave the two of them her sweetest smile.

Walt wondered why Gino had two black eyes and a bandage strip across his nose. *They certainly weren't there last night. Did he try any funny business with Marie? I'll go up during the first intermission and ask her if she had anything to do with it.*

Gino brought the boy back and hoisted him up so Walt could pull him over the plexi and set him down on his seat. He stayed standing and waved to the players and the crowd once more. The crowd responded with the loudest cheering yet and the Greyhounds skated by him with their sticks lifted in salute. They then disappeared down the gangway for the coaches' last instructions to the players before game time.

The boy's parents took advantage of the break and came down to admire the jersey, puck and stick. They thanked Walt again and he told them that he was glad for the good company, and happy for the boy.

Marie told her dad at intermission that she sure did have something to do with Gino's new shiners, and that she'd tell him all about it on the way back home from the game. During the second period intermission, Marie came down to tell her dad that they wouldn't be going to Herb's after all for a beer. Apparently, Gino wasn't feeling well. She smiled wickedly, shrugged her shoulders and walked back up to the news box.

Winter Roses

They never made up, but every time she interviewed him, she tried to at least be cordial. At first, all she could get out of him were grunts, yes's and no's. But he loosened up, and when he learned she was engaged, he actually congratulated her.

At the time, I had a position as an office clerk in the Metropolitan Life office for eastern Upper Michigan. Marie, being new in town, caught my eye and she told me later that I'd also caught hers. She thought I was the most conceited man on either side of the border and I thought that she was a complete snob.

Then I met Ann at a friend's party. We started dating, and I soon learned that Marie was a bright, warm and caring woman. She told me that she was happy to find out that I wasn't a stuck-up asshole after all. I returned the compliment and told her that I didn't feel sorry for Gino. His womanizing was legendary on both sides of the river and I was happy that he'd finally more than met his match. I asked her what he said to his friends when they asked how he broke his nose. She said one of his teammates asked him and he just growled, "You should have seen the other guy."

All of his teammates noticed a sudden cooling between him and Marie, and put one and one together. But none dared say anything to him about that.

Three

Marie Meets Frank

In the spring of 1962, I took a break from my studies at Michigan State University to get myself in shape for Infantry Officer Candidate School at Ft. Benning, Georgia. My training cycle would begin in January of the following year. I was a sergeant in the Sault Ste. Marie National Guard's combat engineering (float bridge) company, and I wanted to get my commission.

I had joined the Guard In 1960 after washing out of a Regular Army three-year enlistment because of a bad shoulder. There, I could at least do something for my country. Surgery in 1961 and a comprehensive rehab program corrected the problem—at least temporarily. My surgeon said it should get me through the considerable physical demands of the Infantry OCS program.

Ann was back at Michigan State during this time, completing her junior year and targeting June 1963 for her graduation and a degree in Psychology. We were engaged in 1962 and scheduled our wedding date for August of 1963.

Marie and I still kept in touch while Ann was away, and one night she called to let me know that the local Chamber of Commerce had chosen her to script and stage a spring fashion show as a means to spark additional traffic and business

Winter Roses

for the retailers. Without knowing much about the task, at least I knew that it was a big undertaking and told her so. I suggested that she had every right to refuse the assignment. But she correctly pointed out that the merchants in town would not be happy with her, which would make her job of selling them air time on the Canadian TV station just that much harder. Maybe even impossible for the few who could and would hold a grudge.

After grousing about the lack of volunteer help from local retailers —some of whom were the Chamber members who'd commandeered her services—she said that she was also having trouble lining up male models.

When I suggested that the men I knew were not likely to put on clothes that they'd rarely wear, let alone stumble around a stage in them and turn red with embarrassment from their buddies' hooting, she countered that my "Macho friends weren't likely to be in the audience at an event that will draw mostly women. But enough debate," she continued. "Let's get to the real reason why I called. I want you to be one of my models, and so does Jerry Nelson."

"Marie, I'd rather not. Jerry's a good friend of mine and this is taking unfair advantage of both of us."

"Well, he's a good friend of mine, too, and of course I'm taking advantage of you, silly. Do you think I'd just ask you without making sure that first I had some leverage?

"Hey, you wear clothes from his store every day. Why not model one of his new suits, complete with new shirt, necktie and shoes? He told me that you can keep the clothing and shoes as your modeling fee."

Jerry smiled when I walked into his store the next day for a fitting. The opportunity for a free new suit, shirt with necktie and shoes was a powerful incentive for a young man who was taking home $70 a week in those days, and he knew it.

Marie had told him I'd surrendered and they both had a good laugh over my feeble arguments. He knew I was uncomfortable, however, and told me that Ray ("Rocky) McFarland—a very tough young man in town who constantly picked fights for no good reason and usually won them—had also agreed to model for him. This sealed the deal for me. Rocky and I were friends who could and did kid each other without me having to worry about a rearranged face. Later, I realized his real reason: my older sister, Kate. She was a knockout, and he knew if he started a fight with me, he'd have no chance with her.

The night before Marie's big night, she called and suggested that the two of us go out to the Delmar Hotel's lounge for a celebratory drink after the show. I thought this would be a welcomed break for the both of us and it seemed to me that a stiff drink before the show would be an even better idea.

The Guard armory's huge gymnasium was the venue, and the "stage" was an old boxing ring platform found in the basement of the local college's gymnasium that had hosted amateur boxing in the '50s. Hundreds of colorful paper flowers concealed the canvas sides and wound around a white lattice entry arch from the town's high-school prom inventory. Marie had wanted faux spring décor for the entire gymnasium but the cost would have blown the lid off her budget, which was already strained.

A coup that cost nothing was a large children's wading pool complete with a wooden surround that masked the pool's cheap vinyl walls.

Her florist sponsor contributed fake reeds and marsh grasses, and a dozen swimming, peeping baby ducklings from my uncle's farm were added to charm and delight the children in the audience.

Marie and her team believed that the meager decorations would be enough for spring-starved Sault natives to welcome any diversion that smacked of warmer temperatures and sunshine after another long cold and grey winter. They were right. The place was packed.

Winter Roses

All of those smiling, chatting faces made me even more nervous. As I recall, the on-stage experience seemed as if it lasted a half an hour instead of the three minutes I spent walking around the stage, smiling and sweating. But I got through it. Marie and Jerry were waiting backstage to tell Ray and me that we'd done a fine job. While I doubted their sincerity, I accepted the compliments and vowed never again to model anything.

The show closed on a happy note for Marie, with the president of the Chamber of Commerce taking the mike and passing out kudos for all who supported the show. Marie received the loudest applause of all, because everyone knew she was the event's prime mover. He presented her with a dozen beautiful, red roses and I watched the tears well up in her eyes. But she swallowed hard and managed to get through a brief and gracious presentation that thanked her sponsors, teased Rocky and me for our reluctance to model as an example of what she had to put up with in staging the show, and thanked the audience for making the event a success. Her recognition was well deserved because she'd personally contacted nearly every retailer in town to enlist their support and coordinated almost all of the events by herself.

We stayed around to help the clean-up committee and then drove to the DelMar for that well-earned drink. The DelMar was probably the nicest entertainment venue in town, and its regular lounge floorshows drew a good mix of young and old alike.

Entering the lounge from its red-carpet steps could make you feel like a film star from the '30s making a grand entrance into a world of plush red velvet curtains and a wild panorama of yellow walls offset with orange and red leather booths, chairs and barstools. Somehow, this crazy quilt worked by adding a feeling that exciting things happened there, which they did.

The lounge was busy, since many of the fashion show's patrons were there. The moment we entered, Marie got another round of applause. Our table became the focus of attention as the patrons came over to offer their congratulations to her. When the accolades finally stopped coming, she got down to the real business she'd planned.

"Do you see that man sitting at the end of the bar? Don't turn your head quickly, he'll know we're talking about him."

I waited a few seconds and then slowly turned to see a good-looking man, maybe in his 30s. He was talking with my uncle George, who often tended bar to help on busy nights and fill in when one of the hotel's full-time bartenders couldn't be there. I caught his eye and we exchanged waves.

"Who's the bartender? Do you know him?"

"I sure do. That's my uncle George. I'll bet that the guy at the end of the bar is a flyboy from Kincheloe and that they're sharing war stories.

"How do you know that?"

"George was a signalman attached to an infantry brigade in General Slim's 14th British Army throughout the entire Burma campaign. I never saw the guy he's talking with and I know almost everyone in town about his age and younger."

"He's a B-52 pilot and his name is Frank Delaney. I found this out when I was dating another base officer, who pointed him out to me when we were having a drink at the officer's club. He's a widower with a couple of children. I want to meet him and you are going to help me."

"Great, I just walk up to him, introduce myself and tell him to come over to our table? That's a little naked for bashful me."

"You just told me how to do it. Go over and say 'hello' to your uncle, order a beer and then introduce yourself while he's getting your beer. Ask Frank if you could buy him a drink."

I thought this over and realized that her plan just might work; at least I'd have good opening lines. Closing the deal would be another matter, but I'd have time to think of something before the all-important introduction.

"Damn, Marie, between the modeling and now this ploy, you'll make an actor out of me yet. You are one foxy lady."

"Thank you. You say such nice things. It's no wonder Ann wants to marry you. If she didn't, I might, but you're a bit too young for my taste. Now please go over there and introduce yourself while I head for the lady's room."

"Can do." I finished my beer, took a deep breath and walked over to say hello to George.

He greeted me first, asking who was the pretty lady and where was Ann? I told him that she was back at Michigan State, and that the pretty lady is her older sister, Marie.

"I thought I'd seen her in here before—usually with a couple of other women."

"You probably have. Hey, I didn't mean to butt in on your conversation. I just wanted to say hello and get another beer. The waitresses can't keep up with the crowd."

"Sure. By the way, meet Lieutenant Frank, who's a bomber pilot at Kinch. Frank, meet my nephew John. You can tell him your last name and I'll get that beer." We shook hands.

"Good to meet you, John. My last name is Delaney."

"And mine is Bingham. Good to meet you, too, Frank. Can I buy you a refill?"

He nodded and I signaled to George that our new friend needed a drink.

"That's a sharp suit you're wearing, John. You looked good up on the stage. I give you credit for having the guts to do that. I don't think I could have done it."

I couldn't help but laugh.

"Marie gets full credit for that. She's a very persuasive woman. There were more men in the audience than I ever dreamed would be there and I obviously didn't spot you in the crowd. Then again, the experience was more like a mad blur of color and loudspeaker noise. I was oblivious to anything or anybody, and I focused hard on pretending that I was enjoying myself. Anyway, you saw my first and last performance as a model. But enough about me; what brought you here?"

"My son and daughter need new spring clothes and the fashion show was the best place to see a good selection. A friend of mine took them back to the base to spend the night with his family.

"So I came over here to relax and struck up a conversation with your uncle. He's a good troop. From what he told me about his Army service with the Brits in Burma, he's been through hell."

"Yes, he has. I was just a boy when my family went down to the railroad station to welcome him home from the war. I recall that he was very thin, but had no reference point at my young age to know why. As I grew and began to know him better, I learned that he still suffered from the malaria he'd contracted in the Burmese jungles. When our families vacationed together at our summer cottage, he'd often have to lie down and shiver and shake his way through severe malarial attacks. I'd bring him glasses of cold water and wet compresses to help break his fever."

Winter Roses

George rejoined the conversation and I noted that Marie was with a friend, a woman I didn't recognize. So she had company and I didn't have to be too concerned about hurrying and botching her introduction to Frank.

Frank turned to George and asked him to finish his story. George scanned the bar to make sure his customers' glasses were full and continued.

"Sure. We'd just taken Mandalay. The slaughter was so bad that every bloke standing was ordered to burial detail without a chance for rest. After tending first to our dead and wounded, we started on the Jap bodies. We tossed them in mass graves dug by the engineers and emptied bags of lime over them as our final blessing. Finally, we were able to stagger back to our tents and get some sleep.

"Sometime before dawn I was rudely awakened by my CO, Brit captain Oliver Rigby. He also led our battalion's HQ company, so he could regularly tap its members to help me lay my commo wire and coordinate communications with our HQ, rifle, and heavy weapons companies. As the only Yank in the outfit, I did my best not to let him down. He recognized and appreciated this. Anyway, I thought surer than hell that we were expecting a counterattack and he was making sure that we were awake and ready for it. But I was wrong.

"He whispered hoarsely in my ear that I had to get up—quietly—if I was to make the C-46 'Commando' flight to Calcutta for a little unscheduled R&R with other regiment officers and sergeants. "Don't bother shaving, just bring your kit and wear your cleanest dirty khakis. We depart at daybreak. Keep it quiet; otherwise, we'll have the whole bloody regiment storming the aircraft. If anyone wakes up and asks, tell him you're on a special, top-secret detail." You can bet that I packed in a hurry for that surprise, and I soon found myself standing in line to board the Commando on the tarmac with about 40 other officers and noncoms. We stood there quietly in our torn and filthy bush shirts and shorts, not willing to wake our chums. Leave it to the Brits to maintain strict order in any situation. It struck me that we were the most raggedy-assed bunch of soldiers that I'd ever seen and that I was no exception. Months of life in the jungle and frequent battles will do that, even to the Brits."

George left for a few moments to serve a couple that had just sat down at the bar and I glanced at Marie who was still with her friend. *George's stories can go on forever, and I hope that he can finish this one while my window for introduction is still open. When Marie's friend leaves, she'll turn the evil eye on me.* George returned to finish his story.

"We entered the aircraft and made our way around a row of secured containers to the sling seats on both sides of the aircraft. We were packed in arsehole-to-elbow. It was probably a good thing that the smell of aviation petrol overcame our B.O. To the well-scrubbed pilots, we must have smelled worse than a herd of goats.

"It didn't bother anyone that we couldn't talk for the racket of the engines revving for takeoff. We were so exhausted from burying our dead, slogging through the jungle and the constant terror of nonstop alerts, patrolling and combat that everyone closed his eyes and fell sound asleep. The engines' roar became our lullaby. But sleep became impossible at altitude. I can't recall ever being as cold, even though I was raised here in the land of nine-month winters. I guess that the months in a sweltering jungle had thinned my blood.

"Fortunately, there were no Jap planes around that day and the plane's engines behaved.

"Except for the chattering of our teeth, the flight was what we all hoped and prayed for—uneventful. We started to warm up as the plane began its descent to the Calcutta airport and now we only shivered over the prospect of getting some decent rest, female companionship for the singles and cheaters, and booze.

"A dilapidated bus was waiting for us as we rolled off the runway and on to the tarmac.

Winter Roses

"Even in the still-early morning, the heat and humidity sucked the breath out of me, although I should have been used to the same weather in the bloody, rotting Burmese jungle. But there, we at least had jungle shade and daily downpours to help cool off during the monsoon season.

"The bus rolled up to the hotel and we bailed out as fast as we could. After the bus's heat and diesel fumes, the huge lobby with its slowly turning ceiling fans felt and looked like heaven. I thought this was appropriate, because we'd left hell behind us, at least for a few days.

"The bellhops stood well behind us in a line, one per officer and one for a non-com peon like me. I thought this was curious, but I was more interested in getting just plain drunk. From the booze and beers lined up on the bar, it was apparent that everyone else shared my interest. To start, I ordered a shot and a beer. Then another. And another. And so on.

"We toasted ourselves, the king, Churchill, Roosevelt, Generals Slim and Stilwell, Chiang Kai-Shek, our 'Inja' regiments, the Ghurkas, the Karen and Kachin guerrillas (who scare the Nips shitless), and more. The noise level of the conversations rose from a murmur to a steady roar, and the first man to pass out fell off his barstool and crashed on the floor. The bellhop behind him rushed over, checked him out to make sure he wasn't injured and then lifted him and carried him like he would a baby out of the bar and up the stairs to his room. Now that was room service at its best!

"A short time later, the commotion of more men falling woke me from my little nap at the bar. We were so skinny that scooping us up in their arms and carrying us up all those steps must have been a snap for those big fellows. I'd switched to straight beers just to see if I could stay sober enough to walk upstairs to my room and decided that I could. Making it to the loo a little while before hadn't been too hard as long as I stayed close to the wall for support. I lurched off the bar stool, which drew my rescuer over to take my arm and steady me during the long march ahead. With my very own Man Friday faithfully at my side to keep me from falling and guide me, I made it, collapsed on the bed and passed out.

"I woke up and stumbled over to the curtain and drew it back. It was evening. I thought I'd slept just a few hours. Wrong. I'd slept right through the next day and right into the following evening.

"We spent the rest of our unexpected 'R&R' drinking, sightseeing, buying new socks, underwear, boots, and combat fatigues, and dining like kings. Some visited the whorehouses, but I stayed away. My fiancé and I would be married as soon as I returned home and the thought of that was good enough to keep me going. Besides, I had enough to worry about without adding guilt and the threat of an exotic social disease nagging at me.

"Our flight back to our unit was uneventful. We slept through it, only this time we were exhausted from too much Calcutta."

With that, George excused himself and headed for the men's room. Now I had my opening for Frank's introduction to Marie. Before beginning my little speech, I'd spun on the barstool and nodded to her.

"Frank, I won't bullshit you. A major reason why I came over to join you and George was to introduce myself and let you know that Marie would like to meet you. She asked me to be the go-between so I could properly introduce you to her. Please understand that even if she wasn't here, I'd have come over to the bar to George and we would have met anyway. And meeting you has been a real pleasure. That said and if you'd like, I'll be happy to introduce you to her. You won't regret it. She's as nice as she is pretty, and she's also smart."

"Sure," said Frank. "I'd like that. Let's go meet her."

We walked over, I introduced them and we sat down, one on each side of her. Marie asked, "What took you two so long?" Before I could reply, Frank said,

Winter Roses

"That man went through the meat grinder during the war in Burma and he has stories to tell. Important stories. It was important that we listened to him."

With that, I knew Frank was a good troop, a stand-up officer who'd look after his men. I could only add that George's tales were also funny.

"I should have come over to the bar and joined you," she said. "But I'll meet George another day. Meanwhile, I'll be the envy of all my friends, sitting here with a fashion-show model and now a handsome Air Force pilot to keep me company." We laughed and I stuck around for a little polite small talk before heading home. When Frank took a trip to the men's room, I asked Marie if she wanted me to take her home this time before soloing with him.

Ever succinct, she said, "Hell, no. In fact, you can leave anytime now."

I said my 'good nights' when Frank returned.
Years later, I enjoyed kidding them and telling our friends about how they met—that Marie didn't just throw herself at him, she threw me first.

Frank never had a chance.

Four

Run-up to marriage

Ann came home from State after she finished her term finals. By this time, Marie and Frank had started dating but neither was quite ready yet for a serious relationship.

We learned this when he tried to hit on Ann. She had just started her summer job as a sales clerk at a local jewelry store when he walked in. He didn't know she was Marie's kid sister and that she was my fiancé. But she suspected immediately who he was from Marie's description and mine. There was no doubt when he introduced himself and told her in the next breath that he was a pilot stationed at Kincheloe. She politely declined his offer to join him for coffee during her break, telling him that she was engaged. He asked who the lucky guy was, and she told him. He immediately knew he'd stumbled into a trap, since he was very interested in Marie and wanted to see more of her. There wasn't much he could say, except to tell Ann that it was nice to meet her and that maybe we could double-date sometime.

Marie laughed when Ann told her that evening about her encounter with Frank. She allowed as how this seemed only fair since she'd first learned who he was from one of his fellow officers at the base. Marie let him off easy on their next date. After seeing a show, they drove up the main street past the jewelry store where Ann worked. She told him that she knew he was "window shopping" and complimented him on his taste. "You had the right family," she joked, "but the wrong sister."

He stammered a bit before telling her that he wasn't ready yet to get serious. The memory of Elizabeth was still too fresh. Marie accepted this and didn't push him, knowing that this man could not be pushed into anything. She remained encouraged, however, by the prospect of a deeper relationship—perhaps even marriage—because she knew he wasn't dating anyone else, unless he'd found someone in one of the nearby small communities, which wasn't likely. Not that there weren't attractive and bright single women in these towns, but she felt that Frank would be more comfortable with a woman who had more street smarts. A woman like her, of course, and there was no denying that she had street smarts.

She was much encouraged when Frank invited her out to the base for a dinner dance at the O-Club. This was a formal affair, so she bought a new dress for the occasion. She drove to the base and met him at his home. The children—Frank, Jr. and Jennifer—were awaiting the baby-sitter so the evening was also a good opportunity to meet them. While Frank was in the bedroom putting on his mess whites, Marie had a good talk with the children. She told them about her own two children and how much fun it would be if they all got together for a beach picnic. The children enthusiastically endorsed this idea and Marie was happy since such an outing could only strengthen their families' relationship. When Frank came out to join them, the children told him about the beach outing and he bought into the idea. They decided on the following Sunday for their outing, with Marie suggesting a little-known public beach on Lake Huron, near the tiny town of Detour.

Marie couldn't help but note the huge oil portrait of Elizabeth on the living room wall and wondered how she could possibly compete with a memory. Clearly, Frank had been badly wounded by her too-soon passing, and she decided that it was also too soon to ask questions about her death. Instead, she told Frank how beautiful Elizabeth was. He agreed and the faraway look in his eyes spoke volumes. He was lost in a memory.

The doorbell broke the awkward silence; the babysitter had arrived. She was the daughter of the base commander and clearly was no Air Force brat. She was warm and personable and the children loved her. With the children's hugs for daddy—and for Marie—they left for the O-club.

Marie was impressed by Frank's 1955 mint green Ford Thunderbird that was in showroom condition. Clearly, the T-Bird was also his love. The evening was pleasant enough to drive with the top down and Marie felt more and more like Cinderella with every passing minute. She certainly had her handsome prince, at least for the evening.

Frank commented on the children's favorable reaction to her, saying that he'd never seen them take to someone so quickly. Marie responded that, besides having their parents' good looks, they were very warm and caring, and that she couldn't wait until they met Mark and Mike.

They drove up to the O-club, where off-duty airmen were making extra money as parking valets.

A fine-looking young man ran up to the car, welcomed them, opened the door for Marie and ran around the back of the car to salute Frank and get his hands on the wheel. There were bigger, fancier cars in the lot but there'd be only one mint-green T-Bird. Frank laughed as the kid drove all the way around the lot to find a parking space and then went around again. "They all do that," he explained. "They can't wait to get their hands on the wheel and don't want to take their hands off it. I feel the same way."

"Lucky wheel," she said with a smile. He gave her an odd look.

Winter Roses

She smiled again and took his arm as they walked up the red-carpeted steps to the club dining room. They dined and danced the night away with Marie drawing more than her fair share of requests from other officers for a dance, including the base commander. When he returned her to Frank, he told him how lucky he was to have such a pretty, bright and personable companion for the night. Frank replied that those were the reasons why he asked her to join him for the night.

"I always knew you were a smart man, Frank—may I call you Frank? Let's drop the formalities for the night." "Of course, sir," Frank replied, as if he could have addressed the colonel by his given name. *Just one of the men, right, Bill? Yeah, sure, and pigs can fly, just like we do.* Frank's new "buddy" Bill read him like a book. With a cool handshake and a well polished 'thanks' to Marie and Frank for brightening his evening, the colonel returned to his wife, who was charming a small group of junior officers in the hallway leading to the ballroom.

Frank told Marie that for a few short minutes, she was closer to the colonel than he'd ever get and he was jealous. She responded with a laugh and told him to stick close to her because she could do that to men and was especially effective with handsome lieutenants. With that, they both laughed and called it a night.

When they pulled up the driveway and parked, he told her that he'd bring the babysitter home and then return to join her in a nightcap if she so pleased. She agreed. They walked into the house and Frank took the babysitter's report. All was well, she and the children had a lot of fun together, they were well behaved as always, and they went to bed at 10 as usual without a fuss. Frank paid her and Marie walked out the door with them, gave Frank a quick kiss on the cheek, whispered in his ear and then thanked him out loud for a wonderful evening. He caught on immediately; the colonel and his wife did not need to know more about his personal life. An Air Force base was too much like one big family and personal secrets had a way of becoming base gossip.

John Bingham

To complete the charade, Marie said "Good night" to the baby sitter and walked over to her car as if she was headed back to town.

Knowing Marie would be waiting for him when he returned made Frank shiver. It had been a long, long time, as it had been for Marie. With the children in the house, they were as quiet in bed as they possibly could be, which was no small achievement.

Driving home in a pre-dawn mist, Marie smiled and thought that their night of love-making without waking the children was good practice. There'd be two more pairs of ears listening in if she had her way.

I suspected Frank was also thinking "marriage" when he told me a couple of weeks later that he'd had a vasectomy. All I could think of to say when he dropped that one on me was "Congratulations. Your mother didn't raise any dumb children." He laughed and I did too, but I was surprised by his candor.

They spent the rest of the summer traveling to local beaches and tourist attractions with the children, and sometimes getting away for a weekend of their own. We often tagged along for the beach outings and always had a good time.

One night, Marie and Ann decided to surprise us with a candlelight lasagna dinner complete with a good chianti, Caesar salad, hard rolls, homemade apple pie for dessert, and fresh flowers from their mother's garden. The meal was superb and we couldn't compliment them enough. The chianti was the smoothest I'd ever had and the floral arrangement provided cheap entertainment when a small army of green inchworms emerged from the flowers and began to rappel down their silk threads onto the table, where they continued their journey over the edge with that cockeyed fold-up and straighten-out motion. The candles on the table had warmed them and they'd crawled out of their cocoons to join us. Their movements seemed to be timed to the classical music playing on the stereo, so we had our very own inchworm ballet. For years after, we remembered that night and the inchworms' stellar performance. Frank and I also remembered how good the food was, a real production for even a highly experienced cook. There was little doubt in my mind that Marie's lasagna had speeded along Frank's decision to ask her to marry him.

Sometimes we triple-dated, most often with Frank's fellow pilots and their dates. One of them, Tom Dirksen, was particularly memorable. He was quick-witted, bright, good-looking and as personable and positive a man as you'd ever want to meet. Frank envied him because he flew fighters instead of the B-52s, which in Air Force jargon were called "BUFFS", standing for "Big Ugly Flying Fuckers."

Tom was dating Sarah Craig, who'd graduated from high school with my older sister. I'd dated Sarah once, taking her to a beach party at our old family cottage near Sault Ste. Marie. She was sweet, pretty and very bright, the girl everyone wanted to date. Tom was equally bright, only he had the street smarts that she lacked at the time. Most often, we'd see a movie at one of the town's two theaters or go out for dinner and then come back to the house, where Ann and Marie's parents had a wet bar in the basement.

One such evening, Ann suggested that we play Scrabble, and everyone thought this was a fine idea. The men would play against the women, and during the game I first saw Frank's ferocious desire to win.

Ann, Sarah and Marie were beating us badly and we were frustrated because we couldn't seem to get the tiles we needed to score big and catch up. Of course, the girls teased us, which Tom and I took as good-natured table talk and we teased right back whenever we'd get a rare, high-scoring word.

I wasn't paying attention to Frank's silence until he suddenly grabbed the board and flipped it over, scattering the tiles across the room. The fire in his eyes immediately changed to one of contrition. He knew in a second that he'd behaved like an asshole, but he didn't apologize at first. He simply said that he was "tired of playing." Marie called him out for all of us, telling him that we weren't tired of playing and that he had no right to do that. He mumbled an apology and that was the end of it. He and Tom decided that it was time to go home after helping to pick up the tiles. I decided to do the same. Ann offered me a ride, but I told her I'd walk instead. I wanted the fresh air to clear my head.

On the way home, I thought about Frank and wondered if he had blown his still-budding relationship with Marie with his childish behavior. I knew that she felt deeply about him and that a break-up would be a very hard decision to make. But that was none of my business and I decided to drop the subject. Besides, Ann would keep me informed if anything happened. She knew the two of us were quickly becoming close friends, with Frank being the big brother I never had.

The early-September air already held the sharp edge of another Sault Ste. Marie autumn. No matter this year. I would return with Ann to East Lansing the following weekend so I could get in another term before leaving for Fort Benning. It was nice to be with her again on campus.

The term passed quickly, and Ann and I took every opportunity to be together. She lived in an all-women's dorm while I was across campus in a men's dorm, so I stayed in shape by running back and forth.

Especially nice were our study picnics on warm fall days in Okemos on the bank of the Red Cedar River. University entertainment offerings and lecture series (including Count Basie, Peter, Paul and Mary, and the Reverend Doctor Martin Luther King delivering a version of "I Have A Dream") were among our more memorable activities.

Frank and Marie came down for a home football weekend. He especially enjoyed himself since he was a Michigan State alumnus. That evening, we celebrated a Spartan win at our favorite Lansing restaurant, The Tiki Club's "Boom Boom Room."

Winter Roses

A better cause for celebration was Frank's announcement that he and Marie were engaged and wanted us to stand up for them. They set January 3rd as their wedding date. Following the wedding, Ann would come back to campus and I arranged to depart that evening by train to make my January 4th reporting date in Fort Benning. They returned to the Sault the following day, and Ann and I went back to our studies.

Then came October 14, when a U-2 reconnaissance aircraft flying high over Cuba photographed the Soviet missile sites. The crisis had officially begun with unmistakable evidence that Cuba could now hit strategic targets on our mainland with nuclear missiles.

I knew immediately that every combat military and support unit at home and abroad would be on full alert with aircraft waiting on the tarmacs and runways and airborne troops in full combat kit, ready and waiting to board. SEALS, Marine Force Recon, Green Berets, and Rangers were likely already there. Our troops stationed at Guantanamo would also be on full alert and were probably the edgiest of all. My unit—the 1437th Combat Engineers (Float Bridge)—was a reserve component of STRAC (Strategic Army Command) and perhaps on alert if Cuba's inland waterways would be candidates for heavy bridging and/or infantry assault river crossings. I remember a sinking feeling in my stomach and cold, sweaty palms. Whether I'd be incinerated by a nuclear blast or machine-gunned during an assault river crossing didn't make much difference; dead is dead.

Because the Soo Locks enabled the huge lake freighters that carried iron ore and other bulk commodity materials to navigate the 21-foot drop from Lake Superior to Lakes Michigan and Huron—and vice versa—Sault Ste. Marie was a major nuclear target during the cold war.

A nuclear strike on the Locks would bring steel manufacturing--along with America's capacity for making war--to a standstill.

Frank, of course, would be on full alert, standing to in the ready shack with his fellow pilots and crews, and the BUFFs lined up on the runway, ready for all-out nuclear war. Rather than ride this one out with classmates, Ann and I decided to take a bus home for the weekend to be with our loved ones.

When we arrived late Friday afternoon, Marie asked if we'd like to drive with her out to the base that evening to see Frank. This was fine with Ann and me, but I knew that the base would be on full alert and wondered how we'd get through the main gate. Marie said that he had made arrangements with his CO and the guard's OIC (Officer In Charge) that night to let us through. When the guard called the ready shack to tell him we were through the gate, he'd walk out to the cyclone fence and meet us.

We left after dinner in a light squall that blew wispy sheets of snow across the highway but showed no sign of turning into a major snowstorm. A light or heavy snowfall was no big thing to us, since any amount was possible on an October evening in Michigan's Upper Peninsula.

During our ride to the base, each of us thought about the very real possibility of a nuclear war and whether this evening would be the last time we'd ever again see Frank. Or see each other, for that matter. We turned off the highway and drove to the front gate, where we immediately noticed the stepped-up security. The guard shack now had three MPs on duty instead of the normal two. M-2 fully automatic carbines were slung on their backs with 30-round banana clips locked in place and .45 Colt pistols holstered on their web belts. The third had a guard dog on a leash. The dog sat quietly, staring at us and likely awaiting his own attack command.

One of the guards stepped out of the shack and asked if we were "The Delaney Party." Marie replied that we were and asked for directions to the ready shack. After checking our IDs, the guard told us to wait a few moments until our escort arrived to take us to the wire outside the ready shack.

Winter Roses

Frank would come out to meet us. We pulled over to the side of the road.

Two more well-armed MPs showed up in a covered Jeep. One got out and walked over to us and I rolled down the window. He saluted and I returned it. "Good evening, sir, and good evening, ladies," he said. "We ask that you follow us to the exact point along the security fence where you will be able to meet and talk with Lieutenant Delaney. You will park there along the side of the road. I will call him and advise him that you are here. He will then leave the ready shack and walk over to the fence. You may then get out of your vehicle, walk to the fence and meet him. While you are talking with him, we will be observing you from our vehicle, which will be parked 100 meters up the road. When you are finished, walk back to your car and wait for us to escort you back to the guard shack. We will stay there until you have left base property. Under no circumstance are you to depart from these directions. Have I made myself clear?" "Very clear," I replied, and he said "Good. Now follow us." We exchanged salutes again and he walked back to the Jeep.

The snow was falling faster and harder as we followed our escorts to the fence-line meeting's location. They stopped and pointed to our rendezvous point. Through the fence you could see the bombers on the flight line and on the tarmac. Each had two "Hound Dog" nuclear air-to-ground missiles slung under its wings. The missiles looked more like sharks than hound dogs, but they earned their nickname with a capability of steering to their target and hitting it within two miles, plus or minus. This accuracy was "perfectly acceptable" for their nuclear warheads, which quickly gave you a good idea of their destructive power.

We saw Frank leave the guard shack and walk towards us, silhouetted in the bright lights illuminating the tarmac. He arrived at the cyclone fence at the same time we did and he put both hands on it. Marie did the same and their fingers intertwined as they tried to kiss each other through the chain links.

He broke off with a chuckle and said, "That kiss may have looked unromantic, but considering what could happen to our world at any moment, it's the most romantic kiss I could ever ask for." Marie agreed and held up the red rose that Frank had passed to her through the fence. "Look," she said. "A beautiful winter rose."

She passed it to Ann for safekeeping and we seconded Frank's sentiment. Later, we'd be able to lose each other in a goodnight embrace and be grateful that we weren't on opposite sides of a cyclone fence and under surveillance. We'd quickly learned to live for the moment when the possibility of nuclear annihilation was so close to reality.

He and Marie talked about the children's adventures during the past week and what their feelings were about the crisis. Especially poignant was Frank, Jr. and Jennifer's dread that they may never see their daddy again. They would leave in the morning with Elizabeth's mother and father to stay with them at their northwestern Michigan home until the crisis was over. He had reassured them as best he could before he left that he would be home as always after flying. When the baby-sitter arrived to spend the night with the children, he hugged and kissed them as he always did before a mission and drove to the ready shack for his orders. He told us after the crisis was over that during the short drive from his home to the ready shack he wondered if the children's concern would turn into a nuclear nightmare of reality. *No matter if that happens,* he had thought. *The world as we know it will disappear in seconds. If I have to, I'll contribute to the slaughter.*

I heard a noise behind us and turned to see what looked like a miniature train on rubber wheels coming down the road that led to the tarmac gate. Each one of the cars in tow carried what reminded me of a big beer keg with rounded corners nestled in a wooden cradle. Each had a small cap protruding from its top. *Probably the H-bomb's electronic arming device,* I thought.

There were too many "kegs" for me to count in a glance and I didn't care how many anyway because of the sudden, sinking feeling in my stomach. I'd guessed immediately that they were H-bombs on their way to the BUFFS that

Winter Roses

sat with their bomb bay doors wide open, ready to be filled with mankind's most destructive weapons -- spawned by the insane race with the USSR that had reached the point of Mutually Assured Destruction (MAD) of both countries, a race of annihilation that no one could win. This would serve as a nuclear stalemate until the USSR's fall decades later. Meanwhile, everyone knew that night that the destruction of civilization as we knew it could begin at any moment.

All Frank could officially say was that he hoped like hell he didn't have to use them. The bomb train disappeared around the corner and all I could think of was their targets; what were they and where were they? I wondered the same about the Soviet bombs and missiles that were aimed at us. Certainly the Sault and its surrounding small communities would be annihilated in the first wave. No one knew if the warring parties would have anything or anyone left to mount a second wave.

Ann saw the faraway look on my face and gave me a kiss on the cheek while taking my hand in hers. I was grateful that she'd returned me to reality. I put my arm around her waist and returned her kiss. Marie told us to "Knock it off, you're making Frank and me jealous." Ann told them to go back to the fence since kisses through chain links were better than no kisses at all. She also said that anything more would just have to wait a few days. They laughed at her retort and returned to try another kiss through the fence. If the sight was romantic, it was also funny. Ann and I averted our eyes and concentrated on one another.

Humor didn't have much of a chance through a cyclone fence, but it sure beat worrying about nuclear incineration.

Now the snow was falling harder, so fast that we could barely see the road. The drive home would be a slow one.

Frank said that we'd better call it a night since he would "have to leave shortly." We didn't ask where he was going because we knew he couldn't tell us.

For all we knew, he wouldn't know his targeted destination until he opened his orders after he and his fellow airmen were on their way. Assuming that they wouldn't be shot down before reaching their targets, death would be waiting for those unfortunates who were trapped in the bombardier's sights.

We walked back to the car with Ann and Marie stepping in my tracks through the snow, and we didn't look back. The escorts saw us and drove up to take us to the main gate.

Marie said through welling tears that she wished she could be on base at Frank's house with all four children gathered around her for mutual comfort. But she was grateful that at least his children might have a chance for survival if Traverse City was spared. No one raised the specter of what would happen to all of us who were living in the Sault.

The drive home was somber and long since we crawled along at 20 mph during the 15-mile return trip. To shake us out of our funereal mood, Ann told us about her pet duck Ichabod terrorizing Wolfie, the family dog. Whenever Wolfie saw Ickie charging straight at him with neck and beak lowered, Wolfie ran for the back door and barked and whined until someone rescued him from his tormenter.

I shared one about my family's foul-tempered duck, Donald—caught early one morning quacking down the street by my father who was dressed only in boxer shorts and a T-shirt and wielding a long-handled fishing net.

Dad must have thought no one would see him at that hour. He learned otherwise when a patrol car turned the corner and stopped alongside him to wonder what in hell a half-naked, grown man was doing at this time of night holding a highly pissed-off duck ensnared in the net, quacking even faster and louder over its plight and striking dad in the shoulder with its beak. The officer couldn't believe the sight and broke into a laughing fit.

Winter Roses

Dad tried to explain the chase by saying that the duck was his daughter's pet that had escaped from its pen in the garage.

Instead of ticketing him for disorderly conduct and disturbing the peace, the officer told him to start walking fast to our house while he slowly drove alongside. Which dad was more than pleased to do, considering the awkwardness of his situation.

Ann and I returned to campus the following Monday. When President Kennedy came on TV later that week to announce that the crisis was over and that the Soviets would dismantle the missile bases and take the missiles back to the USSR, we cheered, hugged and called home. Marie was not there. She'd taken a call that afternoon from Frank inviting her to come out and celebrate with him at the O-Club. The entire base had received orders that morning to stand down. He and his fellow pilots spent the day supervising the disarming of their BUFFs and they were all more than ready to celebrate.

Ann and I rejoiced with dinner at Lansing's White House Inn, a quiet venue that we liked for its privacy and good food at student-friendly prices.

The rest of the term passed quickly and we came home again for the holiday break. We spent a lot of time with Marie and Frank, who had completed their plans for the wedding. It would be simple and short; Ann and I would stand up for them and be the only guests. We'd celebrate with champagne and dinner at the Capitol Park Hotel's dining room. The night before the wedding, we would have a pre-wedding party at Oade's, a small off-campus bar that was a favorite. It featured a great jazz combo, which Frank remembered from his own days at Michigan State. The décor was mostly beer cases stacked up against the block walls that doubled as seating and insulation on Saturday nights. An added touch was a huge aquarium that was home to a school of piranhas. Sometimes overserved customers tried to feed them food scraps or even pieces of their forearms; they were escorted out with a warning to never return. Regardless of the décor and the club's sometimes-rowdy patrons, the music would be good and the company would be great.

The only downer for me would be leaving for Fort Benning right after the wedding. But I knew I'd trained hard for the program, which would be the most challenging I'd ever faced. I took some comfort in knowing that I'd at least be physically ready.

Ann and I alternated our Christmas Day time between my home and hers, with small gifts for our parents and the children. Frank, Frank, Jr. and Jennifer had come into town on Christmas Eve to spend the night and Christmas day with Marie and Ann's family. Their brother Ron was in San Francisco and couldn't make it home for the holidays, which was a disappointment.

On Christmas Eve, Ann presented me with the best present I ever had, a color portrait of her that was taken when she was chosen as Miss Sault Ste. Marie and would compete for the Miss Upper Peninsula title. I took the portrait to Fort Benning and I was happy that I did for a reason: my tactical officer pretended to fall in love with her. He never missed the opportunity to tell me that I was too stupid and ugly to have such a lovely fiancé, and that the two of them were now writing to each other and she was ditching me for him. Moreover, if I didn't start dusting her portrait every day, he'd see to it that I'd never graduate. When I laughed the first time he shouted this crap in my ear, he ordered me to "Knock out 50 (pushups) for laughing at your tactical officer, who owns your ass!" When the rest of the platoon started laughing, they got 75.

Good, clean fun.

During the break, Frank had the chance to meet my father when we decided to have a "men's day," shooting pool in the afternoon at the local Elks Club. I was a decent player, having been coached by dad since I was in grade school.

Winter Roses

Dad was a former men's pool and billiards champion at Michigan Tech who would run the table on you before you'd get a chance to shoot. I mentioned this to Frank on our way over to pick up dad, and he replied that he'd shot some pool himself. Remembering his temper tantrum over the Scrabble game, I sensed that his always-fierce desire to win would surface again if dad or I started winning. Agreeing on a ten-dollar bet to go to the "last man standing" in a nine-game shootout fueled the competitor spirit in each of us; ten bucks was no small sum in those days.

The club's combination bar and poolroom décor was a step back into the early 20th century, with dark, paneled walls and an ornate, stamped-metal ceiling. A well-intentioned member had put up what he must have thought were classy "don't do" signs on the wall, such as "Do not spit in the potted plants." Some wag had changed the "p" to an "h" and no one had changed it back to the original. Maybe they hadn't even noticed. "Players must keep both feet on the floor" was a good one, but the one we liked best was, "No sleeping allowed on tables." Fairly new fluorescent light fixtures provided good game lighting vs. the old incandescent bulbs in green hanging lampshades that tipsy shooters whacked with their cues when they got excited and started waving their cues around. There were even new cues instead of the old, warped relics of the early 20th century—some of which dad swore you could have used to shoot around corners.

Dad started slowly, and Frank got hot during the first game. I opened a beer and sat down on a stool to watch and wait for my turn to take on the winner. Frank dropped the eight ball after a good run and dad and I complimented him on his game. He was especially pleased when dad's ten-dollar-bill went on the table--not that he wanted or needed the money, but the bill was tangible evidence of a victory.

The second game, I turned up the heat and ran the table after Frank had sunk only two balls after his break. He was not pleased, but he complimented me through tight lips. The ten-spot came to my side of the table and dad stepped up to play. Frank didn't say a word as dad and I quickly worked down to the eight ball. Dad dropped it in a side pocket with a beautiful bank shot and the bucks went back to him as Frank took his turn. His smile was gone and I readied myself for his balls-out effort with no telling what would happen if he lost. Lose he did and neither he nor I could touch Dad for the rest of the series.

To Frank's credit, he didn't smash his cue over the edge of the table.

Instead, he gritted out the loss with a red face and very few words other than a muttered "damn" or "shit" when he'd blow a shot. My play had gone to hell after my lone win and a near-win over dad, which gave him more chances to win. Dad was as graceful as he could be, complimenting Frank on his good shots and even giving him chances to shoot by subtly missing a few of his more difficult shots.

Thankfully, Frank didn't catch on and realize that dad was playing with him as he always did with me, like a cat does with a cornered mouse.

If he knew that, there was no telling what he'd do…flip over the table as he did with the Scrabble board? Which didn't happen, maybe because Frank knew it was too heavy. Still, he just might try.

Frank and I relaxed when dad took the money and bought us a beer. Frank's temper had cooled and he even asked dad to show him how to play billiards, which was a game he'd always wanted to learn. Dad obliged and both Frank and I tried to make some shots without much success. But we were at least satisfied that we'd both learned more about pool and billiards from a master.

Frank had been asking me to play handball with him. I'd begged off because I had a plantar wart on the ball of my right foot that really hurt. That was true enough, but I could get by pretty well with a large bunion pad that cushioned the shock of running and quick starts and stops. So I agreed that we'd get in a game before the Christmas break ended. Besides, I knew he was a very good player and beating me would make him feel better. Of course, I'd play as hard as I could; faking it wouldn't work for either of us.

Winter Roses

He was even better than I imagined and had me running all over the court to hit his returns while he moved only to get better ball placement. I didn't have a chance. We hadn't bet on the match: winning was more important to Frank than money. My compliments on his fine play were enough payment.

In the shower, he said he knew from Marie that I liked to play tennis and suggested that we play a match. From his subtle challenge, I gathered that he could play tennis well. I could, too. I'd beaten a former Northern Michigan University champion the previous spring, so I felt confident that I'd give Frank all he could handle and hopefully, then some.

The Christmas break passed quickly and Ann and I returned to campus January 2nd, the day before the wedding. She did some advance work, including ordering flowers for Marie and personally checking out the chapel and confirming arrangements for the candlelight ceremony. She also ordered a bottle of champagne and a box of chocolate truffles for their honeymoon suite at the Capitol Park. The ceremony would be short; after, Frank and Marie would drive me to the railroad station and Ann back to her dorm.

Marie called that afternoon and said that they wouldn't be able to come down until the wedding day. Baby-sitting arrangements had fallen through, so they'd take Frank, Jr. and Jennifer to their grandparents' home near Traverse City where they'd spend three nights, thus allowing Frank and Marie a short honeymoon. Mike and Mark would stay with Walt and Louise in Sault Ste. Marie.

I passed the big day by carefully packing my duffle bag, reviewing my orders and the must-read advance information about the OCS program that the School had sent along with my orders.

Late that afternoon, Frank and Marie picked us up at Ann's dorm. We drove over to my dorm, where I picked up my bag and put it in the trunk of their like-new 1962 Lincoln. They'd traded the T-Bird for luxury and a Volkswagen Microbus. Frank must have bled T-Bird mint green during that exchange, and neither Ann nor I brought up the subject other than to say how nice the Lincoln was and how practical the VW would be for their new family of six.

Later they would discover the hard way that the underpowered VW--when fully loaded with children and luggage--was not the best choice for climbing mountains en route to a new base or when on vacation.

The snazzy Lincoln also had problems; chief among them was a habit of stalling under fast acceleration. Marie said that few thrills matched a stall when trying to pass on a busy two-lane road and that playing chicken with friends in her teens at least had the potential for more predictable outcomes.

The wedding was held in a small stone chapel built into the side of East Lansing's Presbyterian Church. It was a candlelight ceremony, and the flickering shadows in the dark chapel gave the appearance of a medieval castle. The room was chilly from the January cold, which contributed to the Middle Ages ambience. Ann gave Marie her bridal bouquet and pinned on Frank's boutonniere. He in turn gave me the rings and we were ready to go. Considering the somber surroundings for the otherwise festive occasion, I expected the minister to show up in a coarse brown robe complete with a hood over his head and intone the ceremony in Gregorian chant.

Instead, a short, ruddy-faced rotund man dressed in a suit with tie walked in, shook hands all around and went immediately into the ceremony. It couldn't have lasted more than 10 minutes. After Marie and Frank kissed and we all hugged, they went into the church office, paid the minister and signed the marriage certificate. Ann and I went outside and smoked a cigarette.

The wedding dinner at the Capitol Park was delicious and I especially savored it knowing that I wouldn't taste beef like that—let alone champagne—for some time.

Winter Roses

Ann felt the same way since her dorm food wasn't likely to be much better than Army food. Frank and Marie laughed when we shared this thought. Like parents, they urged us to eat more and kept the champagne flowing. It was difficult to avoid a full stomach and a swimming head, but I finally said "Enough!" Ann followed suit.

They refused to let us help with the bill, knowing our limited college income. I worked as a student cook in my dorm complex kitchen during the term and the pay was just enough to cover my books as well as keep me in cigarettes and dates with Ann. More often than not, we'd go "Dutch treat."

Five

Benning's School For Boys

While Marie and Ann drank a Coffee Kahlua and Frank settled the bill, I went out to the car, got my greens out of the trunk and put them on in the men's room. My suit stayed with Marie and Frank; they'd return it to my parents when they got back to the Sault.

En route to Lansing's railway station, Frank said that the program would be difficult but that I should ace it. His confidence boosted mine, but I told him that I didn't expect to ace it. I'd be pleased if I just passed without washing out. He said he'd like to pin on my bars on at my commissioning ceremony. Since Ann would be finishing her term work and finals at MSU, I told him I'd be pleased and honored if he'd do that.

We arrived at the station and said our "goodbyes" and "good lucks" after I hugged Marie and shook hands with Frank. Ann walked with me to the train while Marie and Frank went back to the Lincoln to stay warm in the frigid January air.

After the conductor checked my ticket and wrestled my duffel bag into the luggage compartment, he said that we'd better make our goodbyes short since the train would leave at any moment. We had time for a bear-hug embrace and

Winter Roses

a too-short kiss. A blast of the locomotive's whistle cut our dream world short. I climbed the steps into my car, then turned and told her one more time that I loved her. My voice was hoarse and choked with emotion and I stepped quickly into the car. The conductor walked me to my berth and I leaned over to look out the window as the train started a slow roll out of the station.

There stood Ann, waving and blowing kisses, which I returned. I can still see her standing there in that cold January night. It was a scene right out of a vintage detective or spy film but without the huge clouds and hissing of steam from the locomotive. Reliving the departure later, I thought it was too bad that the diesel locomotive couldn't quite capture the romance of the steam locomotive, but that its mournful whistle made up for part of the loss. It fed my loneliness, since I wouldn't see Ann again until spring.

I opened up my orders to reconfirm my reporting date and hour and did a mental checklist of my uniforms and personal belongings to get my mind off Ann. My official reporting orders also included a reminder that all candidates should be in good physical condition before reporting and I fell asleep satisfied that I was in the best condition of my life--even better than my high school football and basketball days.

During a stop in Atlanta, I got out my duffel bag, re-folded my newly tailored and heavily starched fatigues to avoid as much wrinkling as possible and found a nice surprise from Ann. It was a Longines wristwatch, the same one I had pointed out in the jewelry store's watch case when I picked her up from work one day the previous summer. I recalled telling her I needed one like it that would take a beating, but that I couldn't afford it. Instead, I told her that I'd buy an inexpensive Timex at Benning's post exchange. On her slim budget, I wondered how she paid for it. Later, she told me that the store's owner had sold it to her at cost with interest-free time payments.

There was also a letter inside, one I kept for years after. Reading her heartfelt message of promised love for our coming years together was the best motivational tool I ever had. It still is.

John Bingham

Late the next day, I was one of the 220 men who reported to the Student Brigade's HQ and got swarmed under by too many tactical officers to count, all screaming and shouting at us with conflicting orders as well as many insults about our sorry mental and physical fitness to hack such a difficult and demanding program.

All we could do is stand at attention and wait for the next "TAC" to have us drop down and knock out uncountable push-ups and run races around the barracks to see who was in shape and who was not.

The laggards were being marked already for wash-out. We were then told to report to the base barber shop for a haircut, followed by a dash to the PX (post exchange) to buy a package of diapers, a bottle of rubbing alcohol and a large can of floor paste wax. I recall thinking at three the next morning as I sat and spit-shined the floor with my roommate, Oothniel Oomituk of the Alaskan Scouts, that I'd kissed Ann goodbye at the Lansing railway station and kissed my ass goodbye at Fort Benning's railway station.

I was saddened when Oothniel disappeared one night. I knew he hadn't run away because he was already one of the top troops in our company, behind only the 38 Green Beret NCOs who were the first of their breed to go after their gold bars.

My tactical officer told me the next morning to report to sick call because Oothniel had contracted tuberculosis and that I needed to be tested. I sweated bullets for the next two days, until I learned that the test results turned out negative. I never saw him again, but I always hoped his TB was in remission, and that he was enjoying life while his sons took over the seal and whale hunting.

The program's high degree of difficulty completely absorbed my body and mind and time passed faster than I originally thought it would. Ann let me know that her term would end three days after my graduation date. I wrote back and told her that I'd meet her on campus and suggested taking a bus home the evening I'd arrive.

Winter Roses

Graduation day came and we received our diplomas from the Infantry School's chief training officer, a brigadier general. He gave a congratulatory presentation and also pitched the joys of coming back to Benning for advanced infantry training, Ranger school and jump school.

Because of my bad shoulder, I knew that I'd never qualify for Ranger or parachute training. In the hand-to-hand combat phase of our training, a Ranger had worsened the shoulder. I was able to hide the injury, even through some difficult and painful physical training exercises. By biting the proverbial bullet and with luck, I wasn't washed out of the program.

Successfully completing "Benning's School For Boys" made me think of applying for service in the regular Army. When I sent Ann a copy of a field manual that detailed the Army's expectations for a good officer's wife, however, she balked in a hurry. After I had the chance to read it back home, I understood immediately why she refused.

Her independent nature would collide head-on with the Army's need for regimentation and control and I wasn't about to make a choice between the two. In a subsequent conversation with Marie, she confirmed my decision as the right one for both of us.

I caught a lift with a classmate to Gary, Indiana, and from there took a bus to East Lansing. The trip was uneventful except for a stop to tour the Chickamauga battlefield, which helped us get off our graduation high. All we'd done was to get through a demanding training program. What these men did was to answer duty's call and pay for it with their blood and with their lives.

I arrived in East Lansing late that afternoon, just in time to walk over to the Psychology Department's lab and wait for Ann to finish her afternoon's work. I had no civilian clothes with me, so I wore my khakis. A bearded man who had to have been a professor came up the sidewalk carrying an overstuffed briefcase that must have weighed 20 pounds. I smiled and wished him

John Bingham

a good day. He returned the greeting by staring at my uniform and growling something unintelligible, a likely reaction to the escalating Vietnamese conflict. I wondered how he'd felt about his employer's secret training of the South Vietnamese in police administration, government policy and economics, but didn't bother to ask. I didn't have the time or patience for a harangue, especially one from an amateur.

Ann came running out and came straight into my arms for a huge hug and a long kiss. I swung her around and she grabbed my hand and told me that I had to come into the lab and see her final term experiment. The experiment was conditioning rats, and her pair had learned how to find their way through a complex maze and then press levers to first get a drink of water from a suspended tube and then a food pellet. I was impressed and remarked that the rats reminded me of what I'd been through in the past few months. We laughed and then walked back to her dorm so she could pack and we could get some dinner before catching our bus.

Our trip home was a lengthy one, which was fine with us. We used the time to share our school experiences, plan the wedding and catch up on the family news, then fell asleep in the reclining seats. The last I remembered before daybreak was Ann's head nodding on my chest and her arm around my waist. The pleasure of her loving warmth was indescribable and helped me bury my still-fresh memories of 13-mile runs in combat gear; hoping I wouldn't screw up in the student chain of command; tactical officers screaming and shouting in our ears; the chest-fluttering blasts of tank fire, antitank missiles, artillery fire, mortar fire, recoilless rifle fire; incessant sharp barks and chatter of rifles, machine guns, pistols, grenade launchers: in short, learning many, many ways to kill people without being killed.

The School tried its best to make the training realistic and largely succeeded. Through it all, the fear of board reviews and flunking was foremost in our minds.

Winter Roses

I was happy to have graduated, but I was much happier to be going home.

Shortly after reporting back to my unit, I received my orders to report to battalion HQ in Ishpeming for my commissioning ceremony. My reporting time was 1700 hours, so Frank and I would have plenty of time if we left by 1300 hours. I wore my civvies and brought along a starched and ironed pair of tailored khakis. I'd change into them in a restaurant men's room just before my reporting time so they'd still have a sharp crease with no wrinkles.

The drive was pleasant. We traded stories of our training and I remembered that he had enlisted right after high school in the Air Force and was then sent to Korea.

He said he was happy that he'd landed in supply as his MOS (Military Occupational Specialty) because it taught him the value of taking good care of the troops, be they privates or generals with no favoritism for the latter—even if they demanded expedited service and equipment, which they invariably did.

After he returned home, he'd married Elizabeth, his high school sweetheart. He then rather abruptly changed the subject to Marie and their new family, and how well the children had made the transition with their new parent.

I knew that Marie was overjoyed with her new life in officer base housing with Frank and the children; we'd been with them several times for dinner at the O-Club, baby-sitting the children and going to a good film with a drink later at a local club. I'd never seen her happier and if anyone ever deserved it, she did after suffering the physical and emotional abuse of her first husband.

The Del Mar remained their favorite club and Marie never failed to re-tell the story of how she and Frank had met and how angry she'd been with me for stalling their introduction with the "old soldiers" conversation at the bar with uncle George.

We'd sit at the bar when George was bartending, and he enjoyed sharing the story from his perspective along with others from his service in Burma and telling them what a mischievous brat I'd been in my childhood.

Frank also shared a story that had become one of his favorites: George telling him about an Air Force pilot who'd just been transferred to Kincheloe from a tour in Alaska. The man had trudged in covered with snow from an early-November storm and George told him to go to the end of the bar where he could shake the snow off his parka and warm up next to a heating vent. He ruefully told George that he had no idea that Sault Ste. Marie's weather could rival Alaska's in cold and snowfall. "Damn," he said. "I'll resign from the Air Force if I draw another base like this in my next tour." Frank delighted in telling George that the officer bitched so much that he was promoted and then immediately transferred to Minot AFB in North Dakota, and didn't know if he'd made good on his promise to resign.

Frank and I arrived at 1645 hours and went right to HQ rather than the restaurant. I opened the front door and looked around to find that no one was there. He waited outside the men's locker room while I ducked in and changed into my khakis. I stepped out and there was the battalion CO, a bird colonel, with a tall and cadaverous first lieutenant whom I guessed was his driver and orderly. I saluted them, they returned the salute and we introduced ourselves.

The lieutenant's hand was cold and wet, which turned out to be a mirror of his personality. Frank didn't tell him that he was a USAF captain and senior pilot. I resisted the temptation to wipe my hand on my pant leg.

Their first concern was how we managed to get in when the front doors were locked. I replied that we just walked in and that the doors were not locked.

Winter Roses

Perhaps there was a janitor on duty who'd neglected to lock up for the night? They said that was not possible. There was nothing more Frank or I wanted to say other than that someone had screwed up, which they already knew and would probably shoot the messengers if we said so.

The colonel told his aide to wait with Frank and me while he went into his office to make a couple of phone calls. So we did, and the conversation became strained when wet-hand turned to me and asked me what made me think I was qualified to become an officer? This took me by surprise since I'd been told I was there for my commissioning, not to be grilled over my credentials. Frank coughed while I gathered my wits and replied: "I just completed one of the toughest programs a man could go through and I was damned proud of it because I'd graduated 39th in my class, just behind the 38 Special Forces NCOs who were the first of their breed to enter Fort Benning's Infantry OCS program. Of the 220 who started, 108 graduated. My performance tells me that you, my company and my battalion should be quite happy to have me in the officers' ranks."

He wasn't ready to let go. "Very good, but you only completed the Infantry OCS. What about your engineering training?"

"Sir, I've had Advanced Combat Engineering training along with OJT. I'm well grounded in the basics and I'm also proficient in training, which is our primary mission. To supplement that and qualify for promotion in future years, I will enroll in Ft. Belvoir's Officer Engineering program. Meanwhile, my training at Ft. Benning gives me the ability to accomplish our secondary mission, which is to fight as infantry."

Frank cut off the lieutenant before he could open his mouth again. "Why don't you cut out the crap? John's already been through a hell of a lot more than you're throwing at him. He's earned his commission and we're here now to award him with his new gold bars."

This got the lieutenant's attention in a hurry. "Who in hell are you to tell me what to do?"

Replied Frank, "Glad you asked. I'm USAF Captain Frank Delaney to you and I'm telling you to back off. I came all the way here because John asked me to pin on his bars and I'm not leaving until I've done just that. I strongly suggest that we see the colonel right now and get on with the commissioning."

Now it was the lieutenant's turn in the barrel. He didn't know what to say to Frank and he finally came up with, "Well, sir, since you aren't in uniform, how was I to know you outrank me?"

"You didn't, but would knowing that have changed your rude behavior?"

He ignored the question and instead told us that the colonel should be free to see us now. After he made sure the colonel was ready, we followed him into the office, where I formally reported as ordered. The lieutenant told him that Frank was an Air Force captain, a B-52 pilot and aircraft commander stationed at Kincheloe AFB. The colonel commented that he knew many of the officers who were stationed at K.I. Sawyer AFB, another B-52 base that was close to both Ishpeming and Marquette. He asked Frank why he was there. The lieutenant started to answer, but the colonel cut him short, telling him that he had asked Captain Delaney, not him.

The lieutenant didn't say a thing, but his flushed-red face and neck shouted that he was boiling inside. I almost felt sorry for him.

Frank said he was pinning on my bars because my fiancé was still at Michigan State, finishing her final term before graduation. The colonel answered that this was a good alternative because not many young officers have a captain there to do the honors, let alone one who's a pilot and aircraft commander. He reached into his desk drawer, took out the gold bars, the Corps of Engineers castles, handed them to Frank and said, "There you go, captain. Let's get started, I have a dinner date tonight with my staff." Frank pinned the bar and castle on my collars, and stepped back. I stood at attention and saluted him. He snapped to attention, returned my salute and we shook hands. I then pivoted and exchanged salutes with the colonel and the lieutenant.

The colonel offered his congratulations along with a handshake. The lieutenant said nothing, which prompted the colonel to ask him if he'd like to say something appropriate before he left. The lieutenant then offered his congratulations. I thanked him and shook his cold, slimy hand once more. The "ceremony" was over.

Six

Another AFB, Another Wedding

*F*rank described it best on our ride home, saying that Mickey Mouse could have done better, and what kind of example did their boorish behavior set when they should be concentrating on words and ways to fire up a good young officer with plenty of potential? I agreed and still remember the experience for all the wrong reasons. But that didn't matter. Ann and I would be married in less than three months. I had my commission and was enrolled at the Sault branch of Michigan Tech. There, I'd completed my two-year major in business administration and then transferred to Michigan State the following year.

We looked forward to having Marie serve as Ann's maid of honor while Frank would be my "second best" man behind my kid brother Bob.

I was concerned that Frank couldn't stand to be second best in anything, but he agreed to this arrangement and he jokingly asked if we were having a formal military wedding.

He said he needed another excuse to wear his mess whites besides putting them on for base dinner dances and receptions for visiting high-ranking officers. I replied that I'd be lucky to save enough for our honeymoon, let alone pop for dress blues. A tux rental would have to do, but Frank would be welcome to wear his whites if he wanted to. At least our jackets would be the same color.

Winter Roses

Then in June of 1963, he was transferred to Puerto Rico's now-closed Ramey Air Force Base and Marie and the children were going with him. When the Air Force tells you to move, you move quickly; they were gone within the month with Frank leaving only a week after getting his orders. BUFF squadrons had to be kept at full staff level and mission-ready no matter what the inconvenience was to the pilots' families.

This left Marie with the responsibility of packing, making all of the shipment arrangements and scheduling the family's commercial flight. A Kincheloe lieutenant and his staff were available to help her, and their experience in military moves proved to be invaluable.

Ann said her goodbyes to them with a phone call from Michigan State. She couldn't make it home because the week they left was her finals week before graduation. She also had to complete her thesis, which consisted of a major study that dealt with stereotyping behavior among various ethnic groups. This turned out to be a major piece of new research, one of those successful college assignments where the professor takes the credit and earns tenure points while the student who designed the methodology, implemented the study, tabulated the results, and wrote the final report is lucky enough to get a credit in the preface. At least she could use it as reference for a future job.

Ann's parents called me to let me know the Delaneys had safely arrived and that Marie was throwing a fit because there were rats the size of cats infesting their base home's screened-in back porch that was planned as the bedroom for two of the children. Apparently there weren't any rat eradication specialists on duty that night.

Frank was on full alert and could be in the air for all she knew, so she and the children slept together in the master bedroom after dragging in three single beds for the boys while Jennifer slept with her in the double. They all wished that they were back in their ratless Upper Peninsula home, except for Mike, who thought he could make pets of the furry critters.

John Bingham

Ann and I were married as planned on August 17, and Marie and Frank's presents to us were memorable. Knowing our love of music and that we had an ancient record player, they gave us a very good stereo system which Frank had purchased through the Ramey AFB base exchange and had it shipped to Ann's parents so it would be waiting for us when we returned from our honeymoon. We couldn't play it anywhere near its maximum volume because our tiny apartment was connected directly to our landlord's home via a small covered walkway that channeled the sound right to their back door.

Our second gift from Marie and Frank was a hardbound edition of the Kama Sutra, which prompted us to ask them in our thank-you note if they thought we were gymnasts, contortionists, or both.

Marie also told us that she was taking flying lessons because Frank wanted her to be able to take the controls of a small aircraft should he suffer a heart attack or stroke and be unable to fly it. She was thrilled by this idea because she'd always wanted to learn how to fly.

A pilot friend of Frank's who taught flight lessons in his off-duty time volunteered to be her instructor pilot (IP). After breezing through her pre-flight training, she could hardly wait for her cockpit lessons. Her IP thought she was well on her way to earning her license and told her so, which fueled her confidence.

Her cockpit training got off to a good start, and she quickly got the feel of the controls. She did so well that her IP accelerated her training by scheduling her first landing after only three hours of basic flight practice. Assuming a successful landing, she'd then solo.

Her first attempt at landing brought everyone's hopes crashing to earth. At least it wasn't the aircraft that crashed. Later, her IP told Frank that her kamikaze descent had taken him by surprise and it was the first time he'd ever tried to stand up in the cockpit, uttering the classic pilot's epitaph of "Oh shit!" As the runway raced up at them, he had grabbed the controls just in time to level the aircraft for a touch-and-go.

She had zero depth perception, which her IP realized after he had narrowly averted catastrophe.

Frank was disappointed to learn that she'd never be able to fly.

Years later, Ann and I experienced our own "Oh Shit!" Marie moment one night in downtown Phoenix, when she was driving us to a restaurant that still permitted smoking on the premises. She was an inveterate chain-smoker who'd drive for miles to find a restaurant that still allowed smoking, because those restaurants were becoming few and far between. I was seated in back with her friend Jim, while Ann was in the front seat with Marie. En route, she said that the children had been after her to quit driving and she told them she was a better driver than any of them. She then turned and asked Ann whether she thought she should stop driving. Ann couldn't answer because she was frozen in fear.

At that second, Jim and I saw what Ann saw. We were bearing down far too fast on a minivan that was stopped at a red light. Ann screamed, "Marie, look out!" Marie stood on the brakes and wheeled suddenly into the left-turn lane, stopping just before we smashed the mini-van through the stoplight and into the next block. With that maneuver, we all let out a sigh of relief and fell off the adrenaline cliff. All Marie could do was manage a nervous giggle and state the obvious: "That was a close one!"

Jim couldn't contain himself. "Goddammit, Marie, I keep telling you that you shouldn't be driving but you won't listen. If this doesn't scare the hell out of you like it did to us, then I'm never riding with you again. Now for our sake and yours, pay closer attention to your driving, OK?"

Marie answered, "My depth perception must be getting worse."

She turned into the downtown Phoenix traffic flow as soon as she thought she had an opening, which forced the screech of brakes and a blowing horn as she cut off a driver coming faster than she'd thought.

Jim hissed between his teeth. "She'll be damned lucky if she doesn't kill herself and all of us with her." I later asked him what he and the family were going to do about her atrocious driving, and he replied that he'd call a family meeting as soon as Ann and I returned to Michigan. "Hopefully," he said, "We can all meet with her to express our concern and ask—make that demand--that she surrender her keys. I'm also thinking of playing a card that she used on her dad to stop his dangerous driving and that's enlisting the help of her insurance company. If she won't listen to us, maybe the threat of losing her car insurance or paying sky-high insurance premiums without remedial senior citizen training will convince her." I wished him luck.

After we'd returned to Michigan, we called him and asked him if Marie had agreed to stop driving. He said that she hadn't, so he no longer goes anywhere with her unless he drives. Ann also told me after we'd returned that she had told Marie to slow down and pay attention to her driving because she was afraid to ride with her.

Following Marie's flight training wash-out, Frank decided to see if any of the children showed an aptitude for flying. He began taking them up for short hops with basic maneuvers to see how they reacted and coached them through brief intervals at the flight controls. One way or another, he was determined to have a back-up pilot onboard should he become incapacitated in mid-flight. He also vowed to have back-up should he ever fly two-seater military aircraft.

The results of this test were mixed. While the children all loved their recreational flights over lush Puerto Rico, Frank, Jr.'s stomach rebelled during his turn at the controls. Whether he had airsickness or was simply overstressed by trying to both emulate and please his dad was moot; he had suddenly vomited, spraying the cockpit and even his dad.

Winter Roses

Frustrated by his experiment's inability to test the pre-teens' aptitude for flying—which Marie had warned him would be a futile effort—Frank swallowed his pride and cleaned the cockpit with Marie's help. She told us later that, with Frank retching while wiping up the mess, she would wait for a better time to remind him that she'd warned him.

She did ask him if he had put the Piper Tri-Pacer through more aggressive maneuvers than the other children experienced, perhaps because his expectations for young Frank were higher? He responded with a glare and a half-coughing, half-gagging fit that drove him out of the cockpit to get some needed fresh air.

Never again did he try to make pilots of his children and instead resigned himself to taking fewer recreational flights without a backup. Instead he depended upon the results of his stringent Air Force flight physicals, knowing that his chances of sudden incapacitation by heart attack, stroke, or other sudden medical emergency were small.

A good friend of ours from the Sault, Dave Lundeen, was also in Puerto Rico and he visited Marie and Frank often. He was with the engineering firm that designed and built the gigantic Arecibo radio telescope. He had plenty of street smarts when I knew him in the Sault and they served him well in Puerto Rico. Since he'd been in-country for almost a year before the Delaneys arrived, he knew the "respectable" rum shacks—"respectable" meaning that you weren't likely to be killed or mugged while you were there, although you sometimes had to pay a parking attendant protection money if you didn't want to walk home.

At first, Frank held back from joining Dave on his jungle adventures since the shacks were off-limits and no exceptions were made for their quality and kind treatment of Air Force guests. Marie, however, got bored and joined Dave in trying to persuade Frank to go to at least one so they'd get a better understanding and appreciation of their Puerto Rican hosts and their shared zeal for adventure. Her persistence carried the day and she looked forward to a weekend night out, a refreshing break from the same faces and bar dice at the O-Club.

Frank, on the other hand, looked forward to getting in and getting out of the shack before he got caught. He'd made sure with Dave that the Air Police didn't regularly sweep the shack to bust errant airmen. Dave replied that he'd never seen them raid the shack they'd visit. This was a good sign, meaning that there were plenty of juicier targets for the APs on a Saturday night. Dave also said that he'd seen and met officers and their wives or dates in there, which made Frank feel better.

Off they went in Dave's company-furnished car, and their adventure did not disappoint. Entering the side door and inhaling the fumes of raw rum made Marie dizzy. She whispered to Frank that the smell reminded her of jet fuel. He agreed and made her laugh when he said that the Air Force would know where to come should there ever be a fuel shortage. "Be careful when you drink that stuff, " he added. "You might become a human flame thrower when you light your cigarette."

Frank was pleased to see two other officers there, along with several airmen from the base. He was able to chat with them over a rum Bacardi. Marie loved the daiquiris and ambience, especially the jungle atmosphere and a Latin music combo.

"This shack is one of the classier ones," Dave told her. "Instead of a tin shack with a dirt floor, what we have here is one made of concrete blocks with a tin roof and a dirt floor. You can even get a decent brand of rum instead of taking your chances with the bootleg stuff," he explained. "That was the smell that hit you when we entered." Marie asked Dave if it was dangerous to smoke in there, and he laughed, saying that there were plenty of cracks and holes in the structure to aerate the shack and dissipate the smoke and fumes.

Frank kept a wary eye on the barefoot patrons standing at the bar, some of whom were leering at Marie. A few reminded him of characters he'd seen in the

Winter Roses

pirate movies of his youth, except they had no weapons that he could see. All of them were dressed in colorful shirts and presented a dizzying blur of moving colors.

Dave noticed Frank studying the shack's regulars and told him not to worry, that they know the risk of starting a bar fight over Marie; it would land them in prison, which would be a fate worse than hell. "Besides," he added, "They already know that I'd kick their asses all over the floor. I've been here with a pretty woman myself and they found this out the hard way. One even tried to pull a knife on me and I flattened him with my chair before he could make a move and then kicked him in the balls while he was still down.

"By this time, the owner had brought out an antique shotgun that must have been stolen from Moro Castle. No one knew if it still fired or would blow up in the owner's face, but it managed to quiet the bar in a hurry." Both Frank and Marie allowed as how they felt better with Dave's comforting remarks.

The hookers who were working the bar for tricks were intriguing; Marie had never seen women ply their trade so earnestly and so obviously. Watching them score with young airmen who'd take them to their cars and then return in just a few minutes suggested strongly that the johns were not getting their money's worth. She asked Dave about this and he replied, "How in hell would I know? The last thing I need is a social disease." Dave was always direct. He was also 6' 3" and built like an interior lineman, which further helped improve Marie and Frank's perception of security.

Dave and Marie cleared the dirt "dance floor" by trying to mambo. The locals laughed, cheered and clapped as the two gringos stumbled through their steps and bowed to their appreciative audience when the music ended.

When Frank told Dave that he danced with the grace of a buffalo, Marie chimed in to say that he was amazingly light on his feet. He laughed and said, "A Fred Astaire I ain't, but thank you for your kind words." The house brought them a free round for their efforts and they settled down to enjoy the music and the daiquiris. Dave pointed out that this shack was so upscale that it even had ice.

They didn't have much time to relax. The front door burst open and three APs rushed through the front door, blowing their whistles and shouting to everyone to stay in their places.

Big Dave saved the evening for Frank and for all of the base personnel who were still in the bar. With a booming voice that quieted everyone, he stood up and announced that he was the boss for the final construction phase of the giant radio telescope and he was treating his crew and their wives to a night out. "They've been working damned hard," he said. "This is our first stop on our way to dinner at the Sheraton.

"We were just getting ready to leave so we can get there before they cancel our reservations. C'mon, boys and girls, let's go, I'm hungry enough to eat the south end of a northbound skunk!"

With a sweeping motion of his big right arm, he headed for the door and all of the gringos fell in behind him. Marie went out the door hanging on to Frank's arm, laughing at Dave's audacity and stumbling over the wooden stoop. They went to their waiting cars and drove off to their "dinner rendezvous at the Sheraton" while the APs stood there slack-jawed in stunned silence. Dave honked the horn and saluted them as he drove by. They returned the salute, prompting even more uproarious laughter from Marie.

Even Frank had to laugh at the situation, which by then seemed like a rum-fueled zany dream. "Dave," he said, "You deserve the base BSA Award of the Year!" Dave asked, "What's the BSA...Boy Scouts of America?"

"The annual Ramey Bullshit Award, which is an honor bestowed by the NCO Club on people who save their bacon from the frying pan." Dave thought for a moment and said, "You know, I was always good at bullshit. A good BSer can go a long, long way in this world; just look at Congress for proof of that." Marie said, "Maybe you can run for Congress." "Naw," answered Dave. "I don't have other necessary qualifications like lying, cheating, backstabbing, and talking out of both sides of my mouth at the same time. I'd sooner become a priest. My congregations would love my sermons and I'd enjoy saving souls, not bacon. But I was a buck-ass sergeant in the Army National Guard, so maybe that would help qualify me for the award."

Frank's chief mechanic nominated Dave, and he won by unanimous vote of the base's enlisted men. Only a few of them had been there to witness Dave in action, but that was enough. The word spread quickly throughout the entire base and no one could think of any better-qualified candidates.

The following Saturday night at the NCO Club, he put two men in the base hospital for back injuries sustained while they were carrying him around the club on their shoulders.

While he appreciated this hero's welcome, he was concerned about their injuries and sneaked in beers to help ease their pain and speed their recovery, pissing off the head nurse because the combination of beer and painkillers could have proved deadly.

Dave didn't argue the point. He simply bellowed in his best sergeant's command voice that the beers were on him when they recovered. The whole ward erupted in cheers and whistles, thus cementing his legendary status as the best winner ever of the coveted and prestigious Ramey BSA Award. He was even awarded a plaque to prove it.

———

Marie's adventures continued with one she'd particularly wanted—a romantic weekend getaway at a local golf resort. She told Frank that she'd played golf with her father and wanted to take up the game again. This was a stretch; all she and her dad had ever done was hit a couple buckets of balls and putt on a practice green behind the golf club in Deadwood, South Dakota. They then played nine holes, where she learned the basic rules and showed an aptitude for the game by beating her father.

Frank bought two sets of hardly-used clubs from one of his crew who would soon be rotating back to the mainland. They booked a golf weekend package at a local ocean-side hotel that had a beautiful, 18-hole course which Frank believed he could at least par. Friends had recommended it as very player-friendly, perfect for novices and more experienced golfers alike. Having played a little golf with his crew members, Frank felt he belonged in the latter category.

After a relaxing evening of drinks and dining on the hotel veranda under the stars, they went upstairs to their room. The champagne on ice, a red rose and chocolate truffles Frank had ordered were waiting for them. The champagne hit Marie hard and she giggled while they helped each other undress and climb into bed to enjoy the best sex they'd had since their honeymoon. They fell asleep in each other's arms and woke up refreshed and ready for a good breakfast, followed by nine holes of golf to ease back into the game. In the afternoon they'd try the next nine and then the full 18 early the following morning.

Following breakfast, they went to the locker rooms and dressed in their new golf togs that they purchased at the pro shop the previous afternoon.

From the first tee, Marie knew she was in for a long morning. She chalked up her straight drive to the cup as a lucky shot and Frank's huge slice into the rough—accompanied by a teeth-clenching "Goddammit!"—as just a shot that everyone has to deal with, especially for someone who hasn't played the game for a long time.

When Frank tried to hit the ball out of the rough, he rapped it off a big palm that had partially obstructed his view and watched it ricochet across the green into the rough on the other side of the fairway. As if to punish the tree, he slammed his four-iron into its trunk, sending a sharp, vibrating pain from his hands right up into his arms. More cursing followed.

Winter Roses

After five more vicious swings, he finally put the ball on the green. Marie sank her putt—six feet from the cup—and then watched Frank putt the ball past the cup from 15 feet away, sending it 20 more feet down the backside of the gently sloping green. Two more tries and he finally sank the ball. By that time he was completely frustrated and mad as a wet hornet. He picked up his golf bag and slung it up the fairway as far as he could, sending the clubs flying. Marie couldn't stand it and looked away, not daring to say anything about his play. Encouraging to him to calm down and relax would only make him angrier.

By the fourth hole and two more club throws, she was ready to head back to the clubhouse with or without him. He had taken so many bad shots that the foursome behind them finally ran out of patience and asked if they could play through. Marie waved them to come up while she and Frank sat on the benches near the tees. As they passed, he forced a quick, sick smile while Marie commented on the beautiful weather. He concentrated on fixing a broken nail with the file on his Swiss Army knife as the foursome teed off, all with good lies. One was on the green and the others were close enough for long putts. He correctly suspected that they knew as he did that his wild play had caused the hold-up and that they had likely seen his club-tossing antics.

When the foursome passed, Marie said what should have been obvious, that she'd never play golf with him again unless he promised that he'd play as a gentleman and not as a complete jerk. With that, she shouldered her bag and began her long walk back to the clubhouse. Frank was too angry at himself to walk back with her and too proud to say he was sorry and ask her to come back. He knew that she'd be too upset to be anywhere near him, especially when he was still in a foul mood. He sat on the bench until he cooled down enough to head back to the clubhouse and apologize for his boorish behavior. *Besides,* he thought. *I learned that I can't stand playing this goddam game. At least I learned something today.*

He walked into the clubhouse through the lounge door and found Marie at the bar nursing a Bloody Mary. He walked over, took the barstool next to her and signaled the bartender that he'd have the same. Marie broke the silence. "If

I'd have known you'd get so angry just because I was beating you, I'd have slacked off and let you win a couple of holes."

The golf clubs went into the hall closet. Soon after, when Frank was somewhere else on a training mission, Marie sold them to a couple who wanted to take up the sport. He never asked where they'd gone. But he did ask Marie if she'd like to play handball with him. She told him that she wouldn't play tiddlywinks with him.

The Strategic Air Command CO's secretary alerted the base commander that the command and staff officers would conduct a planning conference at Ramey in mid- January. The conference would last a week.

Both Frank and Marie thought that the top doggies would enjoy much more credibility among the troops if they scheduled their winter conferences in winter climates, such as Alaska, Minnesota or North Dakota. Someone in a high command position must have realized how a week in Puerto Rico looked like a top brass boondoggle to the enlisted personnel, so SAC's sergeant major and his wife came along as the figurehead who'd represent the enlisted men and women. His duty was to make sure that the rank-and-file knew the brass was working day and night on issues of great strategic importance, which was true enough.

Recalling his own days as an enlisted man, Frank wondered how the sergeant major of the entire Strategic Air Command could possibly communicate what transpires during a VIP powwow to the enlisted men and women, let alone relate it to their needs. He left this train of thought behind by realizing that they probably didn't give a damn, anyway.

Winter Roses

Marie regularly took the children to the base beach so they could swim, play and search for seashells. Jennifer in particular became a strong swimmer and soon graduated to the base pool where she started winning medals for the swim team and was scouted as a candidate for the Junior Olympics. This was not to be, because Frank and Marie couldn't afford the cost and they'd soon be transferred, anyway.

Frank's orders for jet fighter training and qualification at Williams AFB in Mesa, Arizona, finally came through. He'd wanted to be fighter-qualified since a pilot's unique perspective and point of view was a must for his upcoming Vietnam duty as a Forward Air Controller (FAC)--which his orders now stated would become his primary MOS (Military Occupational Specialty). He rationalized the move because it got him out of SAC. Since a FAC's primary mission was one of search-and-destroy, his end of the bargain would be to fly a slow and unarmed two-seater Cessna modified for combat FAC duty, the O-1E "Bird Dog."

Flying the O-1, he would seek out enemy ground forces and their equipment, weapons, and munitions, and destroy them by coordinating and directing USAF fighter-bombers to the targets he'd mark with white phosphorous rockets. His directives to "Hit my smoke!" and "Cleared in hot!" would release the fighter-bombers that came from USAF bases in Vietnam and USN aircraft carriers in the South China Sea to dive and bomb or strafe the enemy. Another of his important FAC roles would be close-in air support for friendly ground troops who were under attack from enemy ground forces and needed the "airborne artillery" that he could provide.

After FAC duty, he reasoned, perhaps he'd be given a chance to become a full-time fighter jock and even get a shot at a senior flight command position.

Meanwhile, along with the rest of the base's personnel, he began to prepare for the top dogs' visit. Base operations were turned upside down as the emphasis switched from training to cleaning and painting, with special arrangements for lodging and guarding the senior officers and their wives in the same luxury hotel where Marie and Frank had stayed for their golf weekend.

He saw to it that his B-52 was factory-clean with chipped paint touched up and even an Air-Wick deodorant bottle tucked into the map pocket. This turned out to smell even worse than the years of sweat that permeated the seats, so he got rid of it. He thought that the smell of hard use was preferable and at least wouldn't make any inspector's eyes water. Bad decision. The inspector—a major—told Frank that he ought to stick some Air-Wick into the map pocket, because the stink of who-knows-how-many sweaty butts in the seat's fabric was overpowering.

Frank resisted the temptation to ask the major if he went around sniffing the pilot's and co-pilot's seats during all of his inspections and instead nodded, took his notepad out of his shoulder pocket, pretended to write it down for future action, and recalled his tour of duty in Florida when a huge cockroach on his B-47's instrument panel got his attention in a hurry. He'd heard that these "palmetto bugs" were big, bold and everywhere. He became a believer after that experience.

When Marie took the children to the beach early one morning, she learned that the brass had probably arrived the night before even though the arrival date had been kept a secret for security reasons.

A sizeable portion of the beach was now roped off. Several new "lifeguards" walked the perimeter and tried to send her further down the beach where the real lifeguards had set up shop. Before she and the children departed for the "new" beach, her journalist's instinct kicked in. She walked over to one of the men and asked him what he was guarding. "I can't tell you, ma'am," he replied. "It's supposed to be secret."

"That rope is useless protection for a secret Air Force piece of beach property. Where's the razor wire, weapons and guard dogs?"

Winter Roses

"Please, ma'am, no more questions. I'm not at liberty to answer them. All I can tell you is that the rope will be gone by noon."

She persisted. "Can you tell me if this has anything to do with the grand pooh-bah's visit?"

He surrendered. "Ma'am," he answered, "I swore that I wouldn't tell anyone about this, but no one said anything about showing people what's inside our perimeter." Marie laughed, and he did, too. He escorted her and the children inside the enclave, where they walked down to the wet sand and saw dozens of seashells scattered about. She recognized the cowries, conches, and miters, and saw others that were equally beautiful and very likely prized by collectors. The children were awed and asked if they could take some home.

The guard told them they could each select one, providing they left the area immediately and swore that they wouldn't tell anyone where they got them. He urged them to be quick, because the gate to the beach where they'd entered was about to be closed and the area declared off-limits. He said that the gate should have been closed before they arrived but no one had anticipated early-morning visitors and swimmers.

Marie caught on quickly. She knew from Frank that the senior officers' wives would be with them, and that entertainment for them would be a must. What could be better than a seashell hunt on the base beach, especially one that guaranteed a good selection of some of the most beautiful shells in the world? She also guessed that a seashell expert would be there to tell the ladies all about their "lucky finds," and how to care for them when they returned home with their treasures.

She shared her thoughts with her new lifeguard friend about what was really happening for whom that morning and he denied any further knowledge of the plans and the happenstance of good-looking, well-built lifeguards.

He did say that the ladies would arrive and depart by command and staff cars and a seaside cabana would be set up and open for light seafood lunches and cocktails after the "hunt" was completed. Once more he asked her for secrecy, since the carefully staged seashell search could soon become a bad base joke.

Which it did, even though Marie had kept her word and not told anyone except Frank, who wouldn't risk his career by being tagged as the source of the leak. Perhaps one of the "Beach Boys" had told his wife or girlfriend about the big shell hunt scam and she ratted it out. What no one had thought about was pacifying the two ladies who argued over possession of the same shell, each claiming she found it first. It didn't help when one of the women tried to pull her husband's rank and the poor lifeguard had to somehow please both. He got them to agree to a coin toss, a solution about which they weren't happy but at least they accepted. Of course, this story also got around the base quickly.

One more glance at the well-muscled "lifeguards" on duty strongly suggested to Marie that their torsos and biceps would not only discourage any interlopers from entering, but they also provided eye candy for the ladies. To be fair to the generals and colonels, she thought that a bikini bombshell or two or three might be nice for their viewing pleasure, but they'd be in conference or on the golf course and likely wouldn't have time for such pleasures. Later, she told her lady friends that the brass should have put girls on the course at selected tees, where they could scrub the generals' balls. Her friends blew their drinks through their noses at that one.

Whatever, the base commander and his PR officer were glad that the "news" didn't make the newswires as an example of wasting taxpayer dollars on spoiled senior officers' prima ballerinas. Not as juicy as thousand-dollar toilets, but enough to piss off the President, the Pentagon, the White House, Congress, and maybe even a few alert taxpayers.

Marie knew that there were hundreds of dollars' worth of seashells on that beach. A rumor was going around the base to the effect that the base commander had the good sense not to order a contingent of airmen to comb all of the island beaches for exotic shells. It would have been far easier to quietly divert O-Club operating funds and send a team of sharp young officers and NCOs to Miami and buy the shells they needed from beachside souvenir shopkeepers.

She wondered at the time what other ginned-up activities awaited the ladies but then thought maybe she'd rather not know.

The formal reception and dinner dance at the O-Club to close the conference was an event that eclipsed anything the base personnel had ever experienced. Neither bar whiskey nor inexpensive beers and wines were served; every beverage was top shelf. Dark and light rum drinks were the house specialty and guaranteed a lively event. The base band helped the festivities along by playing to near-perfection their Latin numbers for the few who ventured out on the floor to show off their Arthur Murray mambos, cha-chas and sambas.

Frank thought that learning to dance these intricate numbers was a waste of time, especially for senior officers who had more important things to do such as preparing for nuclear Armageddon. But that was Frank in those days. He was determined to get ahead, get out of SAC and become a fighter pilot, and he worked and studied hard to achieve his goals, even getting his master's degree in business administration from Inter-American University in Puerto Rico. I responded that perhaps nobody needed a break from such a burden like these men and women, including getting away from their dark reality every now and then by boogying down on the dance floor. He grudging agreed that this line of reasoning was a possibility but drew the line at hundred-dollar seashells.

Instead of dancing, Marie was drinking and chatting on the veranda with the ladies while their husbands were busy schmoozing. While Frank's favorite euphemism for social networking was KBA, short for "Kissing Brass Ass," he knew it was a must for advancement and discovered that he was getting quite good at it even if he hated it. He particularly resented his commanders asking questions about his personal life, but also knew they considered this in their evaluations for promotion as a means of determining a candidate's stability in the cockpit and at his desk. Unlike some of his peers, he never once considered encouraging his beautiful wife to flirt with the generals in the hope of scoring promotion points for him. Besides, he correctly reasoned that fiery Marie would have punched him in the nose if he ever dared to try. The ancient jokes about the colonels with the lieutenants' wives and the lieutenants with the colonels' wives held some truth, in every branch of the armed forces.

It was probably a good thing that Frank didn't golf with them during the day's big tournament.

He was getting along just fine with the guests, several of whom were interested in his Korean War service as an enlisted man and then his subsequent commission through ROTC. They were particularly interested in talking about his B-47 flying days, especially those who'd also flown them. Some ventured that his experience as an enlisted man was a real asset in understanding the needs of the troops in the ranks. He didn't argue with them because he knew their observations were true. To them, he'd say that he used the words "Good Troop" as the best compliment he could give whether to an airman or SAC's Commander-In-Chief.

They liked this, and he knew it when General Powell, the SAC CIC, came over, introduced himself and told Frank that he understood that he'd called him a good troop and wondered what he'd done to deserve such high praise from an up-and-coming officer. They chatted for a few minutes about their mutual service in Korea where the four-star had first piloted the P-51 Mustang and then the Lockheed Shooting Star before moving up to the F-86 Sabrejet.

The let-your-hair-down camaraderie of pilots and their tales flowed along with the drinks until Marie came over and tugged at his sleeve, whispering to him that it was important that they talk for a moment. He excused himself and they went over to a corner of the ballroom where she told him that a three-star had propositioned her. While he noticed that she was a little tipsy, he couldn't ignore her story.

He would never hesitate to go in harm's way and a face-off with a general—even a three-star--would be no exception. He took a deep breath and walked a fast and straight line to the offending officer to let him know what he thought of his inexcusable behavior.

The general—who was wiping something from his pants and shoes with paper napkins from the h'ors d'ouevres table—glanced up to greet Frank. He extended his hand while telling him that a woman who'd obviously been over-served had spilled her drink on his dress pants and mirror-shined shoes after sharing her pride in her husband, who was an enlisted man in Korea and was now a BUFF pilot here at Ramey. "She told me that his enlisted experience had taught him a lot about leadership, and I told her that I couldn't agree with her more, especially since I also came up through the ranks. With that, she must have got a little excited. She started to talk and gestured with her drink hand, and that's when I got the rum bath. Well, no damage done and I was glad to learn how proud she was of her husband. We all need spousal support like that. Maybe with a little less enthusiasm and a few less drinks."

The officer smiled at Frank and asked how he liked his tour in the subtropics.

Frank was completely disarmed, but still managed to stammer out why he'd come over to see the general in the first place and ask the general if he'd made any such advance.

The three-star replied, "I appreciate your direct talk, your honesty and your guts, captain, which I consider to be leadership qualities I look for in my officers and NCOs. But I'll tell you flat-out that I made no such advance. Even if I'd wanted to, my orderly was with me when your wife and I were talking. Go ask him if you don't believe me. He's right over there by the foyer, talking with my wife."

Frank glanced over to see a tall, good-looking captain engaged in conversation with a pretty blonde woman who immediately reminded him of Elizabeth. This rattled and further disarmed him. "Sir," he said, "I appreciate your honesty and apologize for my wife's behavior. I'll be glad to cover the cleaning bill." The general chuckled and told him there was no need to apologize, that the incident was over as far as he was concerned.

With that, Frank saluted the general, who returned it and then wished him good luck. "No offense intended," he added, "But I hope for your sake and your family's sake that your wife doesn't have a drinking problem. Being a SAC pilot's wife can be a very lonely and often unnerving life, and I've seen a lot of spouses turn to alcohol to help calm their fears. If you'd like, I'll be happy to have my secretary arrange a good contact for counseling and help."

Frank answered that he didn't think that offer was necessary at this time, but he'd certainly follow up with the general's kind offer if Marie started drinking more and more often. He thanked the general and then returned to Marie, who was now seated in an easy chair in the lounge and nursing another drink.

"You were talking with him a long time," she said. "What did he tell you?"

"He told me that he did no such thing and that his orderly was there with you to verify it. He did say that you managed to spill your drink all over his dress pants and shoes, and that you appeared to have been over-served, which is a nice way of saying that you're drunk, which I can plainly see. I think that it's best to take you home now so you can sleep it off and avoid embarrassing yourself, me, and any more generals."

"Oh, bullshit," Marie replied. "The general's bootlicker was not with us. You just don't get it, do you?"

Winter Roses

"Get what?"

"See, I told you that you didn't get it. Fine, let's go home."

She stood up and wobbled on her high heels. He took her arm to steady her and they managed to get across the room, out the door and into the car without her stumbling. When they arrived home, Frank told the babysitter that Marie got sick and had to come home. He half-carried her upstairs into the bedroom, made sure she could undress and get into her pajamas without help and then got her between the sheets. She fell immediately asleep. More likely passed out, he thought.

He pulled the coverlet over her and left the bedroom without a bedtime kiss.

After making sure that the babysitter could stay for another hour, he returned to the club just in time to hear General Powell finish his after-dinner speech by thanking and complimenting the base brass, the pilots and their air and ground crews for their hard work on behalf of their country by serving with "the mightiest deterrent force in history…the Strategic Air Command!"

Everyone in the room stood to applaud, and Frank wondered why the general had not bothered to recognize the base's fighter squadron and its pivotal role in making sure that the BUFFS could carry out their mission. Without them there'd be no success and the base might be burnt toast, and the general knew well this hard-learned axiom of aerial warfare. Was this just another example of SAC-TAC rivalry? His fighter-pilot buddies would be pissed and justifiably so, he knew that much.

Before leaving, he cornered the general's orderly and asked him whether he was with the general and Marie "during their conversation." The captain quickly—too quickly?—said that he was and that Marie had spilled her drink on the general's uniform. As to the alleged proposition, he confirmed there was none.

He wondered on his drive home who was telling the truth....Marie or the general? The orderly's response sounded a little too rehearsed, a well-oiled response in defense of his boss, who could have briefed him on the situation as soon as Frank was out of sight.

He thought about this for a long time.

Thinking about Ramey's fighter pilots reminded him that his orders for training should be coming soon and he wasn't disappointed. He was called into his squadron commander's office a couple of weeks after the top brass had left. The colonel told him that SAC needed top pilots like him and that he'd be missed, but wished him the best of luck and success in both his fighter qualification training and in combat as a FAC in Vietnam. Frank thanked him and told him truthfully that he'd enjoyed serving under him because he put the needs of his officers and enlisted men and women on equal footing when it came to making sure they had everything required to accomplish the mission. They exchanged salutes and Frank executed his best "about face." He left feeling as if he was already in a fighter cockpit.

On the way home, he stopped at the BX (Base Exchange) and bought two bottles of Dom Perignon and two big lobsters to celebrate. For the children, he brought two large pizzas. While Marie and the children helped him celebrate his new career direction, they had mixed feelings about leaving their island paradise. Their memories of sun-filled summer days at the beaches and their other activities—Jennifer's competition swimming, karate, judo, Little League baseball, horseback riding, judo, tennis, golf, even the pet rats—last to this day.

The kids learned they'd be going to Phoenix where their parents would buy a home, so they read all they could about life in the Valley of the Sun. While they knew it would be hot, at least they wouldn't have the cloying humidity of their Puerto Rican home. There'd be plenty of year-round activities, such as volleyball, baseball, golf, and tennis. For relief from the constant heat, they could even escape for a weekend of skiing at Flagstaff, and Arizona's spectacular natural wonders provided the family with unlimited sightseeing opportunities. Marie especially couldn't wait; for her, Puerto Rico's dripping subtropical climate was becoming insufferable.

Frank would be busy training for his fighter pilot qualification, and he relished the thought of the work ahead as pure pleasure, especially his cockpit time in the F-100 Super Sabre fighter--affectionately known to USAF fighter pilots as the "Hun," which was short for the aircraft's 'One hundred' designation. Following his qualification, he would move on to his FAC training in Florida. After a short leave, he would depart for his one-year tour of duty in Vietnam.

After brief visits in Sault Ste. Marie with Marie's parents and Frank, Jr. and Jennifer's grandparents in their home near Traverse City, Marie and the children flew to the Valley of the Sun and went on a house-shopping tour arranged by a local realtor who'd worked for the base families and had a good idea of their needs as well as affordable price ranges. They bought a nice ranch in Phoenix, in a well-kept neighborhood. Ann and I didn't have the chance to see them when they visited with Marie's parents in the Sault. We were in East Lansing, living on-campus in a married housing apartment.

Ann had taken a job as a social worker with Michigan's Department of Social Services while I was a full-time student. This was a HHT (Help Hubby Through) program supplemented by MSU's general scholarship fund and my meager income from various part-time jobs. A treat for us was frequent visits with Ann's older brother Ron, an ex-Marine who was working on his master's degree. He and his wife Janet lived in a married housing complex across campus. Work, study and our limited income in those days precluded trips to Phoenix to visit the family; our Saturday night celebration often consisted of sharing a couple of quarts of beer and extra-sharp cheddar on Ritz crackers with Ron and Janet while watching "Star Trek."

John Bingham

Marie kept us informed with her breezy letters, learning the adventures of the children in their oven-hot environment, and Frank's flying adventures in his F-100 Super Sabre, including a thundering pass complete with barrel rolls through the Grand Canyon, which was strictly forbidden. He got caught since he was the only pilot in the vicinity at the time reports started coming in about the wild man in the fighter who was trying to split visitors' eardrums and upset the Havasupai Indians who lived at the canyon's bottom.

His spur-of-the-moment flight of fancy understandably offended the tribal elders since canyon lands were sacred to their people. After landing, he was passed through his practice mission debriefing and ordered instead to report directly to his commanding officer, who was waiting for him along with his instructor pilot.

Frank said his ass-chewing that day was the worst he'd ever been through and he considered himself fortunate to still be in the program. He admitted his guilt and his only defense was that he'd always wanted to fly through the canyon in a hot fighter, that his wish got the better of him and that he'd never again pull a stunt like that. He also promised to personally go down to the canyon's floor and apologize to the tribal elders.

He managed to prove once again that honesty is the best policy; his CO grudgingly forgave him and kept the incident out of his personnel file. Instead, he got off with a warning which also included his CO's promise to his instructor pilot that he'd also be held responsible should there be any more flight rules broken.

Frank, Marie and the children took the donkey ride down to the canyon floor several weeks later, bringing gifts of good cigars for the tribal elders, quality costume jewelry for their wives and candy treats for the children. The elders were especially pleased that he'd taken the time to visit them and they gladly accepted his apology, telling him they were happy that he was helping to protect them

Winter Roses

and prophesizing that someday he would be a great sky-warrior and chieftain. The tribe's chief then took out the peace pipe, broke the expensive cigars into tiny fragments, packed them into the pipe and lit it. After a chant that mesmerized Marie and the children, he passed the pipe to Frank, who barely kept from choking on the sharp-edged cigar tobacco. He didn't even inhale the cigarettes he pretended to smoke, let alone suck unfiltered cigar tobacco into his lungs.

He never forgot this encounter and gained a new appreciation and respect for the ways of native Americans. He thought the experience—along with his memory of working with South Koreans during his tour in the Korean War-- would be a good reminder to treat the South Vietnamese peoples with as much dignity and respect as he could possibly muster. He hoped he could reconcile this desire with the fact that he'd be there to direct the bombing of Viet Cong guerrillas and invading NVA.

Causing collateral damage on friendly soil—if there was such a thing in South Vietnam--would likely be unavoidable.

The visit was also big medicine for Marie and the children, who were wide-eyed at the experience of meeting real-life Indians, their wives and their families—who were a far cry from the stereotypes they'd seen in motion pictures.

After completing his fighter qualification, Frank moved on to Florida for his FAC training while the family stayed behind.

He qualified on both the O-1 "Bird Dog"--one of the FACs' primary light observation aircrafts during the Vietnam War—and the O-2 ("Oscar Deuce") twin-boomed, light observation aircraft that had both conventional and pusher propellers.

He learned the related tasks of managing his assigned airspace during the simulated heat and chaos of combat, often while simultaneously communicating on three radio frequencies: one for directing the Air Force and Navy fighter-bomber strikes and then assessing their effectiveness in accomplishing the mission; another to provide liaison, air cover and support for ground forces in contact with the enemy; and the third to communicate and coordinate with the orbiting tactical air command aircraft that obtained and directed the fighter-bombers to the FACs for their targets and strike orders, and request Air America rescue helicopters.

The FAC had to effectively utilize his radios all the while flying his aircraft, finding targets of opportunity, trying to evade small arms, heavy machine gun and antiaircraft artillery (AAA) ground fire, and watching out for his fellow FACs.

His instructor pilot—who had served a year's tour of duty in Vietnam as a FAC—also taught him how to harass the enemy with standoff fire using his leftover white phosphorus (WP, also known as 'Willie Peter') marking rockets after his interdiction and ground support missions had been completed.

WP wasn't only good for marking targets, it was a deadly weapon that would not stop burning until it was either dug out of the flesh or smothered. The rockets also served as good ignition devices for enemy ammo dumps.

Seven

With Tigers And A Battleship

In April of 1967, he left for Vietnam. But not before he'd arranged the delivery of a single red rose every month to Marie until he returned home after his year's tour of duty.

When Frank arrived in-country, he was assigned to the 21st Tactical Air Support Squadron (TASS) and drew the Republic of Korea's (ROK) Capital Division, more widely known as the ROK Tiger Division, as the primary unit he'd support. That was fine with him. He'd learned to appreciate the ROK units he'd seen or heard of during his tour of duty in the Korean War. They had the reputation even back then as being ferocious warriors, although poorly led at the time because of a shortfall of qualified officers and NCOs. Because of top brass tactical errors and inadequate intelligence, the Tigers were completely surprised by a North Korean attack early in the war and suffered terrible casualties. They were forced to retreat and thus shortened the whole defensive perimeter by ceding more South Korean ground to the enemy.

For this, the Tigers were deeply shamed and not only lost face, they lost the ears of the Tiger insignia they once wore with great pride. Advertising their shame with their earless shoulder patches infuriated them and their new commanding officer told them to take it out on the enemy. By showing other units and the top ROK commanders how well and how hard they could fight, they would win back their once-fine reputation and be able to proudly wear their patches with ears once more.

Frank told me in one of his letters about the Tigers' combat MO. "When they secure an area against enemy attack, you know it's secure. They have a unique way of fighting, surrounding the enemy and slowly closing the ring, squeezing them tighter and tighter as the firefight increases in intensity and not stopping until the last Viet Cong (VC) or North Vietnamese Army (NVA) is killed, too wounded to fight, or captured. The key is to gain fire superiority before the enemy has a chance to. The Tigers achieve remarkable kill ratios. One example after a firefight last week was twenty-nine enemy KIA to one Tiger. Another key to their success is good intel, which they achieve by patrolling day and night along with their interrogation of prisoners, which I stay away from. The patrols I can handle, but interrogations are their business."

A story sent to me by a fellow FAC of Frank's, Dusty Eberhart, was about a joint hammer-and-anvil operation with the Tigers in M-113A1 armored personnel carriers (APCs) chasing a battalion of NVA (North Vietnamese Army) soldiers across a river (the "hammer") and into the waiting ambush of an ARVN (Army of the Republic of Vietnam) battalion, which was the anvil.

Frank flew cover for the Tigers while Dusty stayed on station to watch over the ARVN troops. The two FACs had four F-4 fighter-bombers on call for close-in air support; two of them flying cover for Dusty's ARVN troops and the other two for Frank's. The attack aircraft were ready, each carrying six HE (high-explosive 500-pound bombs) and 300 rounds of 20mm cannon strafe.

The operation began with the NVA battalion trying to escape the Tigers via several fordable stretches of the river.

Winter Roses

The Tigers could have chased them down on the same fords and shot them at point-blank range, but they didn't know that. Instead, they entered the river in line with their .50 caliber machine guns firing at the enemy soldiers, who were struggling to wade faster and escape the deadly rain of bullets. The Tiger soldiers riding on top of the APCs also fired at the enemy with their M-16s. All were concentrating so hard on shooting enemy soldiers that they hadn't noticed their APCs were stalling and sinking into the riverbed. Some were partially buried in the muck.

No one had told the Tigers that they had to put in fording plugs before entering the water, to prevent drowning the engines. They would not cross the river that day.

Unfortunately for the enemy, the Tigers were still able to keep firing at the NVA troops. By then, the NVA soldiers were frantically clawing their way up the river bank, trying unsuccessfully to avoid the intense and accurate heavy machine gun and rifle fire that raked them. 40mm grenades from the Tigers' M-79 grenade launchers—each round with a kill radius of five yards--exploded among them, speeding their panicky climb.

The enemy soldiers scrambling up the riverbank reminded Frank of ants swarming out of a broken nest. He fired a marking rocket into their midst and then unleashed his F-4s to hit his smoke, first with their 500-pound bombs and then followed up by two strafing passes each.

The unfortunate few who crested the ridge after making it through the Tigers' fire and F-4 strikes ran right into the waiting ARVN's firing line. Their greeting card was a deafening blast of Claymore mines positioned to hit the enemy's lower bodies and backsides from the trees behind them.

The NVA troops who survived the Claymore blasts lost complete control in the shit-storm of the ARVN's interlocking machine gun and rifle fire, and scrambled back down the riverbank only to be shot to pieces by the waiting Tigers.

John Bingham

Frank told his F-4s to stand down and report back to their base at Phu Cat.

Looking at the complete rout of the enemy, it was clear to Dusty that he wouldn't need his F-4s circling above, so he directed them to check in with Tactical Air Control Party and see if their services were needed elsewhere.

A week later, Frank and Dusty were standing down in a Saigon bar and agreed that, despite the fording plug problem, the operation was a huge success and that the ARVN unit now had a nice feather in its cap—a much-needed victory against the dreaded NVA, which didn't happen very often.

They then toasted the ARVN, the Tigers, the fighter jocks, themselves, the Air Force, and the president. When the toasts ended, they found themselves shit-faced drunk.

The story hadn't ended for the Tigers. They still had to retrieve the sunken and stuck vehicles, all the while making sure that neither Charlie nor the NVA were lurking nearby and ready to ambush them as they worked with their combat engineering battalion and mechanics to free the vehicles and get them running again.

There was also a strong possibility that enemy sappers would booby-trap the vehicles. Already, a Tiger night patrol had reported that NVA scouts had been seen sniffing around the sunken APCs. They let the enemy soldiers go, thinking that their recon might lead to even more death and destruction…their own, not the Tigers. The Tigers' regimental CO, Colonel Pak, seized the opportunity and decided to set up an ambush with Frank playing an integral role. The Tigers would use a classic L-shaped ambush set up in the tree line above the river to rake the enemy with withering fire once the main body of enemy troops had entered the kill zone.

If the enemy resistance proved to be too heavy, Colonel Pak and his officers would blow their whistles to get their troops out of the tree line, quickly. They

Winter Roses

would dash to the river and stay down behind the APCs while Frank marked the enemy's position with a rocket. Tigers firing the .50 caliber machine guns that had been re-mounted on the APCs would cover the ambush teams' dash to join them. At Frank's command, two F-4 fighter-bombers on station would dive and unleash napalm hell on the tree line that the Tigers had vacated. In case any enemy troops survived the napalm, he would direct the fighter-bombers to strafe with their 20mm cannons. All the while, the sharp-shooting Tiger troops would be picking off any enemy soldiers who dared to show themselves.

Two days passed without a move by Charlie or the NVA. On the third day just at dusk, an outlying observation post alerted the ambush teams that a reinforced NVA patrol was headed straight for the L, taking the point for a rifle company in column and a company of explosives-laden sappers followed by a rear guard.

The Tigers waited until all were in the kill zone and then opened up by firing a line of Claymores that formed the L, spraying the NVA troops head-on and from the side with thousands of steel fragments that shredded their ranks. The shock of the blasts froze them where they stood, opening a window of opportunity for the Tigers' .50 caliber and M-60 machine guns to cut them down. The NVA sappers who were behind the decimated riflemen were able to collect their wits, dive for cover and return fire. Rather than risk Tiger lives in the firefight, their officers blew their whistles, signaling them to break off and run for cover behind the APCs.

Seeing the Tigers now in the open and running to beat hell for cover behind the APCs, Frank dove and fired a marking rocket into the tree line.

"Red Dog Lead, this is Warlock One. Hit my smoke! You are cleared in hot! Do you read me?"

"Loud and clear, Warlock One. Roger that, lead diving in hot to hit your smoke with nape."

Frank turned away from the F-4's dive path and watched from a safe distance as the pilot pickled off his two canisters of napalm. The tree line erupted with a roar and a huge fireball that leapt through the trees like a flame-spitting dragon incinerating all before it. He told the pilot to go back to 10,000 feet and wait for his BDA (Bomb Damage Assessment). Three slow passes over the charred and smoldering trees drew no fire, but he took no chances. He called for the second F-4's napalm and for two strafing runs by each of the F-4's 20mm cannons, one parallel to the tree line and the other at a right angle to catch any survivors running back into the jungle.

Both Frank and the Phantom pilots noted with satisfaction that the strafe had triggered secondary explosions, likely explosives that the sappers were carrying and couldn't shed in time. In discussing the damage, they concluded that they'd sent the sappers straight into hell via the napalm's all-consuming furnace of fire.

The Tigers sent a reinforced rifle platoon into the blackened landscape to make sure there were no enemy troops waiting with a reverse ambush. There were none. The Tigers' planning and near-perfect execution had paid off again with a body count that turned up 218 enemy dead. Eight ROK troops had been killed. Rather than follow the survivors, the Tigers set up a defense perimeter complete with outlying observation and listening posts, M-60 and .50 caliber machine-gun kill zones along with Claymores set around the perimeter in the remote chance the enemy would return in force. The Tigers also manned the APCs' .50 calibers.

Now protected, the ROK engineers were free to retrieve every one of the APCs out of the river and operate them again without enemy interference. Between the hammer-and-anvil operation, the ambush, the napalm and the strafing, the NVA had quite enough of the Tigers.

Word got back to Frank that the ARVNs were making fun of the Tigers for neglecting to put in the engine fording plugs. He asked Dusty if he could pass the word to them that their fun was not funny to the Tigers, who hated loss of

Winter Roses

face nearly as much as they hated the communists, and that the one thing no one should do—whether friend or foe—is to make fun of them. The ARVNs quieted down in a hurry when Dusty told them that the last soldiers in the world they'd want to piss off were the ROK Tigers. "Even the NVA know that," he said. "And that's why they stay away from the Tigers. They'd much rather kill you or Americans."

Flying low and slow one morning over hilly terrain to see if he could draw fire that would give away the enemy's position, Frank glanced down and thought he saw a couple of soldiers walking near the base of a hill. *Probably NVA.* Rather than give the enemy any hint that they'd been discovered, he kept on his flight path and decided to hold off double-checking for three days. In the late afternoon of the third day, he flew well away from the hill at an oblique angle to avoid alerting the enemy of his presence. He used his binoculars to scan the hill's base. Sure enough, he saw what must have been a reinforced patrol of NVA troops emerge in column from a door in the hill's base and disappear into the jungle. *They're moving out to choose a path and set up their ambush while there's still daylight.*

He could only guess who and what else might be hidden inside. More troops would be a good guess, as would ammunition and food supplies. Perhaps a headquarters company. He had heard of caves concealing trucks, tanks, even field hospitals. Regardless, he now had a good target and thought about the best way to take it out. Fighter-bombers' 500 pound —even 1,000 pound—bombs would hardly scratch the surface. Artillery was out of the question unless eight-inch guns might be within range. He doubted it; most were firing into Cambodia and Laos, targeting enemy supply and weapons caches.

Then the idea hit him. *What about the New Jersey's 16-inch guns? Hell, the battleship's only mission here is fire support for the ground troops, and I've heard that it's been very effective for the Marines up in I Corps. If the jarheads haven't tied her up and she's still open for business today, I've got a dandy fire mission for her.* He called up Tactical

Air Control and asked the OIC (Officer In Charge) if he could get him in touch with the New Jersey.

"That would be a first for me," the OIC replied. "I've always wanted us to use those 16-inch guns. I'll find out if the ship is open for business. If so, I'll send them over to you for fire mission details. You must have a whopper of a target."

"You bet I do. I have a small mountain I need to take out. I believe NVA troops are in there along with who knows what supplies, munitions, vehicles, weapons, maybe even a field hospital, you name it. I have good coordinates for the ship's gunnery crew, so they can't miss."

The OIC signed off to call the New Jersey and ask if they'd be interested in taking out a big NVA stronghold that needed big firepower. The answer came back quickly; yes, they would take on the fire mission. Five minutes later, the TAC OIC alerted Frank that the mission was on and then cut him over to the gunnery OIC.

"Good afternoon, New Jersey, this is Warlock One, a FACer flying with the 21st Tactical Air Support Squadron in support of the Korean Tiger Division. I was trolling for enemy positions three days ago and came across a big hill—or small mountain, if you prefer--that's home for a NVA unit and its weapons and supplies. Short of a tactical nuke, there's no other way besides the mighty New Jersey that I have of blowing it off the map. Want to take a shot at it? You'll save a lot of American and friendlies' lives.

"Affirmative. It's about time we supported the Air Force, anyway. Give me the coordinates so we can begin the fire mission."

Frank read the coordinates and asked his contact to read them back to him to make sure they were correct. His contact then relayed them to the ship's chief gunnery officer, who alerted the ship's skipper and asked for approval.

Winter Roses

With that, the top gunny briefed the fire control officers in the two forward turrets, who ordered the gun crews to load the shells.

Frank got impatient. "How long before you can fire? I need to alert any friendlies operating in the area to get the hell out of there. Also, the sun's going down fast and I need to be back at the brag bar so I can tell my buddies about how the New Jersey blew a NVA fortress all to hell. With a little help from Warlock One, of course."

"Of course, Warlock One. I will hold until you give me the all-clear. It won't take long, I can tell you that. The two forward turrets will already have their shells loaded in their breech blocks, all eight tons of them. We'll fire HC for High Capacity; they make the biggest craters. With your coordinates, the gun crew will also load the propellant bags."

"Whoa, eight tons of high explosives packed in six shells? This ought to be quite an experience. By the way, what's your call sign?"

"Call me Ishmael. Just kidding, I always wanted to say that. I'm Hellfire Three. You are definitely in for an experience that you'll never forget. Now we're holding up your fire mission and bar time. I'll sign off until I hear back from you."

Frank banked into a circle and came back around to see if there was any more enemy activity near the cave entrance. Once again he depended on his binoculars to spot without getting spotted. He radio'ed Tactical Air Control to chase away the friendlies. TAC came back to say that the target area was clear and wished him good shooting. He called Hellfire Three and gave him the all-clear. All was quiet for the next couple of moments. *The place probably becomes a beehive of activity after sundown. What a surprise we have in store for them. When the battleship's shitload of shells lands on the hillside, that NVA reinforced night patrol will consider themselves to be the luckiest people on the planet.*

"Warlock One, this is Hellfire Three. We have a fire mission. We advise you— strongly advise you—to start climbing right now at full throttle. You want to be as far as possible from the blast's shock wave.

No doubt you've felt explosion shock waves before. They're like your sweetheart blowing you a kiss compared to 16-inch shell explosions. Confirming, we will fire a salvo of six rounds and we will tell you when the rounds are out and on their way. Keep climbing."

"Roger that, Hellfire Three. After the shells hit, I'll fly down to check out the BDA—that's 'Bomb Damage Assessment'—and give you the report for your record."

"Roger that, Warlock One. We appreciate feedback."

"Over and out."

Frank continued to climb as fast as his Bird Dog could climb, which was about 1,100 feet per minute and not fast enough. When he heard the call from Hellfire Three—"Rounds out, time to target is one minute!"--he acknowledged, took a deep breath, and hung on to the stick with an iron grip.

A blinding yellow-orange flash swept the landscape below, traveling as fast as a bolt of lightning, only in all directions. A couple of seconds later, an invisible force that felt like a gigantic hand reached out, ripped the Bird Dog's control from Frank's grip on the stick and hurled the aircraft straight up into the air, giving him the altitude he'd tried to reach in the first place. A thunderous boom followed, so loud that he thought his eardrums were ruptured and he felt the familiar flutter and "thump" in his chest from the shock wave. He struggled to regain his bearings and control of the aircraft; for a moment he had been upside down, then in a side slip, followed by the beginning of a graveyard spiral. With his eyes finally focused and his head cleared and eyes leveled on the horizon, he managed to reorient himself and flew the plane out of trouble.

Winter Roses

"Hellfire Three, Hellfire Three, this is Warlock One. Do you read me?"

"Read you loud and clear, Warlock One. How was the carnival ride?"

"I'm still dizzy, my ears are ringing and I have the shakes, but I'm back in control. Good thing you warned me about gaining altitude. Too bad that my Bird Dog isn't built for fast climbing. BDA to follow."

"Roger that."

Frank had little visibility on his way down to assess the damage. There was too much debris in the air even at altitude and he hoped the particles wouldn't get sucked into his intakes and seize the engine. He opted to hold for a few moments until the detritus drifted away. Finally, it cleared enough for him to drop down and get a better view of the damage.

"Holy shit!" he exclaimed when he realized the extent of the devastation.

"Hellfire Three, Hellfire Three, this is Warlock One. Do you read me?"

His headset crackled. "Loud and clear, Warlock One. Did we get the bad guys?"

"Get the bad guys? The whole damned hill is gone. You have just created the biggest NVA cemetery in-country. There's no telling what's buried with them—guns, ammo, food supplies, vehicles of all sorts? We'll never know without a bulldozer and an excavator to dig out what's under all that dirt. All I can say is 'mission accomplished' and great job."

"Without your good eye and accurate coordinates, we'd have blown up the wrong hill. You get to take a bow, too. If your CO doesn't believe your after-action briefing, have him call me."

"Thanks, Hellfire Three. It's been a pleasure working with you and the mighty New Jersey. Maybe we can blow the shit out of some other target someday. Until then, amigo, smooth sailing or whatever else you sailor boys say. Over and out."

"Happy landings, Warlock One. Over and out."

Flying back to Nha Trang, Frank wondered if his buddies—and his CO—would believe that he'd blown up an entire hill full of NVA, their supplies and weapons. Maybe even trucks and tanks, for all he knew.

What he did know is that he was more than ready for a cold beer or two to steady his still-shaking hands. Maybe a scotch chaser from the squadron's medicine cabinet if the beer didn't work. He left the dirt that had infiltrated the cockpit and covered his face and clothing as further proof of his story. Hellfire Three was right, it sure was a tale for his children—and his buddies, who still thought it was bullshit.

All he had to do was to get home in one piece—no small achievement for a FAC.

Eight

Save A Fighter Pilot's Ass

Frank's Bird Dog was badly shot up by enemy antiaircraft fire.

He'd flown lower than usual to get a bomb damage assessment for the two Navy A-7 Corsair II fighter-bombers overhead. The target he'd put them on was a VC compound that was partially hidden in the lush, green jungle growth below: obviously, the surviving enemy troops had been waiting for him. He managed to muscle the aircraft over the treetops and crash-land in them. After coming to a jolting stop in a forked branch that ripped the wings right out of their roots, he unclipped his safety harness, crawled carefully over to the crumpled door and kicked at it until he forced an opening wide enough for him to crawl through. Sticking his head out and looking down, he guesstimated he was around 60 feet from the brush below.

Whistles from several directions signaled that the VC were locating each other's positions so they could encircle and capture him.

He strapped his CAR-15 over his back with a bandolier of clips, and reached under the seat for a 50-foot length of rappelling rope that a Ranger had given him.

After tying it to the branch, he tested the knot and lowered himself hand-over-hand until he reached the end, then dropped the remaining distance, reminding himself to tuck and roll the second his feet touched the ground.

He crashed through the brush and landed hard, but felt no immediate pain as he struggled to his feet. Spotting sunlight filtering through the jungle, he headed for it. While stumbling and tripping through the heavy underbrush, he pulled out his mirror and activated his beeper, hoping that the A-7s or some other fast movers would still be in the neighborhood to provide suppressing fire and keep the VC at bay while he waited for a rescue helicopter.

He couldn't know that, in the ferocity of TET, every Air Force and Army rescue helicopter was already deployed, ferrying troops, ammunition, water and rations to the troops in contact with the enemy and carrying out the wounded and dead to their home bases. The A-7 pilots knew that his best chance of survival was a Navy helicopter, but he didn't. They had already taken the initiative and one was on the way.

Just as he reached the tree line, he spotted the two fighter-bombers coming in fast, low and directly at him, and he knew instantly they were coming in hot. He flashed his mirror at them and hoped they'd marked his position to avoid blowing him to hell during their bombing and strafing runs. He knew the Navy pilots were good—damned good (or "shit hot" in pilot lingo), as good as the best of the USAF fighter-bomber pilots--and that the VC wouldn't dare follow him into the clearing when the rescue helicopter showed up. Not with those hunter-killers around.

The A-7s roared overhead and pickled off two more of their 500-pound bombs well behind his position in the tree line. The concussive waves of the blasts hammered in his chest and ears and he tried hard to breathe, thinking that the air had been sucked out of his lungs. It hadn't. He was hyperventilating and felt a strong sense of impending doom that intensified with the whistling of shrapnel shards that had whacked into nearby trees and slashed through the underbrush like scythes.

Damn, that was close. Thank God they're not carrying napalm.

The lead aircraft started firing just before passing over him and his wingman followed suit. Their 20-mm rotating cannons ripped through the jungle foliage and he heard screams as the exploding shells found their marks. *Jesus, just one of those rounds will tear a man in two. If any VC is still alive after that shit storm, I don't want to fuck with him. On the positive side, he may not want to fuck with me. Maybe they'll all think twice after the 500-pounders and 20mm strafe tear them new assholes.*

The jets climbed rapidly and began to circle far above, staying on station. *They must have called for a rescue chopper and are sticking around to make sure Charlie keeps his head down when it arrives and I make my dash to get onboard.*

Later, he said he'd never heard any music so sweet as the wop-wop-wop of the Navy helicopter that appeared over the far tree line and hovered just above the ground in the center of the clearing. He burst out of the tree line and ran towards the chopper as fast as he could, half-skipping and hopping because of a sharp pain knifing through his left ankle and shooting up his leg. A crewmember in the door manning an M-60 machine gun was pumping his arm up and down, signaling him to run faster. *Jesus Christ, I'm running as fast as I can.* He heard the snap of bullets whipping by and ran even faster, heart pounding in his throat, finally reaching the door. With one hand, the gunner reached down, grabbed him by the collar, yanked him in, and then opened up with the M-60, sweeping the tree line in short, accurate bursts.

The moment he was inside, the helicopter lifted fast.

The gunner turned to him, grinned and continued firing until the helicopter was on its heading west to its mother ship in the South China Sea.

"Welcome aboard, sir. You've just been rescued by the U.S. Navy's best. Now, I know that you Air Force FACs are shit-hot and have saved many a Navy pilot's ass, so tonight we're going to return the favor.

"How does a steak dinner with a glass of wine in the officers' mess sound?"

Frank stared at him in disbelief. "Yeah, and I'll take ice water in hell."

"Hey, I'm serious. The vino and beef are our small way of saying 'thanks' to a good FAC and now a good buddy, and we pre-cleared the meal with the old man on our way over here to pick you up.

"I haven't had a decent piece of beef for months, let alone a good wine. You're on and I appreciate your hospitality."

Frank asked him where they were headed and when they'd arrive.

"You'll be an honored guest aboard the meanest, toughest, baddest ship in-country, the mighty *USS Coral Sea*. Our ETA is 1530 hours."

"Seems to me I've worked with some F-4 Phantoms she carries. The F-4 pilots are shit-hot, just like the Corsairs who helped save my ass."

"Yeah, we're mighty proud of all our pilots and everybody bleeds when one doesn't return."

"I know the feeling."

By that time they were airborne and moving rapidly away from the clearing. He watched in awe as the A-7s swooped down parallel to the tree line and shredded the jungle one last time, then climbed rapidly to head back to their carrier. The chopper's gunner punctuated the Corsairs' strikes with his own bursts to give Charlie even more of an incentive to stay low or bug out.

The gunner asked Frank if he knew how to operate an M-60, and Frank replied that he'd had orientation fire with the weapon.

"Good," he said. "Take the gun while I check our ETA with the pilot and see if you can nail a few Charlies. Payback is a motherfucker, right?"

"Right," said Frank.

"Fucking ay doo. Then get some and I'll be right back. Sir." He disappeared into the cockpit.

Frank butt-bumped over to the gun, tucked the butt plate into his right shoulder pocket and aimed it down at the jungle flying by in a green blur. *I sure as shit can't see any Charlies down there at our speed and altitude and I don't want to hit innocent civilians. But it will be fun to fire this baby again.* He tilted the weapon up so he'd hit nothing and jacked the first round into the chamber. Following the gunner's lead, he cut loose with several three-round bursts.

The gunner poked his head out the cockpit to check on the racket. "You handle that gun well, captain," he shouted. "You've had some training on the M-60?"

"Just practicing. I learned how to fire and maintain the weapon a few years ago during small-arms orientation. I know enough to be dangerous with it."

"Hell, you're supposed to be dangerous with it. Ol' Charlie down there sure as hell thinks so. He now knows that you know how to fire a machine gun the way it's supposed to be done--in rapid, short bursts."

Frank cleared the breech and released his tight grip on the weapon, rolled over to lay on his stomach and propped himself up on his elbows while the gunner hopped off the cockpit bulkhead and resumed his position behind the gun.

"Hey, you can be my spotter. No one can find the enemy like a FAC! What is your name and outfit, captain? I need the information to brag about having the best spotter in-country."

"Frank Delaney, 21st Tactical Air Support Squadron, or TASS for short. And yours?"

"Gunner's mate Chuck Ristorante, the best fucking machine gunner in-country."

"Best at fucking or best at gunnery?"

"Yes."

""I won't argue. You helped save my life today and I won't forget it. I'll buy you a drink when we land."

"I wish you could, sir."

"I'll find a way. I want to buy one for my Corsair pilot buddies, too."

"Heh. Maybe those two can smuggle me a snort. Check with them, OK?"

"I promise. I'll ask the captain himself if I need to."

"Good luck. We have a no-alcohol policy, but there are exceptions, mostly for VIPs like you. But I won't be heartbroken. I'm due for a couple of days at China Beach and will get some soon enough. Maybe even some good whiskey. Meanwhile, I appreciate your trying."

"That's the least I can do besides shake your hand and say "Thank you." They shook hands and Chuck returned to his gun.

Winter Roses

Frank sat up and unlaced his boot to look at the cause of his pain during his mad run to the helicopter. He could only stare at the massive bruise that began at his ankle and traveled up his leg almost to the knee. The ankle was badly swollen and he regretted taking off the boot.

"Holy shit, captain, what a mess! You've either got a bad sprain, a broken ankle or both. It's too bad you took off the boot. Now you won't be able to get it back on. Jeez, with all respect due an officer, when's the last time you showered? You don't smell very good. Sir."

"I'm not surprised. My last shower was over a week ago when I stood down with one of my ROK Tigers companies."

"Wow. I hear the ROKs are real bad-asses and that neither Charlie nor the NVA will fuck with them."

"You heard right. They are meaner than cat shit. When they secure an area, you know it's secure. My primary mission is to provide air-to-ground support for the ROK Capital Division, better known as the Tiger Division. They're up at Qui Nhon and they sure as hell are tigers. I've been on combat night patrols with them several times and it's like a walk in the park. Well, not quite, but I swear that Charlie smells the kimchee from a mile away and puts even more space between them. Of course, the Tigers smell their fish sauce and use that to track them down. It's fun to play cat-and-mouse when you're the cat, especially a big, bad-assed cat like the Tigers.

"I imagine that the ROK brass isn't pleased to know you're out on the firing line with their grunts."

"That's true enough. But I tell them that the patrolling helps me better understand what's really happening on the ground and that makes me a better FAC. This saves even more of their troops' lives and they buy into that premise big-time."

"Betcha the ROKs are missing you big-time today with the TET shit-storm in full swing. Some fucking way to celebrate a new year!"

"Yeah, at our bloody expense. I learned a little about TET this morning before I got whacked. But I'm betting that my ROK buddies have ambushes set all around their perimeters and neither Charlie or even NVA regulars will take any chances with them. Instead, they're attacking the ARVN and American units they've learned they can defeat. No need to name names, you probably know which ones I'm talking about."

"Yeah, we get plenty of feedback from our fast movers and even I can tell who's hot and who's not by listening to the wounded we sometimes pick up. Speaking of naming names, we have another world-class gunner onboard, Silent Max, sitting over there on our port side. He doesn't say much on missions because he's too busy looking for someone or something to kill. Hey, Max, say hello to Captain Delaney, our rescuee for the day and a boss Air Force FAC."

Max turned, nodded with a smile that reminded Frank of the Cheshire Cat, threw him a quick salute, and returned to his gun and binoculars.

Chuck told Frank to stick his head into the cockpit and introduce himself to pilot Lt. Richards and co-pilot Lt. Somerset. Frank scrambled over on all fours and pulled himself up and over the bulkhead into the cockpit. He shouted his name and a "Thank you!" as loud as he could to be heard over the engine's racket. Co-pilot Somerset turned, smiled and shouted right back, "Welcome aboard, sir!"

Pilot Richards gave him a thumbs-up and shouted, "Better get a life preserver on, captain!" We'll be over water in a few minutes and the preserver's a must. We don't want to rescue you twice on the same day!"

An adrenaline crash, the air rushing in and the reassuring sound of the rotor blades made Frank drowsy and he told the gunner he'd like to take a quick nap.

Winter Roses

The gunner tossed him two kapok life preservers, one to wear and the other for a pillow.

He had hardly fallen asleep when he heard the rotor blades change their pitch and the gooney bird touched down on the carrier's deck with a slight bump. He sat up and watched two corpsmen running towards the helicopter with a stretcher. Gunner Ristorante stood up, gently reached down, picked up Frank, carried him over to the open bay door and sat him down with his legs dangling over the edge within easy reach of the corpsmen. As they lifted him onto the stretcher, a cheer erupted and he propped himself up on his elbows to see pilots in their G suits, the ships' officers and seamen all clapping, cheering and whistling their welcome aboard the carrier.

Frank grinned and saluted them; they immediately came to attention and returned the salute.

"Welcome aboard the USS Coral Sea," the senior corpsman said. "Before we get you down the elevator, the old man wants to meet you and shake your hand. So do the two Corsair pilots who stayed on station for you during the rescue."

They carried him over and set him down right in front of the skipper and two pilots in their jump suits. He stayed upright as the ship's captain leaned over, introduced himself as ship's Captain Joe McManus and thanked Frank for his FAC service in getting his pilots to the right places at the right times, and getting them home again. "I want you to meet the two Corsair pilots who were on station with you today, Lieutenants Phil George and his wingman Dick Everts. They tell me that you helped them blow Charlie all to hell today, but that you had a peculiar way of doing it. As if getting them on target to blow away the VC compound wasn't enough excitement, you had to get your Bird Dog hit on your damage assessment run and land in a treetop. Then set a world record for the 100-meter dash to safety in the rescue helicopter that Lt. George managed to find for you today."

Frank replied, "Sir, your pilots, are good, damned good. When I tell them to hit my smoke, they hit it. I'm proud to serve with them."

The captain took a bullhorn from a seaman standing behind him, then told the assembled pilots and crew members, "Welcome aboard United States Air Force Captain Frank Delaney, one of the best Forward Air Controllers we work with, a man who gets our pilots on target while giving them the best, safest angles of attack possible to help make sure they not only accomplish the mission, but return to the the mighty *USS Coral Sea!* Let's give him a welcome worthy of our ship!"

With that, the crowd erupted with a loud roar of approval. Frank flopped back down on the stretcher, waved his thanks, saluted the captain and then asked for the bullhorn.

Propping himself up on his elbow, he said, "Thank you for your warm welcome to an old Air Force FACer like me."

Laughs of approval.

"There's a saying in the Air Force that goes, 'Throw a nickel on the grass, save a fighter pilot's ass'. I'd throw a nickel on the grass any day to save a Navy or Marine fighter pilot's ass. Speaking for me, my wife and our four children, I cannot thank your two Corsair pilots enough for standing by me to save my ass after I was hit and crash-landed my Bird Dog in a treetop and Charlie started to chase me down.

"They showed me first-hand how accurate their bombing and strafing runs were, destroying not only the VC compound I'd marked, but keeping Charlie away from me with their bombs and strafe that found their targets in the bush behind me. I could clearly hear the screams and knew Charlie wouldn't dare try to chase me into the clearing where your helicopter picked me up. Speaking of which, I also appreciate the bravery of your helicopter pilots and crew who took enemy AK fire while I ran and hopped as fast as I could to reach the helicopter. Gunner Ristorante's M-60 fire not only quieted the few Charlies who were left after the Corsairs' bomb-and-strafe runs, he threw me on board and then told me I smelled bad. I kissed him anyway."

Big laughs.

"Could Gunnery Mate Ristorante, 'Silent Max,' and Lieutenants George, Everts, Richards, and Somerset step over here? I'd like to shake their hands." The two pilots came over to him and shook his hand, as did his rescue helicopter pilots along with Ristorante and Max. They all turned to face the crowd, and Ristorante raised Frank's hand with a victory "V." The crowd loved it and surged forward to shake his hand, too, but the skipper grabbed the bullhorn and told them to hold off, saying that the captain had to go to sick bay for treatment. The crowd parted as the corpsmen carried him over to the flight elevator, all wishing him good luck and thanking him. He tried to shake their hands and return their high-fives as they bulled through the crowd but the corpsmen were now nearly running and further hand contact was impossible.

In the sick bay, the doctor cut up the leg of his flight suit so he could roll it up for a better look at the ankle and leg. He whistled and told Frank he'd never seen an ankle and lower leg as swollen and as colorful. He asked him, "How in hell were you able to run across that clearing field to get to the chopper without falling down and crawling the rest of the way?"

"Adrenaline," answered Frank. "I knew the ankle wouldn't hold my weight, so I half-ran, half-skipped and half-hopped with Charlie's bullets zipping by until I reached the chopper and gunner Ristorante grabbed me and threw me in."

"Under fire, a man can accomplish feats of endurance and strength that aren't possible without the adrenaline rush to keep him going. By the way, captain, how long has it been since you've had a shower?"

"Ristorante asked me the same question. Sorry about my fragrance. Over a week. Can I get a shower?"

"Forget the shower for now. We'll get a nurse in here to give you an Army bath as soon as we find out what's going on in your ankle. Bad smell aside, it's either the worst sprain I've ever seen or it's badly broken. Or both. We need an X-ray to tell for sure, but we've got a problem.

"Our equipment went on the fritz and we're waiting for a new, portable X-ray unit. But tell me how this happened and I'll give you a diagnosis from your story along with a see-and-touch exam. OK, let's take a closer look."

Taking it gently in both hands, the doctor felt along the top of the foot and moved the ankle while gently manipulating it, trying to feel for broken bones.

"Tell me when it hurts, OK?"

"You'll be the first to know, doc."

He then rotated the foot with one hand while supporting the ankle with the other.

"Jesus Christ, that hurts!"

The doctor backed off and told Frank that he was going to rotate the foot in the opposite direction, this time with a firmer grip. He felt the bones shifting position as Frank inhaled deeply, hissing in pain through clenched teeth.

The doctor set down his foot as carefully as he could. After Frank told his story, the doctor asked him if Ranger rappelling rope was a standard component in his survival kit.

Winter Roses

Replied Frank, "It may not be in every FAC's kit but I thought it might come in handy in case I ever went down and crashed in a treetop. I know what happened sounds like a self-fulfilling prophecy, but I always liked the old Boy Scout motto: be prepared. If I hadn't brought along that rope, Charlie would be torturing me right now. That, or I'd be dead from a 60-foot-plus fall.

"Well, with your gift of prophecy, you might consider a side trip to Vegas on your way home."

"No, thanks. I've seen too many buddies lose their money, their homes, their wives and even their children because they were addicted gamblers. The house always wins is a good adage to remember. The closest I ever get to gambling is bar dice at the Officer's Club."

"Yeah, I'm no serious gambler, either. Now let's get back to what's ailing you. It sure feels like a break to me. Do you recall rolling your ankle joint when you landed on good old *terra firma*?"

"I don't remember that. I guess I was concentrating on getting the hell out of there because Charlie would have been on my ass in minutes.

"I thought I was pissing adrenaline, but it turned out to be just that, piss. That contributed to my odoriferous flight suit. The adrenaline crash hit me hard when I was safely onboard the rescue helicopter."

"Now you know what the grunts go through when they're being overrun and the appreciation they feel when there's air support and/or artillery available to help them get out of their jam. Not that I know what it feels like to be a ground-pounding grunt.

"That's why I'm in the Navy and not in the Marines. OK, lie back and relax. I'll be back in a few minutes and hopefully, we'll have a plan when I return."

Frank fell back on the gurney and closed his eyes. "Take your time, doctor. I'll finish the nap I started on the chopper."

He woke up with a start when the doctor laid his hand on his shoulder.

"Captain, we have a plan. First, there won't be any dinner party tonight in your honor. Is your ankle broken or sprained? The answer is a probable 'yes.' The ankle feels and looks like it's been broken and the tendons and ligaments are very likely stretched and torn. In short, they are a mess. You'll need multi-view X-rays to help determine what's going on in there and if you'll need surgery to repair it. The good news, of course, is that your run through the jungle probably saved your life. Anyway, the skipper agrees that you have to go to our hospital ship, the *USS Sanctuary*. I'll brief their doc on duty. We're arranging for another helicopter right now. The sooner we can get you there, the better. Don't worry about keeping your 21st TASS skipper informed; our ship's captain is probably in touch with him right now to explain that the *Sanctuary* is a better place for treatment than anything he can get anywhere in South Vietnam and the better the treatment, the sooner you'll be back in action. That is, if they don't decide to ship your ass home."

He told Frank that the corpsmen were on the way with a gurney to get him back to the flight deck for his trip to the *Sanctuary*. He also said that he just learned about huge, simultaneous attacks the VC and NVA had launched all over South Vietnam, even one on the American Embassy. He added, "They're calling it 'TET,' for the Chinese New Year."

"Yeah, Chuck told me what he knew about it. It sounds like the biggest, baddest massed attacks yet by Charlie and the NVA. My buddies must be mighty busy, spotting targets and calling in the fighter-bombers for the kill. Hopefully, many of those bastards will be in the open and we'll have more chances than ever to kick Commie ass."

The corpsmen arrived. Frank extended his hand in thanks and said, "Christ, doc, I don't even know your name."

Winter Roses

"It's Irish, Jack Kelly. If you ever get to the Big Apple, look me up and we'll knock back a few Bushmills together."

"That would be a real pleasure, Jack. Thanks for all you've done. And call me Frank, OK?."

"You got it, Frank." He leaned over to shake Frank's hand one more time and pressed something into his hand. "For luck," he said. "Keep it in your flight suit pocket and make sure you bring it with you on all of your missions. Especially TET missions, if you heal fast enough. Personally, I don't think you will. Anyway, If you do that, you'll be a-makin' it back to yer home and hearth and all of yer loved ones, and almighty glad they'll be! And let's not forget your CAR-15, revolver and bandoleer. They're even better luck." He put the weapons and ammo on the gurney.

"Again, Jack, thanks." He unzipped a shoulder pocket and dropped in his new talisman, a sterling silver trefoil.

The corpsmen carried him to the gurney waiting on the flight elevator. When he was securely strapped in, one gave the "thumbs up' signal to the waiting operator and the elevator climbed to the flight deck where a helicopter sat waiting with its rotor blades slowly turning. *I could get used to this VIP treatment, but I hope my ROK Tigers are getting through this TET shit with few casualties and good air support from my 21st TASS buddies. But if any unit can handle Charlie, even the NVA, the Tigers can. Looking out for my own ass, the Navy may have saved my life twice—maybe even three times. Once when I was shot down, twice when the Navy Corsairs greased Charlie and three times by keeping me here while TET battles must be raging everywhere.*

Frank was lifted onto a stretcher and then loaded aboard the helicopter. As the crewmembers strapped down the stretcher, the rotors turned faster and the engine's whine grew louder. The helicopter lurched, did a 360-degree turn and then moved quickly out over the sparkling blue hues of the South China Sea.

John Bingham

Here we go again. How long will I be on the hospital ship and when can I return to my unit and my Tigers? Yeah, I know. As long as it takes. Go with the flow, asshole. There's no sense trying to rush your healing and get back into action. You have to be able to work your pedals as if they're extensions of your legs and feet and you sure as hell can't do that wearing a cast. You'll have to be checked out on your Bird Dog all over again. The healing and rehab process could take a couple of months and by that time, you may be able to rotate home. <u>I better not even think of that</u>. Damn, that good, red vino with a prime cut of beef at the carrier's officers' mess would have been a treat. But I'll bet the hospital ship menu won't be C-rats or MREs, either. Now relax and get some sleep.

A crew member woke him as they approached the hospital ship and told Frank to look out the open door. He was amazed at the sight of what must have been 30 or maybe even 40 helicopters swarming around the ship in stacked clockwise circles, waiting in turn to land and discharge their precious cargo. They reminded him of bees returning to the hive, and it dawned on him that the choppers were carrying troops who were wounded in the TET battles raging throughout the country.

His helicopter's turn came to land on the ship's stern helipad. The pilot came in fast, spun around the pad in a semicircle and then landed. Two corpsmen were waiting with a stretcher. They ducked under the still-rotating blades and ran to the open bay where Frank sat waiting. They loaded him on the stretcher and began running to an open bulkhead door where a doctor was checking and tagging several troops. This was the triage station and Frank was moved to the back of the line while the corpsmen rushed the patients who needed more urgent care to elevators that would take them to the operating rooms, the X-ray bays, whatever was appropriate for their wounds, injuries and illnesses.

The doctor asked him what his level of pain was on a scale of 1-10 with 10 being unbearable and 1 being a nuisance. Frank felt the pounding ache and stabs of the ankle with the smallest of movements and gave the doctor a level of eight. "Give the captain 5 mg of morphine," the doctor told the corpsman standing next to Frank. "That will keep him relaxed until we can get him into X-ray to see how much damage he's done to that ankle."

The doctor then asked Frank to be patient. ""We're filling up fast with TET wounded, many of them badly. They'll be the first in line for surgery and we won't know if you need surgery until you get X-rayed. But whatever your injury is, we'll need to get that swelling down before we do anything. We'll get you to a bed in a few minutes. Keep that foot elevated and a nurse will pack it in ice to speed up the reduction in swelling.

"Corpsman, get the captain a bed in one of the rooms close to X-ray. Good luck, captain."

He turned away to see a young Marine who had just been wheeled over. He was writhing in pain with his chest bared. From what Frank could see, there was a big, blood-soaked bandage bound around the boy's chest. He was crying with pain and calling softly for his mother. *A sucking chest wound. My hurt's nothing compared to that kid's. I hope to hell he makes it. Damn, here I am with a lousy broken or sprained ankle while these wards are filling up with the worst wound cases, the ones that our field hospital docs can't do anything for. Don't ever whine or bitch about your little problems again, asshole.*

The corpsman slid the syringe needle into his arm. Frank thanked him.

"I don't get thanked very often, sir. I appreciate it. Don't fight the morphine. Relax, let it do its job and welcome to Happy Land."

"It's hitting me already," replied Frank. "Yeah, I'm relaxed."

He woke up when a corpsman and X-ray technician helped him off the gurney and laid him on his back on the granite stone underneath the camera. The cold of the granite had him wide-awake in seconds. Thanks to his morphine nap, he hadn't even felt his ice pack, but then he realized that he was dressed in a hospital gown with his bare back on the stone.

He asked the corpsman where his flight suit, carbine and pistol were.

"Your clothing and all your valuables are locked up in a wall locker behind your bed. The carbine and revolver are locked up in a safe and will be returned to you when you're discharged. Sometimes patients get wild and crazy and we can't have any firearms around. I'm sure you understand why."

"Yeah, I understand. But I'm also concerned about a special token that was in my flight suit shoulder pocket. Did you find a small, sterling silver shamrock?"

"Yes. It came back up from the laundry room and it's with your carbine and revolver. The clean-clothes crowd always finds good luck charms in pilots' clothing. You'll find it in your flight suit's shoulder pocket. You guys must be a superstitious lot."

"In a combat zone, I think nearly everyone has a good luck charm. It may not ward off harm, but it's comforting to have."

"I forgot to mention that the nurse gave you a sponge bath. I'll bet you're sorry you missed that."

"Hardly. I'm a married man who can't walk, let alone chase women."

"Just teasing, sir. A guy gets horny around here with all of these pretty nurses around. Trouble is, they always fall for the officers, especially the doctors. I reckon that they're looking for the big bucks that the doctors will make when they return to civilian life."

"You're really cynical for a young man."

Winter Roses

"You'd be cynical, too, sir, if you lived every day around the dead and the dying, trying not to throw up when you're helping the nurses and doctors repair the worst wounds you can possibly imagine and carrying amputated limbs to a huge, walk-in freezer. They tag them for proper burial should the patient die. There are rumors that they really don't save the limbs because the freezer gets too full to handle them all. Then they're fed to the sharks because no one would be the wiser. I sure as hell wouldn't want to draw that duty."

"I see what you mean. Most of the time I'm in the air directing fighter-bomber strikes and I usually don't see the carnage close-up and personal. When I'm on patrol with the ground troops I support, we sometimes get into firefights. Then it's way too close-up and personal and I wish during those moments that I was back in the air. But you can't have it both ways. Combat patrolling with the troops is worth the risk, at least for me. But back to you, I hope that your officers and NCOs recognize and appreciate the difficult job you're doing for them. They couldn't function without you and I'll be glad to tell them that."

"Jeez, sir, you're not like any officer I've ever been around. Sometimes I think I'm working for the biggest assholes in the world."

"Doctors have tough jobs, too. They often mean the difference between life and death and even seconds can mean the difference between life and death, and they have to make their decisions for the right treatment in split seconds. I'd get short-tempered if I had to do their job."

"Yeah, I guess you're right. Still, it would be nice to hear even an "attaboy" every now and then. They'd have a hard time doing their jobs without guys like me."

"If you're looking for sympathy, you can find it in the dictionary between 'shit' and 'syphilis' and you don't need any of those three."

"No, sir. I'm not a crybaby or a whiner. I'm more like Rodney Dangerfield, just looking for a little respect."

"I sure as hell appreciate the care you're giving me and I'll bet there are plenty of wounded troops you've helped who feel the same way I do. Speaking about appreciation, may I ask for another morphine shot if the pain comes back?"

"The doc said to give you another every six hours if you need it. So let the nurse or corpsman on duty in your ward tonight know that you hurt and you'll get one."

"Thanks and we'll see. I don't want to risk addiction."

"Won't happen, sir. The doctor will see to that."

The technician came in and took four X-rays of the ankle in various positions and told Frank that the doctor may not get the chance to give him the diagnosis until morning because all the staff doctors and nurses were overloaded with more serious casualties. Frank said he understood, and the corpsman got him back on the gurney to return him to his ward and bed.

He dozed off again, then woke up when an orderly brought him a dinner tray. It was the first "home-cooked" American meal he'd had since he'd been in country and realized that he'd been mostly on an all-Korean diet. He missed his kimchee, but thought that the chicken noodle soup was delicious, as was the chicken Kiev with real mashed potatoes and string beans. Chocolate cake topped off the meal. *Sure beats hell out of C-rats.* He also enjoyed the carton of milk and the cup of coffee, which was much better than the jungle swill he and his buddies were used to.

My dinner here was great, but I still wish I could have stayed on the Coral Sea. It's not often you get a dinner party in your honor, particularly one hosted by the captain of a famous aircraft carrier. I'd like to have talked with the chief aviation officer about the

Winter Roses

ship's fast FACs and why they don't get respect. Their recon photos aren't worth shit. Flying high and fast doesn't cut it; the enemy's too good at camouflage to be spotted well above AAA fire range at Hun, Corsair or Phantom speeds. Then again, the pilots' OIC (Officer In Charge) would probably get defensive and blow me off. Besides, he wouldn't have any authority to change the top doggies' mindset that jets are better spotter aircraft than our low-and-slow O-1s and O-2s.

Our little ol' Bird Dogs have to come in low and slow to spot targets: first on the recon runs and then on BDAs (Bomb Damage Assessment) runs. Every dive is a roll of the dice. Will I get hit this time or won't I? I sure as hell did this morning on my BDA run.

Frank got his next two morphine shots on schedule and woke up the next morning to discover his leg was in a cast. He remembered what he'd thought was a morphine dream of a nurse and corpsman wrapping his lower leg. *They must have been for real, prepping for the cast that runs from my toes to my kneecap. Great. How the hell can I fly? Why didn't the doctor give me the diagnosis first, before going ahead with a cast?* He fell back on his pillow, looked around the ward and heard the cries and moans of the wounded, which seemed to coming from every direction. Nurses, doctors and orderlies walked fast and with great purpose to attend to their worst-case wounded, and Frank realized that his broken or sprained ankle must seem like small beer to them. Especially since the ward's beds were filling as fast as the orderlies could wheel the dead to the ship's morgue or other wards for specialized treatment. *Hey, asshole, remind yourself: you don't have any reason to piss and moan about your ankle. Compared to what these guys are going through, you've got no problem at all.* He closed his eyes and thought about Marie and the children and wondered how they were. He smiled when he thought about his son Mike, who'd also broken his ankle the previous year after jumping out of a tree in his neighbor's yard. When Marie had asked him how he did that, he said he was running and he tripped. *Now we have the same injury in common and he'll get a laugh out of that. I hope to hell that I get a laugh out of it.*

By this time, my CO must be wondering what I'm doing and he may be thinking about charges like malingering, loss of aircraft and dereliction of duty. I sure hope that someone's keeping him informed of my whereabouts and letting him know that I won't be flying again for some time.

The doctor startled him out of his daydreaming by lifting the bed sheet and inspecting the cast.

"Good job, isn't it?"

"I'll take your word for it, doctor. I'm no judge of a plaster cast, let alone the injury that's the reason for it."

"As you've probably gathered, we couldn't waste any time in getting you into the cast even if the ankle was still slightly swollen. I hate to sound crass, but we've got to get you out of here to make room for someone who's in a worse world of hurt. This god-damned TET offensive is filling our beds faster than we can empty them and I'm sure you'll understand why we're moving you on."

"I understand completely, doctor. If I were in your shoes I'd do the same. But tell me what's wrong with my ankle before I leave."

"Sure. It's a combination of multiple fractures along with torn and stretched tendons and ligaments. Screws are now holding the joint together. You'll be hurting for some time, so I'm giving you these morphine tablets. Don't take any more than what the label says. When they're gone, that's it. Aspirin will have to get you through if you still have pain. I've arranged for a helicopter to get you back to your base and your CO knows you're coming. He said something about shuttling you to NKP, whatever in hell that means. What a pilot with a messed-up ankle like yours can do is beyond me but I'm sure you'll think of something. Plan on wearing that cast for at least six weeks, OK? After that, keep it wrapped with an Ace bandage. An orderly will bring you breakfast shortly along with your flight suit and weapons. Your suit has the leg cut right to the crotch so you can get the cast through.

Winter Roses

"Your scheduled departure time is 0950 hours. Good luck and Godspeed, captain. It's been a pleasure helping you and I wish we could have met in a world that hadn't gone mad."

"Sometimes I think we're the ones who've gone mad. But I can't let myself believe that. My job may be dangerous and we kill for a living, but we share a common goal—saving our boys' lives. If that's madness, I'll kiss your ass. And by the way, the young corpsman you assigned to me is a first-rate troop, one I'd be proud to have under my command."

"I'll tell him you said that and that I agree with you. Kiss my ass? Heh. I'll remember that, especially in the bad times around here like right now, when you break your ass and your heart to help these brave young men and women and there's nothing you can do to save many of them."

The doctor saluted. Frank returned it. He laid his head back on the pillow, closed his eyes and was suddenly overwhelmed with a bone-deep sorrow. Tears ran down his cheeks. *Doc, we have more in common than you know. Maybe more than you'll ever want to know.*

Frank spent his recovery at the USAF's clandestine Nakhon Phanom (NKP) base in Thailand, reporting to a colonel who needed an experienced supply officer to support the 56th Air Commando Wing--a top-secret, all-volunteer special operations unit that provided close air support for the Lao and Hmong forces fighting the Pathet Lao and NVA. The wing's operations were top secret, since they were in direct violation of the Geneva Accords that, on paper, assured strict neutrality for Laos. Yet the Hmong army was fighting entire NVA divisions streaming down the Lao side of the Ho Chi Minh trail bound for the war raging in South Vietnam, and attacking Laotian and Hmong forces seemingly everywhere in the country. The 56th ACW was one of America's answers to help keep the enemy at bay and slow the flow of enemy troops, equipment and munitions into South Vietnam that would otherwise have been deployed to kill American soldiers and their allies.

Special operations appealed to Frank since his own FAC experience brought him into close contact with many of the pilots and their aircraft he'd directed to hit enemy targets and he did his best to help keep his buddies well-fed and well-armed. He particularly admired the heavily armed, A-26 twin-engine light bombers that had French instrumentation, leftovers from France's disastrous war in Indochina. He enjoyed watching them take off on parallel runways with the F-4 Phantoms and outrace them because their props gave them the acceleration edge until the jet's engines kicked in with their superior thrust. As a FAC, he also appreciated the firepower these aircraft—along with the weapons-laden Skyraiders—brought to his FAC "by invitation only" parties.

His time at NKP passed quickly, and he rationalized his stay back in supply and logistics as a way to meet and work with good officers who might be in a position to help him someday. *Here's hoping that my new bosses here in NKP will remember my services if and when I ever need a job.*

Nine

Back to Battle, Back to Home

Frank passed his checkout flight in a Bird Dog as soon as he returned to Qui Nhon, after the squadron flight surgeon gave him a hurry-up physical that concentrated on the ankle's strength and mobility. Both his CO and the flight surgeon were angry that he flew a rehabbed Bird Dog back from NKP without their approval, but grudgingly accepted his rationale, i.e., his ankle felt good and with him at the controls, they wouldn't have had to pull a pilot off combat missions for a day or more just to pick up and deliver an aircraft.

He decided to see how far he could push.

"By the way, sir, I'd like your permission to make that Bird Dog mine for the duration. I really liked how she handled and her new power plant really purrs, even at altitude."

"Jesus Christ, how high up did you take her?"

"To the max, sir. Maybe even a little higher. The way I figured, I may as well make good use of my flight back and check out the aircraft after she'd been overhauled. This saved tying up one of our FACs. I mean, what the hell, sir, I was flying her back, anyway. I wanted to make my trip a productive one."

"OK, I get it and you're off the hook this time. Not that you've deserved a reward, but you now have a hooch all to yourself and you can finish out your tour in the lap of luxury. You have FAC seniority in the mighty 21st TASS. Check in with our supply guy at HQ for your bedding, a bottle of good champagne, a box of chocolates, and your first all-nighter with a beautiful flight nurse. Don't forget, reveille at 0400 and mission assignments and briefing at 0500.

"Oh yeah, and welcome home. I can't tell you how much it hurt to thank the Navy for saving your sorry ass, but someone had to do it. Don't ever make me do that again. One more order while I'm on a tear. Limp over to the far bay and check out what's left of your Bird Dog. We sent an Army Chinook after it and the damned thing managed to yank it out of the treetop without crashing. I personally checked it over and all the bullet holes support my decision to not hold a hearing on loss of aircraft.

"In the future, I expect that you'll take greater pains to avoid flying through similar shit storms. Have I made myself clear? Good. Now you can go. And don't forget to give thanks for your good luck and many blessings, not the least of which is having a caring and understanding commanding officer like me. Now get the hell out of here. I'm tired of agreeing with you."

"Yes sir, thank you, sir!"

"Don't thank me. Pure, dumb luck is beyond even my ability. That's your domain, but you better not test it anymore."

"No, sir!"

Frank wandered over to the bay to look at his broken and shot-up Bird Dog and walked around it to count the bullet holes for himself. *Holy shit, the colonel wasn't kidding about my luck. It's a minor miracle that I was able to fly this thing even into a treetop landing. It's more of a miracle that my ass wasn't aerated considering the spray of bullets that came through the fuselage and wings from two directions. Never forget what you've seen here, asshole.*

This is the Bird Dog that Frank muscled into a treetop landing after being hit by VC ground fire. He rappelled down a piece of too-short rope and then fell the rest of the way, badly breaking his ankle. A Navy helicopter picked him up after he ran as best he could with the VC firing at him, inspiring him to run faster. The broken bird was picked out of the treetop by an Army Chinook and returned to base for parts salvage. Frank wrote on the back of the photo, "Ain't she beautiful?"

Frank Delaney Collection

He crawled into bed late that evening after catching up on the FAC missions with his best FAC buddy, Dusty Eberhart, who'd flown several missions in support of Frank's beloved Tigers during his absence. Frank was most pleased to learn that every one of his fellow FACs had survived TET even though they had flown more than twice the number of missions than they'd flown pre-TET. Fortunately, all—including himself--had beaten the law of averages.

Dusty brought Frank into an impending mission, which was a major ambush. The Tigers were planning to suck the Viet Cong into a "V"-shaped kill zone using a reinforced platoon on combat patrol as bait. It started with the discovery of a wide trail that Charlie used, often in force. The Tigers had quietly and patiently cut a long path on both sides of the trail in the form of an inverted "V" that would steer Charlie into the kill zone with ambush teams waiting on both sides. They took extra care in clearing the underbrush, shaping the V to gradually steer Charlie so he wouldn't notice a subtle shift into the pathway to hell until it was too late.

Frank learned about a new ally who had told Dusty about the trail, who in turn advised his squadron CO and Colonel Pak. She led them to it, and the colonel immediately saw its ambush potential. Her name was Mai Tran Thi, a young Vietnamese woman who had good visibility of the local Viet Cong units' capabilities through a young and disgruntled VC who had taken the fall for a senior officer's screw-up in a major operation.

She not only spoke understandable English, she was very pretty and led the young VC into believing that he had a chance with her. She kept this hope alive with occasional rewards of black-market American dollars that she smuggled to him, telling him that she would never speak to him again if he got caught with the money and ratted her out as his source. This was a hollow threat, since the VC would have tortured and killed both of them as black marketers and spies if they'd caught him and he squealed. When he thought about the possible consequences and told her he wanted out, she coaxed him into staying with her with a promise of better things to come…namely, that the two of them might have a future together if they stuck together. She also promised him amnesty from the Americans and perhaps even an escape together to America if the war started to go badly for the South Vietnamese.

With her VC contact secure at least for the foreseeable future, she asked for ten American dollars as payment for herself and for her source. She would keep seven and pay her fellow spy three with the promise of more if he continued to cooperate. Dusty took her proposition to his squadron CO, who agreed.

Winter Roses

Thanks to her intelligence, the ambush planning was well underway. Dusty and Frank would provide the air assets while the Tigers finished prepping the V's kill zone.

Since the Tigers expected at least a company-sized attack as a worst-case scenario, they stacked the V with two rifle companies on each side. 50-caliber machine guns on both sides and M-60s in the V's point would sweep the enemy troops with interlocking fire from every possible angle. Claymore mines were set everywhere, above the kill zone in the trees and hidden in the brush along the sides of the V.

To avoid friendly-fire casualties, all agreed that that artillery and air support would be used only when Charlie turned and fled. The Tigers zeroed their preplanned mortar and artillery fire on the wide end of the V, which Charlie would have to pass through to escape. The arty kill zone would also serve as the fighter-bombers' kill zone.

Dusty and Frank requested permission to control and direct the artillery so they could better coordinate it with the napalm and strafing ("nape and strafe") runs from four F-4s they'd have ready to strike seconds after they stopped the artillery barrage. This made sense to Colonel Pak and he agreed.

The operation began with Tran's VC partner telling his comrades that he'd seen a ROK Tiger platoon patrolling on their secret trail when he went in search of his machete that he had lost on their last patrol. He told them that he jumped into the bushes when he heard them coming and hid there while they went by. He overheard two American officers with them say that they'll use it every night. With that, the trap was set for the next evening.

At 1730 hours, Dusty and Frank were in the air and flying well away from the ambush site to avoid tipping the Tigers' hand. The first alert came in from an observation post on a rise above the V: "Lock and load, Charlie's on his way. Looks like a reinforced rifle company coming in behind a rifle squad on point."

Moments later, the firefight started between the Tiger "patrol" platoon and the VC. After a long three minutes of sustained fire, the platoon's rifle squads began breaking off in sequence to maintain covering fire for their "escape." The last squad disappeared into the point of the V. The VC paused for a moment and then continued, unaware that they had slowly closed their ranks as they followed the narrowing brush lines. When they reached the V's midpoint, the Tigers triggered the ambush by detonating the Claymores. The machine gunners and riflemen opened up. In seconds, over half of the enemy troops were on the ground, dead or too wounded to escape. The rest milled around in wild-eyed confusion, firing blindly at the muzzle flashes that seemed to come from everywhere.

A few ran right into the Tigers' positions where they met instant death from point-blank fire. Others started to run back in the direction they'd come from while the Tigers stood and shouted their battle cry, "Mang Ho!" This made the VC run even faster. Just as they reached the mouth of the invisible V, the Tiger 81mm mortar crews and 105mm batteries began firing simultaneously, enveloping the VC in a firestorm of white-hot, razor-sharp steel shards of shrapnel flying everywhere in the kill zone. Every VC caught in the open was chopped into bloody chunks of flesh and bone.

The barrage lifted after 10 minutes, which signaled Dusty to mark his target and call in napalm from the two F-4 Phantoms circling overhead. He placed his marking rocket right in the middle of the remaining troops and cleared the lead Phantom in hot. The jet thundered down, flattened out and released its two canisters of napalm. They tumbled down and exploded in gigantic, fiery splashes that burned the few surviving and barrage-stunned Charlies into charred, shapeless lumps. As insurance, Dusty fired his second rocket into a clump of trees near the first explosion and cleared in the wingman, just in case there were still some enemy troops who had reached an area that they thought might be safe. The jet came in hot, released its canisters and flew back up to his lead to see if strafe might be needed. Frank then repeated the nape strikes from both of his F-4s.

Winter Roses

Dusty flew down for a BDA. All was still in the smoldering kill zone and carbonized lumps of VC bodies were scattered everywhere in the ashes. With no sign of enemy movement, he released the fighters. No strafe was needed.

He reported "Mission accomplished!" to all on his radio nets and the senior Phantom pilot came up on the net with a rousing "Mang Ho!" and his own compliment… "Tigers Number One!" With that, the Phantoms turned in formation sequence and headed back to their NKP home where they would signal victory with a flyover.

When the Tigers walked the kill zones to look for survivors, all they found were bodies and pieces of bodies. The Charlies had succumbed to a near-perfect deluge of death. The jungle was strangely silent and the air hung heavy with the sickeningly sweet stench of burned flesh.

The next day, Dusty and Frank learned the body count. One hundred and eleven VC bodies were tallied vs. four Tigers KIA.

Colonel Pak was satisfied that his Tigers' ears were once more vindicated in battle. In their after-action reports, the colonel and the FAC squadron CO both wrote that the VC had probably come in force to attack the airbase and that the enemy's timing was perfect for the ambush. They also agreed that future ambush timing was too important to depend upon pure, dumb luck. They would need better intelligence before planning any more, and that perhaps the young spy and her turncoat VC could be of help again.

After the slaughter, Frank asked Dusty if he could introduce him to Mai Tran. He correctly believed that her life would be in danger since she'd be a prime suspect by showing the Americans the trail and perhaps even helping them plan the ambush.

Dusty agreed and they got together with her after the ambush to discuss ways they might protect her from VC retaliation. Frank thought that the best way to protect her was to get her moved on base. She told them that she needed protection and worried about returning home because her friends and even members of her own family were VC sympathizers. They might suspect that she had told her American friends about the trail's location. She also said that her VC partner would have to be protected. Frank promised that he'd talk with his squadron commander to see if they could also do something for him; perhaps a nearby American infantry unit would accept him as a Kit Carson scout.

When they parted, Frank asked where she was staying that night since it was too late--and probably too dangerous--to go home.

She said that the cook would let her sleep on his cot in the back of the kitchen, which he used for quick catnaps during the day. When they parted, Mai Tran thanked Frank and Dusty for their concern and their help, and in turning away, she brushed her breast against Frank's forearm. He pretended to ignore the come-on.

Walking back to their Bird Dogs to make sure the mechanics had checked them out for the following day's missions, Frank told Dusty that he was pleased that they had conjured up a story that she could use when she went home the following day. She would tell them that she was held captive overnight by the Tigers because they didn't trust any Vietnamese coming anywhere near their camp. They released her the next day when the cook for the Americans came looking for his dishwasher.

After they'd been satisfied that their planes were mission-ready, Frank and Dusty called it a night. Frank wandered back to his hooch to get some needed sleep; he still tired easily from his broken-ankle experience. He had also crashed from his adrenaline high, which exacerbated his fatigue. Dusty headed for the operations tent to see if he could get a couple shots of scotch from the squadron's medicine cabinet.

Winter Roses

0400 hours would come early and Frank wanted to be sharp on his first solo mission back since he was shot down and saved by the Navy. He smiled when he thought of the Coral Sea crew's welcome and hospitality, and wished he'd had the chance to dine with the ship's captain and the officers who'd saved his life. *As good as that steak and wine would have been, I never want to go through that ordeal again.*

I'll hear those AK-47 rounds zipping by for the rest of my life. Thanks to the Navy, I have a life. Unless I make the same mistake of flying through a lead shit-storm, which won't happen.

He leaned his CAR-15 carbine against the nightstand, hung his pistol belt with its holstered revolver on the bedpost next to his head, peeled off his flight suit and fell into bed. He was sound asleep in a moment.

A hand on his thigh awakened him and he reached for his revolver. The hand left his leg and gently tugged his wrist to signal that he was in no danger. Now he was wide awake, and realized that a woman was lying next to him. She was naked. It was Mai Tran! She stroked his thigh again and spoke to him in broken English, telling him how happy she was that he was back and that she wanted him, and emphasized her desire by reaching into his shorts to grasp his erect penis and softly stroke it. "Now you like me," she whispered. "You try to save me. I want you, you want me, you take me, OK?" Frank couldn't resist. Without a word, he pulled off his shorts, rolled over, placed his arm around her waist and pulled her body tight to his.

He put his finger to her lips and pressed them to tell her to be very quiet, then reached down and rubbed her. She was open and already wet, shuddering and inhaling rapidly, and Frank quieted her again with his now-wet fingertips pressed to her lips. She moaned, opened her legs wider and he mounted her, penetrating deep with deliberate, slow strokes as she quivered with rising excitement. He kept the slow pace as long as he could stand it, and suddenly began to thrust faster and faster as she wriggled and gasped beneath him. He ejaculated when she began to match him stroke for stroke and they stayed tightly clasped together until they could again recapture their breath. "You come fast," she whispered. "Long time no sex. I fix tomorrow night. Thank you for helping me."

She rolled off the bed and he watched her in the gathering light of dawn as she gracefully slipped into her *ao dai*, the beautiful, silken dress of the Vietnamese women. Before disappearing through the wooden door of his hooch, she turned around and blew him a kiss.

OK, asshole, you've gotta get up in 30 more minutes. No sense in trying to go back to sleep. You'd oversleep, miss reveille and probably the old man's briefing. You've been gone long enough and he would not take your late arrival lightly. More likely, he'd announce to all that the goddam Navy has spoiled you rotten. Heh. Which it has.

He was surprised to see Mai Tran seated in the back of the briefing room. She ignored him as he walked by and took a seat closer to the podium so he'd get a better look at the wall map marking the day's mission targets. *She must have more intel for us, otherwise she wouldn't be here. God, I wonder if she's a double agent. I could get compromised with our sudden relationship and I'd better be very, very alert, especially if she starts asking me questions about my missions and the FACs' secrets for finding and fixing Charlie. Go easy, asshole, and don't let your prick rule your thinking.*

The major's briefing was right to the point. He showed the pilots their targets of the day along with any special precautions they'd have to take to avoid enemy small arms fire and heavier AAA if the targets were NVA troop concentrations. All were told to be ready to divert for ground support if friendly troops got into firefights they couldn't handle and warned them not to be stupid like the Army helicopter pilots who fly right through friendly artillery barrages. Frank had heard these briefings many times, and he was amazed that some pilots still forget these basic rules in the heat of battle and pay for it with their lives.

Winter Roses

The major also thanked Mai Tran for her continuing intelligence that had saved a lot of Americans as well as friendly forces' lives. The FACs all stood and applauded her for her courage.

As his finale, he asked the assembled pilots to welcome Frank home after his long vacations with the Navy and the spooks and snake-eaters at NKP.

His buddies applauded, and Frank returned their welcome with a salute and a statement of his own. "You guys don't know what you've been missing. Next time you're wounded and crash-land, make sure you ask TAC to get you a Navy rescue helicopter. The driver will take you to a small piece of paradise in the South China Sea called a 'hospital ship'.

There, you'll find beautiful young nurses galore who will bathe you from head to toe. Trouble is, you won't know it because you'll be stoned on morphine, but that's not a bad trip, either. Anyway, I'm really glad to be back, guys. And thank you for bombing the shit out of Charlie and the NVA while I was gone.

"It will make my short-timer's life a little easier to bear."

The pilots stood and applauded, and the major closed by saying how much they'll miss Frank's Irish blarney when he's gone.

On his way to his aircraft, he thought how easy it would be for Mai Tran to collaborate with her VC turncoat should they prove to be double agents.

He was happy that he had no serious encounters that day, only a false alarm. One was a frightened young Tiger lieutenant who thought his platoon was going to be overrun. He had heard the screams of the enemy growing louder and louder as they charged directly at him and his men. Frank dove down to take a look and laughed when he saw a huge pack of monkeys racing through the treetops on a heading that would bring them right over the troops' heads. He quickly called the lieutenant and told him to hold his fire because his "enemy" was a pack of monkeys.

The lieutenant called back and said that the monkeys had passed and made a stinking mess out of his platoon. Every one of his men was either sick or angry or both, with monkey shit or piss all over them.

Frank consoled them. "Better to get splattered and sprayed by monkey piss and shit than by AK-47, B-40 rocket and RPG (Rocket Propelled Grenade) fire." The lieutenant had to agree and he signed off by asking Frank to tell his CO what happened. He was too embarrassed to admit that his platoon was being overrun—not by North Vietnamese troops, but by monkeys. Frank agreed with a grin; now he had another good story for his buddies back at HQ.

After dinner, he and Mai Tran agreed that their liaisons could not be nightly because of fatigue, his daily adrenaline-pumped missions and a concern that they might be discovered.

They worked out a simple system for on-again, off-again nights. No small rock on the ground to the left of his wooden hooch door, no sex. For that night, the rock stayed at the door.

Instead, they discussed Frank's idea to keep her out of harm's way. He would get her to America, where she could get an education and start a new life. To that end, he asked permission from his CO to periodically use the squadron's radiotelephone net to contact friends back in northern Michigan whom he believed would help finance the money that Mai Tran would need for her air fare, tuition costs and room and board. He also contacted his alma mater, Michigan State, to enroll her in a 10-week crash course in English for foreign students. She would then transfer to a community college in Northwest Michigan for two years of basic coursework that would lay the groundwork for transfer back to MSU where she would pursue her chosen field of study.

Winter Roses

He called me around 0300 EDT one morning, briefed me on his plan and asked me to write and send out a press release that focused on the intelligence that Mai Tran had gathered at great risk to herself that had saved many American soldiers' lives. The release also requested donations to help finance her education at MSU and the community college. I sent the release draft to Frank for his review and comments. He called back two weeks later with minor corrections and his name as the press contact. I sent it out via the PR Newswire.

The response was much better than we anticipated. AP, UPI, Reuters, local and national newspapers, and broadcast media all picked up the story. Many wanted their own takes and quotes from Frank, who was deluged with calls for interviews. This did not make his CO happy, since calls were coming in to HQ during Frank's alert and training mission time.

Worse yet, his superiors were angry because no one had told them of Frank's plan and our release of the story to the media without their blessing. They had no idea what this was all about and couldn't answer the media's questions.

Frank called me during the peak of the media calls for interviews and asked me to shut off the publicity because of the ass-chewings from his CO. I told him that the press rocket had been fired and hit the target, and that the only thing that would stop it was time.

"However," I added, "You can tell your CO that the news coverage will start to peter out soon since the story's been covered. It's now old news, which is no news."

He was relieved to at least be able to tell his CO to cool his jets, that they were over the worst of it. I also gave him my outside-in opinion that the story put the whole damned Air Force in a good light. A heartwarming story about an officer trying to save the life of a young woman who'd saved countless American and friendly forces' lives is good press, despite the top doggies' anger because they weren't informed in advance.

We had to admit that we should have advised them before launching the story. On the other hand, the story might have been stalled to death as it worked its way up the chain of command. I didn't tell him how pissed off the Air Force PR people must have been because we bypassed them.

Someone up top must have decided that the good will of Frank's efforts was worth the embarrassment he and his staff felt when they didn't know what the hell the reporters were talking about.

The publicity was paying off, along with Frank's personal requests for help from friends and relatives back home. A Traverse City couple had volunteered to provide free room and board for Mai Tran, and over three thousand dollars had been received to cover her tuition costs at MSU and the community college. He also learned that both MSU and the community college had accepted her.

Between his FAC duties, telephone interviews with the media, training his replacement in the ways to properly support the Tigers, and the rock by the his door, Frank was exhausted and more than ready to go home to a more stable life, even though it meant he'd be flying BUFFs again.

The day before he rotated home, Colonel Pak gave a staff dinner in his honor with several of his buddies and the squadron's CO and staff attending. The highlight of the evening was the colonel's presentation of a battle-scarred AK-47 mounted on a piece of stained wood. Embedded in the wood was a cloisonné medallion of the Tiger's patch and an engraved brass plate that read, "Presented by Colonel Pak to Captain Frank Delaney for bravery in combat patrolling." Frank asked Dusty to make sure that the REMFs didn't steal his new keepsake, get the breech leaded in so it would be a legal war souvenir, and oversee its shipment home. Dusty promised and made good on his word.

Years later, Mike threw a party when Marie wasn't home and someone stole the weapon and its wooden mounting board. Somewhere in the Valley of the Sun there may be a stolen and valuable family keepsake. Hopefully, no one drilled the lead out of the breech and bore and turned it back into a working, fully automatic assault rifle.

Frank spent his last night in country with Mai Tran.

Ten

Save A Mistress Or A Marriage

He caught an Army Huey helicopter the next morning to Da Nang, where he'd board a Freedom Bird to the Philippines. From there, he'd go to San Francisco for processing and then fly on to Phoenix and home. In Manila, he bought civilian clothes because he didn't want any hassle from the longhairs that often picketed the airports and harassed military personnel returning from the war.

Marie had already told him about some of the children's classmates who shouted, "Your dad's a baby-killer!" The boys got into a pushing and shoving match with their tormenters on school property, and their principal punished Frank, Jr., Mark, and Mike with detentions and a warning that future fighting would result in expulsion.

Marie lodged a complaint with the school superintendent, who promised he'd talk with the principal and rescind the detentions. As for the name-callers, he told her that he'd instruct the principal to tell them there'd be no harassment on school property. This didn't work; the minute the children stepped outside the school's boundaries, the baby-killer chanting started again. This time one of their tormenters made the mistake of taking a swing at Mark and the teasing quickly turned into a brawl. The children beat the snot out of their adversaries and put an end to the harassment.

Marie heard from several anonymous phone callers who threatened to sue because of the fights. Marie told them to go ahead, because there was ample proof that their little darlings started the fights with their name-calling and the first swings, and that all her children had done was defend their dad's honor, a concept about which the parents knew nothing and cared less. She also chided the callers for not having enough courage to identify themselves and asked if they were afraid she would countersue, prompting them to hang up—some slamming the phone down as hard as they could. Considering this behavior, she was not surprised that their children were bullying brats and she told her children she was proud of them for standing up for their father.

The family celebrated Frank's homecoming with a pizza party and a viewing of his slides of the country and the people, including three of Mai Tran. Marie asked who she was, and Frank told her about his plans to get her to America, so she could escape the vengeance certain to come for her collaboration with American forces. Marie noted the passion in his speech and eyes as he described in some detail how she'd provided good intelligence which saved a lot of American and ROK Tiger lives at the risk of her own life. She also couldn't help but note how pretty the young Vietnamese woman was.

Long-overdue lovemaking was the homecoming highlight for Frank and Marie, just like another honeymoon, only better with anticipation and experience. My own CO told us that the very first thing he and his wife did when he returned from Korea was to make love. He then set down his duffle bag.

Since the children were still in school, family activities were confined to weekends, which included trips up the Mogollon Rim to the Grand Canyon and Arizona's other scenic wonders. Everyone especially enjoyed the excitement of riding the donkeys back down to the canyon floor to visit the Havasupai elders that Frank had offended when he'd blasted through the canyon in his fighter. All were happy to see them again and the children enjoyed a baseball game with the Indian children, who easily beat them.

Frank's leave time passed too quickly. A return to SAC and retraining on B-52 upgrades at Castle AFB in California was next on his agenda and he left with conflicting emotions about flying BUFFs again—especially after his fighter qualification and subsequent service in Vietnam as a FAC, where he'd experienced first-hand the adrenaline highs of flying low and slow over enemy-held territory. That, and the recognition and appreciation that came with his primary mission of saving GIs' lives in ground support missions.

He admitted to himself that his need for adrenaline fueled his dislike of the nearly-routine, high-altitude missions of a B-52 bomber…now being called "Monkey Killers" by the pilots and bomber crews alike.

Between classroom and flying instruction, he had little time for himself. What spare time he had was mostly spent coordinating his main interest—getting Mai Tran to America and into college so she could get a good job and live her life without fear. He knew all too well that the danger of VC revenge was growing with each passing day, and that determined guerrillas could get to her. Air Police guards might not be able to be able to stop them and he hoped that she was getting good protection.

His worst fears were realized when he took a call at HQ from a fellow FAC still in-country. Charlie had indeed attacked in the night and Mai Tran had been seriously wounded during a Viet Cong raid to capture her.

She had warned this FAC that she believed an attack was imminent, and he went to his wing CO to seek permission for more guards. The major balked at first, but then remembered how vital she'd been to the many successful FAC missions flown under his command. He suggested that ROK Tigers be placed around her hooch for maximum security; if they couldn't supply the manpower, perhaps a combination of USAF air police and Tigers would work. The major

Winter Roses

agreed and called Colonel Pak to discuss the situation. The colonel agreed that she needed extra protection and sent a reinforced rifle squad with an M-60 and its crew along with four additional troops who would set up in the tree line to lay an ambush for any VC who came after her. They would also serve as listening posts.

The Tigers and APs had also laid a perimeter of sandbags around her hooch and added the ROK flag along with their regimental Tiger pennant to tell the enemy whom they'd be screwing with should they try to attack. The APs were delighted that they'd been paired with the Tigers. It struck them that the miniature fort advertised to the enemy that Mai Tran was probably in there, but their concern was offset by the likelihood the enemy would back off when they saw the ROK troops.

The enemy would also realize that an entire regiment of Tigers was nearby, poised to destroy any number of troops the VC could throw at them.

The major and Colonel Pak wondered if all of this was a waste of manpower and time that could be put to better use. Frank's friend told him that he'd pleaded with them for at least another week of beefed-up security and they grudgingly agreed to extend it for another two weeks.

All was quiet until early one morning, when a Tiger in one of the LPs shouted, "Mang Ho!" and opened fire on four VCs who'd emerged from a tunnel with Mai Tran in tow. They were just a few meters away.

The VC had tunneled near her hooch and crawled out of their well-camouflaged spider hole. Two of them had garroted the AP guards while the other two grabbed her and stuffed socks into her mouth, then taped it shut so she couldn't scream.

After tying her hands behind her, they pulled her down the hole and crawled back to the tunnel's mouth, dragging her with them. They had no idea the LP was close by and weren't prepared for the Tiger's M-16 fire. They'd been ambushed and they dropped Mai Tran so they could escape into the forest before more Tigers arrived.

The other Tigers in their tree-line foxholes jumped out and ran after them, but tracking them in the darkness was impossible: the VC owned the night. They broke off the chase and came back to help get Mai Tran to safety and a doctor. An AP who'd been on duty in the HQ tent and heard the firing had come over to help. He turned on his flashlight and discovered that she was bleeding badly from a wound in her side. The LP Tiger's burst of fire had hit her, along with a VC whose body was a few yards away. The AP called HQ for a stretcher and a medic while the Tigers turned to the forest with weapons at the ready in the remote chance the VC would return and try again to recapture Mai Tran.

Frank's buddy and the major were surprised by the VC's ingenuity in digging a tunnel to capture Mai Tran. Yet they must have known of the VC's prowess in tunneling. Had it not been for the listening posts, Charlie would have succeeded. Frank was appalled at the news and fully understood that his plans for Mai Tran's education in America were on indeterminate hold. More importantly, he worried that she may not survive the attack. His buddy promised he'd keep him informed of the severity of her wound and prognosis.

In subsequent interviews with journalists, Frank told them that she was badly wounded in a VC attempt to capture her, and that there was little or no chance she'd be able to come to America in time for her English language course. With that, press interest waned in the story and it was never revived. This was just as well for Frank, because Marie had learned of his affair. She couldn't resist opening a letter sent to their Phoenix address from Dusty, who was still in country but now FAC'ing for a different unit. When he'd learned of Mai Tran's wounding, he'd gone to visit her at a field hospital in Da Nang. She had told him of her nocturnal visits to Frank's bed and had asked him if he would write a letter to Frank for her, telling him that she was going to get better, and that she loved him and missed him terribly.

Winter Roses

Marie was hurt, angry, afraid of losing Frank, and didn't know what to do. She wondered just how serious that relationship was and whether he was planning to leave her when he returned from Castle AFB where he was on TDY, training on upgrades that had been made to the B-52. Whether he wanted a divorce, she did not know. After mulling over her options, she decided the best thing she could do was confront Frank, ask him what his plans were when she came to the U.S., and go from there.

Meanwhile, she tried to calm herself with a stiff screwdriver. And another. She tried to lie down and steady her shakiness, telling herself that there were plenty of vets returning from Vietnam who'd had affairs with Vietnamese women.

Do I want to leave him? Marie, Marie, Marie, calm down. Be cool and strong when you confront Frank. No. "Confront" is a bad word. What's needed now is plain talk and mature discussion about our future plans together if there is to be a together. Right now, we need to keep this news from the children. Maybe it's not necessary to tell them about it at all if we decide to stay together. We'll find out soon enough.

She fixed a vodka martini without the martini, drank it down fast and fell asleep on the couch.

When Frank returned home three days later after completing his B-52 training and requalification, Marie welcomed him with a hug and a kiss, and his favorite dish, lasagna. She'd found a good chianti to go with the meal and the children were given their choice of lasagna or pizza. They chose the pizza and then asked if they could have a small glass of the *vino*. Frank agreed, considering that the night was one for celebration because he'd be home again for awhile and that the family would be moving again--this time to Wurtsmith AFB in northeastern lower Michigan. The children cheered at the news; they'd remembered well the good times they'd had in Michigan. Besides, they'd be a lot closer to their grandparents again.

During the children's lively chatter and Frank asking them about their studies and school activities, Marie stewed beneath her façade and kept silently rehearsing what she'd say to him. She did her best to avoid tipping her hand until they got the children to bed after doing their homework and playing a game of Monopoly.

They settled down on the couch after the children had gone to bed, and Frank put his arm around her. She told him to wait, that she had something he needed to see. She stood up, went to their bedroom and came back with the letter. She handed it to him.

"This came from one of your FAC friends in Vietnam and I opened it by mistake. With the APO address and envelope, I thought it was one of your letters that had been delayed for some reason. I'm sure you'll find it interesting."

Frank opened it, took out the letter and began to read. Marie could hold back her tears no longer.

"What's wrong, sweetheart? Why so sad?"

"Just read the letter. It says everything you need to know about what's wrong."

He read the letter and a flush crept over his face.

"So now you know. All I can say is that I'm sorry and promise you that this will never, ever happen again."

"What's your real reason for bringing her over here? So you can continue your affair behind my back?"

"Please don't believe that. The Viet Cong has targeted her for capture, probably torture and then most certainly, execution. She saved a lot of American and

Korean lives, maybe even my own, and they'll never forgive her for collaborating with us. And this letter doesn't tell the whole story. She slept with other FACs before I ever got to Nha Trang, hoping to multiply her chances of getting out of there. As it turned out, I'm the only one who's trying. Now she's seriously wounded and we don't even know if she's going to live, let alone be able to travel to the U.S. Honestly, I don't expect to ever see her again."

"You damned well better not see her again if you ever want to see me again."

"No, I won't be seeing her again. I'll send her a letter care of Dusty that will break off our relationship. On the remote chance that she gets here, I'll arrange for a new mentor, a FAC who was also with me at Castle for training on the BUFFs.

He was in another TASS squadron, but he was interested in helping me coordinate her educational plan and follow through to make sure the donations that are still coming in will be enough to cover her tuition, books and living expenses."

"Look, I don't fault her for your affair and I hope for her sake that she recovers and gets here. I expected more from you. You must be twice her age and ought to have known better. You surely must know how vulnerable any young woman would be to a mature, good-looking man like you, who's also an American officer and a pilot. Perhaps all she saw in you was a ticket to get here and escape the Viet Cong's revenge that was bound to come, but her words in the letter sure tell me that she's looking for a long relationship with you.

"Desperate people say and do desperate things and screwing her way to America may have been the only tool she thought she had. But I don't give a damn about her motives. I care about your motives, and if I thought for a second that you love her, I'd start the divorce proceedings. Now enough about your plans for her. What about your plans for me, and mine for you?

"We'd better discuss these and make sure we understand the consequences of everything we decide, positive or negative."

"You're right, Marie. I admit that I was a fool for sleeping with Mai Tran. More important, I've been a damned fool for hurting you and potentially hurting the children, too. All I can do is ask your forgiveness, reconfirm my love for you and assure you that I want to continue our lives together. You and the children mean too much for me to lose all of you in favor of sex with a woman barely out of her teens."

"OK. I don't want to break up our marriage over this, either. I'll even give you credit for caring enough about that young woman to get her out of trouble. The children and I were-- and still are--proud of you for that. With all that press coverage, you must be a hero to thousands of Americans by now, and this will surely mean more to the kids than fighting with classmates because they call you a 'baby killer.' And speaking of babies, it's a damned good thing you had that vasectomy.

"What do you think the press coverage would have been if your affair had been discovered? Talk about crapping in your own nest! Those reporters would have shredded you; I know that because I was one. I also know that the future of your career would be on shaky grounds. You're damned lucky that they don't know it and think that you're still Sir Galahad in a flight suit."

"Marie, getting her over here for sex was not the reason I tried to help her. Please believe that."

"I'm trying very, very hard to believe that. Right now, your credibility with me is in the toilet and it's going to take some time for me to accept that you're now telling the truth."

"Marie, please believe me! I still love you and want to spend the rest of my life with you. Please believe me—please!"

"I need time, Frank. I don't know if I can ever get over this."

"I understand. But for the sake of the children--and our own sake--can we at least try to get on with our lives? Make that 'our lives *together*.'"

"It's a good thing you added the 'together' bit. Now I'm exhausted and need to get some sleep. Don't you dare touch me when you come to bed. I'm still having trouble accepting all this and even thinking about having sex right now makes me want to vomit."

"I'll make this up to you, Marie, I swear that I will. You'll see."

"I'd better see and don't bother swearing for my sake. I've done more than enough of that for the two of us. Now goodnight."

Eleven

BARFLIES

Marie's flight home from Cleveland to Phoenix had a stopover in Houston, and she was more than ready to relax after the stress of her mother's sudden and unexpected death. While her parents were watching TV six nights before at their home in Dover, Ohio, her mother suddenly sat straight up and cried out, "Not yet!" By the time her father had leaped out of his recliner and dashed across the room to see what was wrong, she was dead.

There was no autopsy, so the cause of her death would remain a mystery. Marie thought that her father's decision to forgo an autopsy was a mistake, because it could provide clues to future illnesses that might strike her, her brother and sister—and their children--in future years. But there was no way she'd say that to him, at least not yet. He'd had enough grief without her piling on questions requiring difficult answers at such a vulnerable time. Without the autopsy, the best answer the doctor could give the family was a massive heart attack, an embolism or a stroke.

She walked into the first lounge she came to and went up to the bar where an older woman and a sailor were seated. She sat down and smiled at them. She'd had two vodka martinis during the first leg of her journey from Cleveland, passing on the cold turkey sandwich served for lunch. *I can always eat when I get home. The chance to enjoy a drink or two by myself doesn't come along very often.* She smiled back and the sailor raised his beer glass. The bartender came over and asked what she'd like. She thought for a moment and realized that she was feeling the martinis.

She ordered a White Russian.

"A White Russian it is, ma'am," he said. "But be careful. They're the original 'Sneaky Peteskis'."

They laughed and the sailor told the bartender he wasn't kidding. "In Jacksonville on a weekend shore leave, I had four of them after a few beers and woke up in the Boca Raton city jail. How I got to Boca from Jacksonville is still a mystery, but one clue was that my wallet was gone. Anyone who'd roll a sailor for his pay must have needed the money more than I did. My knuckles were red and sore and my uniform was spotted with blood, so I must have put up a fight. I thought sure that the shore police would be coming to get me, and that on my way to the brig, they'd tell me about the charges I'd face—probably drunk and disorderly, fighting and/or conduct unbecoming a noncommissioned officer. Whatever happened, I was quite sure I'd be wearing at least one less stripe. Lucky for me that I'd had a good record and the charges were reduced to "captain's mast," which is non-judicial punishment. With good future behavior, my record would be clean again, but I sure as hell got tired of swabbing the decks, cleaning the heads and dumping overboard the ship's leftover food to feed the fishies that fed the sharks.

"By the way, my name is Edward. I've been called a lot of names, especially by my shipboard officers. But you can call me "Eddie."

"Eddie," said Marie, "You're funny. My name is Marie. It's a plain-Jane name, but it's worked for me so far and I'm sticking with it.

As long as we're pals for the moment, why don't you come over here and sit with us? We don't often get the chance to sit next to a good-looking sailor, do we?"

The older woman smiled. "Not nearly as often as I'd like. And my friends call me Francie; you can call me Francie."

Marie's come-on didn't take long, the bartender thought. *But she looks like she's been around. She's got street smarts, so she can probably take care of herself.*

"Sure, Marie," answered Eddie. "Nice to meet you two. I don't often get the chance to sit between two pretty women." He finished his beer, came over and took the barstool between them.

The bartender asked Eddie if he'd like another Budweiser. Looking at Marie's White Russian, he said that he'd had enough beer. "Seeing as how I have nowhere else to go for the rest of the day, I do believe I'll have one White Russian--even though I swore I'd never have one again after my Jacksonville-to-Boca blackout. But since I'm still in uniform, I have to be extra careful not to drink too much. The last fucking thing I need is another night in jail. Whoa, sorry for the bad language, I'll be more careful. I guess you know that sailors get really good at swearing; practice makes perfect and we get plenty of practice. Sometimes we forget we're around civilized people, but I promise I'll clean up my act starting right now. Houston is my hometown and this is my first day of a three-day shore leave. My folks are gone and the only relative I have left around here is an ornery older brother who still treats me like a kid. I'd rather spend my time here with friends like you any day."

The bartender delivered the White Russians to Eddie and topped up Marie's since it was almost gone. Francie said she'd also like to have one. "It's been a long time since I've had one of those, too, Eddie. But to the best of my knowledge, I never got into a bar brawl." Marie laughed out loud and told Francine she'd feel sorry for the other guy if she did.

Winter Roses

Francie smiled and said, "We're living dangerously by drinking White Russians with a good-looking, smooth-talking sailor boy. Seriously, today I'd tell a nice serviceman like Eddie that I'd be happy to have him escort me home. I'd treat him as if I was his mother."

Eddie said that he'd like that a lot since he loved home cooking and his sister-in-law was an awful cook. "It's no wonder they go out for dinner almost every night," he continued. "When I go with them to their favorite restaurants--which are always the most expensive joints in town--he expects me to pay my share of the tab. It's easy for him to cover their share of the meal and drinks because he's a big shot at Standard Oil, and he doesn't even think about my lousy pay. More often than not, I just tell them to go ahead without me. There's a good beer-and-burger place that's an easy drive from their home that suits my wallet just fine, providing he'll let me use one of his cars. Just asking for the keys pisses him off, but that doesn't bother me since he's so easy to piss off. He usually lets me use it, but tells me every time that if I wreck it, I pay the insurance deductible. I can't imagine working for that son of a bitch; being his brother is bad enough. I guess I fulfill his need to kick someone's ass when I'm there and he's not at work. I know he browbeats the living shit out of the Mexicans who do their gardening and lawn maintenance and if I was their boss I'd tell that miserable bastard to go fuck himself, that the grief he and his hard-working crews suffer isn't worth the money."

Even though Eddie's language had slipped back into shipboard high gear, neither Marie nor Francie called him out for it.

Francie asked, "Why don't you tell him to go you-know-what-himself?" He replied that he'd thought about that. "But for all his warts, he's still my brother. Besides, I have an escape route via a few good friends here in the Houston area and I crash at their homes when the obnoxious meter goes through the roof."

"Well," Francie blurted, "You can now consider me one of your good Houston friends!" Marie arched her eyebrows at Francie's outburst, then laughed and said if they continued to drink White Russians and Eddie went home with Francie, maybe she should tag along as their chaperone.

They all laughed and Eddie replied that they'd both be safe with him as their guardian and that he's a good cook and dishwasher who'd earn his keep. "You can't say that the Navy didn't teach me at least a couple of useful skills," he added.

The bartender broke in to ask Marie if she had a flight to catch. "You've been here more than an hour and I just wanted you to be sure you can still make your flight." Marie glanced at her watch, and she broadcasted an "Oh, shit!" to everyone in the lounge. After complaining that the airlines never allow enough time for passengers to catch their connecting flights, she stated the obvious. "I guess I have missed my flight and I better go see if I can catch another in time to get home at a decent hour. My husband is supposed to go on alert at midnight and the children will be worried. I'll say my goodbye right now, and I've enjoyed our little get-together. Good luck and maybe our paths will cross again someday."

She stepped down from the barstool and lost her balance, but Eddie had turned to say goodbye and caught her before she could fall. He told her that he'd walk with her. She gladly accepted his offer, now knowing that the White Russians on top of the martinis and an empty stomach had hit her like a rocket. She felt slightly nauseated and very dizzy. *This can't be happening to me; I can hold my liquor.*

Eddie took her by the arm and told Francie that they'd be back as soon as Marie got her ticket for another flight home. Or, if she was lucky enough to find a flight that was departing soon, he'd make sure that she got on the plane and then come back for a last call before taking a cab to his brother's home. He left a $10 bill on the bar and told the bartender that the money covered both his drinks and his word. The bartender thanked him for his honesty.

Francie said she'd stay in the lounge until either or both came back, just to make sure that everything turned out all right. Marie and Eddie thanked her.

Winter Roses

Together they walked down the concourse to the American Airlines terminal. *I hope that she doesn't have to run to board a flight that's departing soon. She's having a hard time walking straight, let alone trying to run. I'll have to get an electric cart and hang on to her so she won't fall out.*

When they got to the ticket counter, Eddie suggested that they sit for a moment in the lounge chairs across the aisle and come up with a story that might save her the cost of a new ticket home. She agreed, but wondered aloud what she could possibly say? Eddie said, "You can tell her that you were in the ladies' restroom during the entire layover time because you were sick and missed the boarding calls."

Marie agreed and suddenly started to breathe heavily. She felt weak. Then she began to gag. "Thaaa jus might work. A-aaas--a matter of fact, I feel like I'm going to—to-- throw up, real soon." Eddie looked down the concourse for the nearest women's restroom and spotted one. "OK, Marie, here we go and hang on to my arm. There's a restroom down the concourse not far from the lounge where we met. Can you make it without puk—without throwing up?"

"Sure, Eddie," she answered. "Less go!" They started out walking at a fast clip and Eddie thought that they just might make it. He was wrong.

They hadn't gone 10 steps when she stopped, leaned over and again started to gag. He picked her up, carried her to a nearby ashtray, set her down on her feet, bent her head over the ashtray and held it there. The sight and sour stench of the butts almost in her face did the trick; she vomited. Passengers walking by shook their heads in disgust, and the airline attendant at the counter immediately called over the intercom for a janitor to report immediately to the American Airlines counter.

"I'm sorr-ry, Eddie," she mumbled after straightening up. "I thought I could make it. Guess I wash wr-wrong, eh?" Eddie couldn't help but smile and got her walking again. "Can you make it without tossing your cookies again, Marie? We're almost there." She dug her nails into his forearm for a tighter grip. They made it to the restroom door, where Eddie removed her hand from his forearm and told her that he'd be right outside the entryway waiting while she cleaned herself up before they returned to the American counter. She disappeared into the restroom.

He leaned against the wall and rubbed the indentations from her fingernails while stealing quick glances at the attendant. *That woman may not buy Marie's excuse for missing her flight. Still, Marie could say that heaving in the ashtray proved she wasn't feeling well. We'll see. At least she'll have the chance to tell her story.*

Long minutes went by and Eddie began to worry. *What's keeping her? I hope she hasn't passed out.* A woman walked toward the entrance and Eddie intercepted her before she could go in. "Ma'am, may I ask a big favor, please? My wife got sick in the concourse and she went in there to clean up. She's been in there a long time and I want to make sure she's OK." "Sure," answered the woman, "I'll be glad to help. Do you know if there are other women in there? How will I be able to recognize her?" Eddie told her that her name was "Marie" and that she was the only woman in there as far as he could tell.

The woman—a large and very buxom lady who looked to be in her forties—assured Eddie that she'd be right out to let him know how Marie was doing.

True to her word, she peeked out and said that Marie was sound asleep in one of the stalls and snoring hard. She also said that the alcohol fumes coming out of the stall had almost knocked her over and asked him how much she'd had to drink. Eddie replied that she'd had a couple of martinis on her flight into Houston and that she probably drank them to ease her fear of flying.

"She can't handle alcohol," he added. "It hits her pretty hard, and it doesn't do much to calm her nerves. To make things worse, I found her in one of the lounges, drinking a White Russian."

"Well, it's no wonder she got sick," she huffed. "I'll see what I can do to wake her up and make sure she looks presentable."

Eddie thanked her and she disappeared back into the rest room.

About 10 minutes later, she came out with Marie holding on to her arm for support. "Here she is, almost as good as new," the helper said. "I brushed her hair after she'd washed her face, helped her put on the lipstick I found in her purse and then gave her one of her breath mints. Now I have to hurry to catch my flight." Eddie thanked her and she replied, "My pleasure." She abruptly turned away and walked briskly down the concourse.

"That was awfully nice of that woman to help you, wasn't it? Can you walk straight without my help or do you want to take my arm for support?"

Marie chose the latter and they walked back to the AA counter. She introduced herself and told her story to the ticket attendant, who agreed that she certainly was sick; she'd seen her throw up in the ashtray. She also picked up the faint smell of mint-tinged alcohol on Marie's breath and asked her if her drinking was the real cause for missing her flight to Phoenix. Marie shook her head and said that she was in the ladies' room the whole time, throwing up and trying to keep from throwing up and that she'd had only one drink on the flight from Cleveland.

That said, the attendant told Marie that she could give her a break and get her a complimentary ticket on the next available flight to Phoenix. Marie and Eddie thanked her, but the attendant quickly added the bad news: the only flight with a vacant seat wouldn't depart until 8: 45 the next morning. "Is that all right?" she asked.

Marie quite soberly replied, "If that's all you have, then we'll have to take it."

"OK, Marie, I'll need to see your ID and your unused ticket for the Houston-Phoenix leg of your journey."

Marie opened her purse to take out her wallet. After a couple of moments of digging, she panicked and whispered to Eddie that the ticket wasn't in the purse and neither was her driver's license. She asked him if he could look to make sure.

He couldn't find it either and began immediately to think of the woman who'd hurried down the concourse after helping Marie.

Aw, shit! Marie's been rolled and she's too drunk to know it. Now what the hell do we do? We can't just leave her here without money or ID. Maybe Francie can help by letting her sleep at her house and loan her cab fare for the trip back to the airport in the morning. She could make a collect call to her husband so he could arrange her pick-up time at the Phoenix airport.

Eddie took over and explained to the attendant that Marie's wallet was probably stolen when she was in the ladies' room. The attendant replied that there'd been an outbreak of thefts around the airport lately and said that she'd verify Marie's ticket purchase with a call to Phoenix's Sky Harbor where Marie had purchased her round-trip tickets, and that it shouldn't take long.

"Meanwhile," she added, "Do you have any other proof of ID on you?" Marie said she'd had her driver's license copied at Sky Harbor when she paid for her tickets by check. "That will have to do," said the attendant. She looked up the American Airlines desk number in Phoenix's Sky Harbor airport and dialed the call, explaining the situation and asking her Phoenix colleague to help find the record of Marie's ticket purchase. Marie worried when she heard the woman say that she'd look for the record, but that she'll have to forward the call to the airport's AA terminal manager. More worrisome silence followed. While they waited, their attendant said there shouldn't be any problem since Marie had bought her ticket less than a week ago and that at least a copy of the transaction and her ID should still be in the terminal's files.

"Just a moment," the attendant said. "Marie, Mr. Anderson, Sky Harbor's American Airlines manager, would like you to verify a few things to help prove that you're who you say you are." She handed the phone to Marie and a warm, friendly voice came on the line. "Marie, I understand that your ID was stolen and I'm sorry that happened. I'd like to ask you a couple of questions to help us confirm your identity, if you don't mind. They won't take long and you should have your new ticket for home just as soon as you answer them. Is that all right with you?"

"Of course, Mr. Anderson. What do you need to know?"

"Let's start with your home address and your emergency contact's name and telephone number."

"My home address is 14780 West Willow Lane in Glendale, my emergency contact is my husband, Frank Delaney, and the phone number is 623-549-7822."

"OK. What's your date of birth?"

"December 12, 1937."

"Last question. What day did you purchase your round-trip ticket to Cleveland?"

"Last Saturday."

"That's all, Marie, and thank you for cooperating with us. Please put me back on the line with your attendant and have a good journey home on American Airlines."

Marie thanked him for his help, but couldn't understand why he was asking for information that she never had to provide when she bought the tickets. She asked the attendant why and she replied that they were to help make sure that thieves or scam artists weren't trying to get a free ticket. She went on. "A thief wouldn't be able to come up with fast answers to them without stumbling, which would trigger the need for additional information and perhaps a personal check by one of our security department's officers. Speaking of which, I'll alert security."

On their way back to the lounge, Marie felt a little shaky but knew that she was finally sobering up enough to get in touch with Frank. Eddie had told her what he thought happened and his news only heightened her anxiety. *Will Frank buy my "too sick to fly" excuse? He knows I've been drinking more than usual lately. But we can discuss that when I get home. Meanwhile, I've got to find a place to stay. I'm sure not going to sleep in the concourse. Maybe Francie can let me stay with her tonight and loan me cab fare to get back to the airport in time to catch my flight. I'll send her a check and a nice bouquet of flowers when I get home.*

They entered the lounge to find Francie still at the bar. "I've been worried about you," she said. "You've been gone a long time." Marie thanked her for her concern and told her the good news; she got her ticket and that it cost her nothing. "The bad news," she added, "is that the flight won't leave until—until what time tomorrow morning, Eddie?" He replied, "Eight forty-five a.m."

She continued. "There's more; a woman in the restroom stole my wallet and got away with all my cash and ID. She must have rifled my purse while I wasn't looking. At least she didn't take my purse because it's a nice piece of hand-tooled leather that my husband bought for me in Spain. It's probably worth more than the cash I had in my wallet."

Francie was shocked by the news and expressed her anger that such a thing could happen in a busy airport that's supposedly protected by round-the-clock security guards. The bartender shook his head in disgust and told her he was very sorry that this happened and that maybe something could be done if they acted quickly.

"We may be able to catch the thief if she's still in the airport looking for more easy marks," he said. "I'll call airport security if you have a good description of her. Maybe she's not a passenger after all, but a thief who specializes in robbing women who are careless about leaving their purses unattended. No offense intended, Marie."

"None taken," Mary answered. "I was careless with my purse and I'm kicking myself for it."

Eddie added that he could give a good description of the woman because he'd seen her enter and leave the restroom. "OK", the bartender told them. "I'll call the security staff now and we'll see what they might be able to do. Eddie, I'll pass the phone to you for the woman's description." Eddie nodded in agreement. "I can't believe that the ticket-counter attendant didn't call Security," the bartender added. "But maybe she was too busy. No matter, as long as someone does it and that someone is us. This isn't the first time I've done this."

The bartender dialed Airport Security and told the sergeant on duty he was reporting a theft and the sergeant replied that he'd been expecting a call concerning a theft; the desk attendant had alerted him. The bartender introduced Eddie as a customer who could tell him the whole story and handed the phone to him. Eddie recapped the story but left out Marie's vomiting in the concourse, her nap in the toilet stall and his overture to the suspected bandit to help Marie clean up a bit and look more presentable. He gave the sergeant a detailed description of the suspect, including the one distinguishing feature that the security men would be sure to notice: her extraordinarily large breasts. Francie and Marie heard the sergeant's laugh and loud proclamation, "Hey, guys, the Big-Boobed Bandit has struck again! Think we can catch her this time?" Eddie covered his mouth to hide a grin while Marie rolled her eyes and Francie giggled.

The sergeant said he'd dispatch two of his best people to walk the concourse area; one would be a woman so she could go into the ladies' restrooms and see if the thief might be hiding out in one of the stalls.

"If the thief comes out of one of the stalls, our gal follows her after she's radioed her location to her fellow officer. He'll come over to join her. They both make the pinch because two officers are better able to handle the thief if he or she resists." "Since we also pick up our officer's calls back here at HQ," he added, "we can and often do send more officers if there's reason to expect trouble. In the 'Big-Boobed Bandit's' case, she's big enough to cause trouble so we'll dispatch more people to help subdue her in case she resists. Hell, she could beat one of my officers to death with those tits. That, or smother him. O death, where is thy sting?"

He roared with laughter and Eddie could no longer contain himself, snorting and coughing while trying to stop laughing. Marie and Francie couldn't help but smile and even their all-business bartender grinned and shook his head at the sergeant's tasteless humor.

The sergeant asked to speak to the victim and Eddie passed the phone to Marie. He didn't ask her to repeat the same story that Eddie had told him and she was grateful for that. Instead, he reassured her that they'd do their best to catch the thief, and that they had a good record in catching thieves.

"How much cash was in your wallet?" he asked. Marie thought for a moment and told him that she couldn't remember the exact amount, but that it was at least $100.

"I had two 50-dollar bills in there along with a handful of dollar bills for tipping."

"OK" said the sergeant. "Did you have any credit cards like American Express and if so, what are their numbers?"

"I have an American Express card but didn't need it for my trip to Ohio. So I left it at home."

"Good thing," replied the sergeant. "Did you have a checkbook in there or anything else of value like jewelry? If jewelry, we'd need a description."

She answered that she had neither in her purse. *Thank God I didn't take home any of mom's jewelry that she'd promised me.*

"Finally, is there anything you can add to the thief's description that Eddie gave to me that might help us find her?"

"I was too sick to pay much attention to what she was wearing. I had the impression that she was wearing a gray-and-blue, V-necked argyle sweater that showed off her breasts but you'd see that no matter what she was wearing. And a matching gray skirt. Her legs were muscular, like a track star's."

The sergeant laughed. "She might be a former track star to escape as quickly as she's been able to do. But the sight of a large woman bouncing through the concourse—if you get my drift—would attract a lot of attention and pretty much guarantee that we'd be able to catch her.

"Ma'am, this woman has stolen money and valuables from several passengers in the past few weeks and so far, she's been able to get away with it. But from your story and Eddie's, she's getting bolder and that means more careless. We may nab her this time and if we do, we'll page you and Eddie to come to the security office across the street from the airport. Thank you, and we'll do our best to help you get back home to Phoenix and maybe even recover your ID and at least some of your money."

Marie thanked him, wished him good luck and told him that she'd be listening for his page if his officers caught the thief. She also told him that she'd be glad to come back to Houston to testify if the thief was caught and prosecuted.

"We appreciate your offer, but it appears that your friend Eddie would be able to provide a more complete description. A notarized deposition from the both of you should be all we need, but we'll get in touch if the prosecuting attorney wants you here. Her rap sheet will be a long one and the more witnesses we can gather to testify, the better the chance of a well-deserved, lengthy conviction."

John Bingham

When they'd hung up and sat back down, the bartender told her that the airport's security had been very good at cleaning out the crooks, prostitutes and con artists that frequent a major airport like Houston's and if anyone could catch the bandit, Sergeant Rasmussen and his team could.

"Good," replied Marie. "I feel like I could use a little luck today. I could also use another drink, but I'd better stay away from White Russians. They sure did a number on me and if I'd been sharper, I wouldn't have been rolled. "What would you recommend?" she asked. " I like something with a little vodka in it."

The bartender laughed and said that narrowed the field to a few hundred choices. He thought for a moment and recommended a strawberry daiquiri—perfect as a refresher and also on the light side. He said he even had some fresh strawberries crushed in their own syrup and told her that if she didn't like it, she didn't pay. "Now there's a square deal," she said to Eddie and Francie. "Anyone else?" Francie said she'd also like to try one because she loved strawberries in season. Eddie said he'd better go back to something that he knows he can handle and asked the bartender for a Bud on draft.

Marie spoke after the bartender had filled their orders. "Mr. Bartender," she announced, "Here's to you for all the help you've been. And here's to you, Eddie. Without your help, I'd have been up the creek without the paddle. Francie, only a kind and caring woman would wait around as long as you did to make sure I'd be all right, so here's to you, too." They all raised their glasses high for the toast, including the bartender with his glass of ice water.

Marie added, "We've been rude to our bartender friend, since we never even asked his name!"

The bartender laughed and said few people ever do, so he was flattered. "Just call me 'Jack,' he replied. "Simple, easy to remember and very common."

Winter Roses

"Here's to you, Jack, with our thanks." Marie raised her glass to him and her friends followed suit.

Francie spoke up by complimenting Jack on his strawberry daiquiri. "This is even better than my strawberry jam. It's so good that I could take one home and have it for breakfast along with my jam on toast and fresh strawberries on my bran flakes.

Marie agreed. "I'd like the same breakfast when the kids are ornery and arguing at the breakfast table. Better yet, make them one, too!"

Eddie said he'd stick with a beer mixed with tomato juice and a little Worcestershire sauce for a perfect Bloody Mary. "It's a great way to start a hangover day," he said. "The mild buzz eases the pain. I drink two and the hangover's gone."

Jack agreed. "Beer Bloody Marys work for me, too, but I save them for the days I'm not working. If I'd sipped them on duty, I wouldn't be here to enjoy your good company."

I admire his discipline, Marie thought. *I've tried for years to manage my drinking but it always ends up managing me. Maybe I should join AA. But right now, I need to find a place to sleep.*

"Francie," she asked, "Could I spend the night at your home? I have no money for a hotel room."

Francie didn't hesitate. " Of course you can and I'd welcome your company. You'll also need money, so I'll cover your cab fare in the morning. You can send me a check when you get home. Now, it's not too late for me to make us a good dinner. All we need is a driver to get us home. I'm afraid I got a little carried away with the White Russians and now this daiquiri is getting me a little bit silly.

Eddie, if you can drive us, I'll be glad to pay your cab fare to get you wherever you're going tonight and maybe you can stay for dinner, too. I have a nice tenderloin which we can cut into steaks and grill outside. I'll serve them with baby redskins and a tossed salad."

Eddie thought for a moment and replied. "Francie, I appreciate your kind offer and your invitation, but I'm a little on the fried side. I don't dare risk a DUI arrest with my record. Can we take a cab?"

Before Francie could answer, Jack jumped into the conversation and saved the day. "My shift's over in 20 minutes. Can I tag along and drive since I haven't had anything to drink except sparkling water? I haven't had a good, homemade meal in a long, long time and I'll be happy to stop along the way and buy my own steak. Yours, too, Eddie, and I'll cover the cab fare home for us both."

"Of course you can join us for dinner," Francie replied. "And that tenderloin is big enough to feed a lumberjack camp, so there's no need to buy your own steaks."

"Two square deals if I've ever heard one," replied Eddie. " Francie, I'd be pleased and honored to be your dinner guest. Jack, I appreciate your offer, too."

Francie suggested to Jack that, before they left, he should check with Security. "Maybe they caught the thief," she said. "If not, we can at least let the sergeant know where Marie can be reached if he has any news, good or bad." Jack nodded, reached for the bar phone and called the sergeant.

"Hi, sarge, Jack here again. I'm here with my friends and checking to see if you've had any luck in catching the lady who rifled Marie's purse. They're about to leave and my shift is over in a few minutes. I can give you a number where Marie can be reached tonight in case you have any news.

Winter Roses

"Francie, can you give Sergeant Rasmussen your telephone number so he can call Marie if he has news?" Francie nodded, took the phone, told the sergeant the number and passed it back to Jack. Marie also gave the sergeant her Phoenix number in case he needed to call her at home.

She thanked him once more and said she'd look forward to his call. After she hung up, she remembered the dollar bills she'd shoved in her jacket pocket and put them on the bar to pay her bill. Jack waved her off and pushed the bills back to her. "Save 'em," he told her. "They'll come in handy tomorrow morning for tips."

Tears welled in her eyes and she was unable to thank him. Eddie noticed, stepped down from his barstool and put his arm around her shoulders. She began to cry. *Stress and alcohol are really getting to her. We'd better get her out of here and over to Francie's house.*

Francie confirmed Eddie's thoughts by telling Marie that she needed some food in her system along with a place where she can relax from the day's tensions and get a good night's sleep.

Jack's replacement arrived as if on cue. Jack briefed him and then opened the till to cash out his shift and reached into his pocket to pay for the last round of drinks. Eddie spotted this and said he'd pay for his beer and Jack said, "Forget it. You, Francie and Marie have made my day with your caring ways, and I don't often see customers who help each other like you have.

"This is just my small way of saying 'thanks'." He took the money to the safe in the back room, peeled off his apron and put on his old tweed sport jacket. *It's a little frayed around the cuffs, but no one will notice. Even if they did, who cares? It's a real Harris and it's been a part of me since I returned to London after the Jerries surrendered. I'll be buried in this jacket.*

John Bingham

He leaned over the bar on his elbows and said, "The thought of a good steak dinner and a nice evening with all of you is enough to make me hitch-hike to your house, Francie. If y'all are ready, let's go!"

Marie pulled her head away from Eddie's chest, reached into her purse for a Kleenex, wiped her eyes and put on her happy face. "Yes," she said. "I'm ready." She stepped down from the barstool. *Good,* thought Eddie. *She can stand and walk on her own but I'll stick close to her in case she starts to stagger.*

They walked out of the lounge into the crowded concourse and joined the flow of people headed for the minibus parking pick-up lanes in the lower level. Marie even navigated the escalator without a slip or a fall, to the relief of her companions. Jack and Eddie had positioned themselves in front and back of her to catch her. They crossed the lower concourse where Jack checked the scheduling board that listed the minibus arrival times. Rather than sit around in the concourse, they decided to wait outside.

Their shuttle bus arrived at the curb on time. They were the first to board, taking the bench seat just behind the driver. When they were seated, the driver called back to the passengers asking them to check their parking stubs for their car's location. Francie didn't need one. She told him that her car was in Section A, Row 1.

"The VIP section," said the driver. "You must do a lot of flying."

"I used to when my husband was alive," Francie replied. "These days I come to the airport every now and then just to re-live old memories. We traveled together all over the world."

"Ma'am, I'm sorry you lost your husband. But I'm pleased that you're on my shuttle bus today and we'll get you and your friends to your car in just a few moments."

Winter Roses

He couldn't ignore the alcohol fumes. *I hope one of them is sober enough to drive.* "Here's the VIP section, ma'am. What kind of car are we looking for?"

She pointed to a gleaming black, four-door Cadillac sedan and said, "That one." Marie, Jack and Eddie were too busy talking to notice the Caddy.

Francie stood as the minibus stopped and the driver opened the door, turned to the rest of the party and said, "Here y'are, folks, and have a pleasant evening!" Francie tipped him with a five-dollar bill and they stepped down to the pavement. Just before swinging the door closed, the driver called out to them to be careful driving because they were hitting the evening rush hour and said, "Y'all know what a rat race Houston traffic is at this time of day."

Jack seemed to be the only one listening to him. The others were staring at Francie's car. Eddie asked Francie what her husband did for a living, saying aloud what Marie was thinking.

"Don was a hard-rock mining engineer and a good one," Francie said as they climbed into the car. "He had such a great reputation that he wound up as a tenured professor at Michigan Tech, one of the few universities in the country that offers a major in mining technology. When we started drinking White Russians today, I thought of him because the Russkis recruited him—with Uncle Sam's permission—to come over and teach them the finer points of hard-rock mining. This was in 1935 during the pits of the depression and the Russians promised him good pay. The offer was too good to pass on and he took it. Neither of us dreamed that we wouldn't be together again until the war started, when his employers said it would be safer if he returned to America. That made good sense to us both and so we were together again almost five years later—back at Michigan Tech."

"The good thing about his long 'tour of duty' in Russia was the pay, but I have yet to convince myself that it was worth the years we were apart. Since rubles could not be converted to American dollars or vice versa, he was paid in gold bullion and certificates. I can't tell you what that gold was worth; all I remember is that the safe that he bought for our home's basement was filled with cash, gold bricks and gold certificates. Uncle Sam balked when he sold the certificates to international commodity brokerage houses, saying they weren't legal tender. The courts disagreed. They ruled that it was fair pay for the years he'd spent in the far reaches of the Ural Mountains. Since he'd earned the gold in a foreign country, he also didn't pay taxes on it. Goodness, how I can carry on!"

She handed the keys to Jack. He started the engine, which was so quiet they could hardly hear it. He drove out of the lot onto the access drive and merged onto the freeway. Francie told him that their exit ramp was three miles north and that she'd give him plenty of time before he'd have to turn off. She continued.

"The gold gave him his start in commodities trading, where he made a killing because he could almost always buy during market downturns and sell during the highs. His few losses were cushioned by his very own gold reserve, which, combined with his professor's salary, gave us an income that we could comfortably live on."

Marie asked Francie what brought her and her husband to Houston. She replied that he dealt a lot in oil stocks and she'd often accompany him on his trips. They liked the more temperate climate and bought a house there, thinking it would be a good place to retire. "Don had every intention of retiring early," she said. "The only reason that kept him in Houghton was his love of teaching. Upper Michigan's nine-month winters—which reminded him too much of the frozen Urals—were also wearing on him. When he turned fifty-five, he gave notice that he was leaving two months before the fall semester began. That gave us time to sell our house and also gave the university time to find his replacement."

She broke off the conversation to tell Jack that the next exit off the freeway was hers. He anticipated the turn and smoothly changed lanes to get into position to make the turn, then exited onto the ramp that funneled him into a residential area. From there, she directed him to drive eight blocks and make a right turn on Gatewood. Her home would be on the right-hand corner of the next intersection.

He glanced in the rear-view mirror. *Eddie and Marie are seated respectably apart but there's no telling what could happen later, especially if she decides to start drinking again. Well, I'm along for the ride and we'll see how things play out.* A second look back told him that Marie was sound asleep and snoring softly. *Maybe "passed out" is more like it. Hey, Eddie wouldn't try to take advantage of an unconscious woman. Or would he? That's none of my business, but I'll still feel better when Eddie and I are in a cab after dinner and headed home. There you go again, you old mother hen. That's what years in the bartending trade will do to you. Some get tougher than hell and some watch out for their good customers and even intervene to keep them out of trouble. At least I'm big enough to be my own bouncer if someone starts any trouble. OK, I'll keep an eye on Eddie under the assumption that he's a horny sailor. Have I ever met one who wasn't? Oops, here comes Gatewood.*

"You said to turn right here, didn't you, Francie?"

"That's right, Jack. Three more blocks and we'll be there. Look for the two-story house on the right, on the corner lot."

When Jack spotted the house, he dropped his jaw. To him, the "two-story house" looked more like Tara. He pulled into the circular driveway and Francie opened the gate by pushing a button under the dashboard. *I wonder if she has a butler and servants?* He stopped in front of the stairway that led up to the huge front porch.

The door opened and a tall man dressed in jeans, cowboy boots and a T-shirt walked down the steps to the car and opened the passenger-side doors. Francie introduced him. "This is my son, Joe. He lives here with me and he's my household handyman." Joe smiled and shook hands with the guests, asking if they were spending the night. Francie said, "Marie is. She missed her flight and got robbed in an airport rest room, so we're helping her out with some good food and a comfortable bed to sleep in." He told Marie that he was sorry she had such a bad experience in the airport and that he and his mother would try to make up for it with some good, old-fashioned Houston hospitality. Marie expressed her gratitude and told Francie and Joe how much she appreciated their thoughtfulness. Jack and Eddie echoed the sentiment.

Joe asked Eddie and Jack if they needed a ride home after dinner. They said they'd planned to take a cab. "No need for that, I'll drive you. Marie, do you have a morning flight to catch?" She nodded. "I can also drive you to the airport." Francie told Joe that driving Marie to the airport wouldn't be necessary if he had to go to work, that she'd cover Marie's cabfare. Joe replied that the airport wasn't far from his office and if Marie wouldn't mind getting to the airport a little early, he could still make a client meeting. "What time is your flight?" "Eight forty-five," she answered. "Perfect," said Joe. "That works out fine for both of us."

"Good," said Francie. "Now all this talk is making our guests hungry. Let's go inside so I can get dinner started." They walked up the steps while she continued the conversation. "Joe, this is a good night for that filet mignon. You carve the tenderloin while Marie and I prep the salad and get the redskins boiling."

"Great. Eddie, Jack and I will fire up the pit and grill the steaks. Maybe have a couple of beers to stay cool; living in Houston is like living in a giant swamp."

"I'll vote for that plan," Eddie replied.

"Roger that," said Jack.

Joe smiled. "You sound like you've been in the service, Jack. The Big One?"

"Yeah, I served in the Army."

"Can you tell me about it?"

Winter Roses

"I was with Patton's Third Army. I arrived as a young replacement just in time to rescue the 101st Airborne at Bastogne. The words 'baptism of fire' can't begin to describe it."

He tried to smile but instead swallowed hard and turned his head away from them. Joe realized that he couldn't go on.

"It's OK, Jack. I understand. Thank you for sharing your story."

Eddie said he'd read about the Nazis' last-ditch effort at Bastogne to turn around the war on the Western Front, and said he admired Patton.

Jack remained silent for a moment, thinking carefully before he answered. "Patton had his followers and lots of them. If ever a man was born to war, it was him. You probably heard him described as 'Old Blood and Guts'. We agreed: his guts and our blood. But I read somewhere that our Third Army suffered the fewest casualties of all in the European theater. So maybe there was something to be said for his MO: keep slamming the Jerries and never stop until they were killed, too wounded to fight, or surrendered. That, and he was one hell of a tactician. Like Stonewall Jackson, the Jerries never knew where he was and how and when he'd hit them. They only knew he seemed to hit out of nowhere, fast and hard."

They stood on the porch, listening to Jack.

Francie interrupted. "Let's go inside. Joe, you take Marie upstairs to show her the bedroom while Jack and Eddie get comfortable and I'll start preparing dinner. Everyone's hungry enough to eat, as my husband used to say, "The southbound end of a northbound skunk." Eddie and Jack laughed and Eddie said he once was sprayed by a skunk and didn't much care about the experience, and that he sure as hell wouldn't eat one.

They went up the circular staircase to the bedroom. She told Joe that the staircase was probably the biggest she'd ever climbed. Joe replied, "Dad's adopted Texas style made him think big in any endeavor he chose, including this house. When it came to building it, the cost of materials and workmanship didn't bother him if they were of the highest quality available. And they were."

After inspecting her bedroom, Marie told Francie that she hadn't slept in many suites before, but hers was the prettiest ever. "Ah'll feel just like Scarlett O'Hara up theah," she said in her best southern drawl. "As long as you don't act like her," Francie said. "Besides, we don't have any Rhett Butlers joining us for dinner that I can see. Not that our three aren't good-looking, but let's face it. No one here is a Clark Gable."

Joe asked the ladies if they would like a glass of wine before dinner. Francine said she'd like a glass of cabernet and Marie asked for the same. Joe went downstairs to the wine cellar, selected the wine and grabbed three Lone Stars from the refrigerator.

After Joe had poured the wine for his mother and Marie, the men went outside and watched while Joe heaped charcoal into the massive stone barbeque pit, neatly stacked the briquets, poured the starter fluid over them, and threw a wooden match into the pit. The soaked briquets ignited with a loud ka-whooompf, which startled Jack. It reminded him of an incoming mortar round and he fought off what felt like an overwhelming instinct to dive for cover. Eddie didn't notice him shudder, but Joe did.

"Just what we need," Joe said. " More heat for an even hotter Houston evening."

"This beer cools me down just fine," said Eddie.

Jack agreed and raised a toast to his host. They clinked their bottles together. Joe went back into the house to cut the tenderloin into thick steaks. His mother and Marie were in the kitchen, preparing a huge salad. "Looks good, mom and

Marie. Perfect for a hot and sticky night. Shall we eat outside on the patio or stay here in air-conditioned comfort?"

Marie said that a Phoenix girl like her didn't mind the heat, but she'd go along with whatever Joe and Francie wanted. Francie said either way was fine with her, and she'd be happy with whatever their guests wanted. "The sun will be dropping fast by the time we eat," she added, "and it will probably be pleasant outside. Not quite as hot and humid, anyway. Still, it would be more comfortable inside." She poured Marie and herself another glass.

"I'll ask Eddie and Jack as soon as I cut these steaks. This tenderloin is a beauty. I'll slice them two inches thick, just like any five-star steakhouse. Mom, you like yours medium. Marie, how about you? Medium rare?" "Perfect," she replied. Francie said she wasn't going to prepare any sides except the boiled redskins, salad and hard rolls. "Unless someone wants cowboy beans. I have some in the refrigerator left over from a cookout the other night. They came from a cowboy deli downtown and they're delicious."

Marie said she'd just as soon pass on the beans because they were "a bit too much for her digestive system, even if they came from a 'cowboy deli,' whatever that is."

Joe laughed. "It's an upscale version of an old-style cowboy steak-and-bean restaurant. Houston's few real cowboys laugh like hell at the place, but the upscale cowboy image appeals to the wealthy dudes. Going there to see them all decked out in their sequined and mother-of-pearl buttons on fringed shirts, too-tight jeans and alligator boots straight out of Nashville is a treat. Oh yeah, I forgot the fringed buckskin jackets and the Stetson hats, of course."

He finished carving the filets and put them into a huge, cast-iron frying pan. "Perfect for keeping the steaks warm," he explained. "I'll cook them right on the grill while I'm heating the pan, then hold them while everyone fixes their plates.

John Bingham

Let me know when the redskins are done and I'll put the steaks on. Meanwhile, I'll check with Jack and Eddie to see if they want to eat on the patio or indoors, and if they want the beans. I'd better get them more beer, too, it's still hot out there." He went downstairs and brought up three more Lone Stars.

After passing the beers to Eddie and Jack and rearranging the searing coals in the grill's fire pit, he asked whether they'd prefer indoor or outdoor dining, and if they wanted cowboy beans along with the salad, potatoes and hard rolls. Eddie passed on the beans and said that air conditioning would be more comfortable than the steaming Houston air. Jack agreed and Joe went back into the house and advised Francie of their decision.

"Good," said Francie. "Marie, please keep an eye on the redskins while I get out the dinnerware and set the table." Marie took the fork and hoped she wouldn't let the redskins boil themselves to mush—or scald herself by stabbing the fork around in the boiling water. *I'm starting to feel the wine. I'll go slow on the cabernet until we eat and then I'll feel better. Hopefully, Francie will get back here in a hurry to check these potatoes. I'd better call Frank pretty soon. Maybe I can sneak in the call while the steaks are on the grill.*

When Francie returned, Marie asked her if she could use the phone upstairs in her bedroom to let Frank know that she was alive, well and in good hands. "Of course," Francie said. "He must be very worried about you by now." Marie replied, "You don't know Frank. Nothing fazes him, except a bad round of golf." Francie laughed and said that reminded her of her husband. "He tried to make up for all the games he missed while he was in Russia. He didn't play well, but he made up for that by playing often and he always said that letting off steam was the best thing about golf."

Marie chuckled and replied, "It's too bad that those two didn't know each other, although I'd worry that they might kill each other out on the course."

Winter Roses

Francie laughed. "Naaaw. They'd each commit *hara kiri* before they'd do that. That wouldn't matter much since we'd both be golf widows anyway. At least you and I would have plenty of time together to do the things we like to do."

"Hear, hear," said Marie. "I'll drink to that." She topped up both wineglasses, raised hers and said, "To our husbands and their golf!" Francie repeated the toast and they both emptied their glasses.

Francie said she was starting to feel the wine, but that was OK because neither of them would be driving that night. "Now you hustle upstairs and give your husband a call."

Marie filled her glass and went upstairs.

She dialed and Frank answered the phone right away. Before he could say a thing, she opened with, "Sweetheart, this is Marie. Don't worry. I missed my flight today because I got sick and had my wallet stolen with my ticket inside while I was in the lady's room. I'm staying overnight with a friend here in Houston who helped me report the theft to airport security and her son will drive me to the airport to catch my 8:45 a.m. flight home."

"I know," Frank answered. "I called the American Airlines counter and talked with the manager who approved your ticket. He explained what happened and I'm glad you're OK. The children were worried, too. I'll be on alert tonight starting at midnight, so I've hired Marcy to spend the night with the children. Take the limo service home, OK? I'll pre-pay her through 10 a.m. which gives her time to get the kids off to school and clean up before she leaves. I'll call you if I can tomorrow, around noon. But don't worry if I can't. You know the drill. Regarding your limo payment, I'll put $20 in your top drawer to cover that plus tip. Do you have any money left?"

Marie remembered the dollar bills Jack had refused and said she had enough to cover any small expenses like a coffee and newspaper at the airport.

"Good," he replied. "I'll sign off for now and prep for alert. The kids may need help with their homework, too."

"Thanks, sweetheart. I'm sorry for the overnight delay and I'll make it up to you in bed."

Frank laughed. "You know the way to a man's heart. Besides, you're a good cook. I'm getting sick of pizza. Tell you what. I'll throw in a bottle of good wine and you make your famous lasagna."

"That's a square deal if I ever heard one. I love you, love you soooo much, hugs to the kids and I'll see you when you come off alert. Or can I come over to the alert shack for a quickie?"

"You're baaaad! Love you, see you soon, have a good flight home."

He hung up and Marie was satisfied that he hadn't realized just how she got sick. *I know he worries about my drinking. I'd better play it cool and cut back when I get home. Let's face it, I could get by on less vodka and be better off for it.* She walked down the steps and told Francie that everything was fine, and that Frank had made arrangements to pay for limo service to get her home.

Francie said she was happy to hear that all's well on the Southwestern Front, and asked Marie to go outside, check on the steaks and tell Joe that the redskins are done.

Marie topped off her wine glass and went outside. *The smell of the steaks is making my stomach growl. It should growl. I haven't had anything to eat except a cup of coffee and a sweet roll in the Cleveland Airport this morning, and what was left of that came up in a concourse ashtray.*

Winter Roses

"Joe, I hope that those steaks taste as good as they smell. I'm salivating like Pavlov's dog and if we don't eat soon, I'll be whining, barking and peeing on your leg."

They all laughed and Joe replied, "I won't even ask how you'd do that."

"Carefully," Marie answered. "Now, why did I come out here? Was it to sit with three good-looking men? No such luck. Joe, your mother asked me to tell you that the redskins are done."

Eddie said that keeping Joe company without attacking the steaks wasn't easy. Jack added, "Eating them will be real easy. Joe knows how to grill a steak, that's for sure."

Joe spoke up. "Your flattery will get you everywhere. Hey, folks, these steaks are so nice that they damned near cooked themselves." He pressed each with his tongs and announced they were done. "To perfection, I humbly add. I'll keep them hot in the big pan if one of you can tell mom they're ready. I'll roll the butcher block into the dining room and serve the steaks tableside right from the pan on the block."

Eddie went back inside to move the butcher block and Marie went with him. Francie put the potatoes, salad bowl and butter on top of the block before Eddie wheeled it into the dining room. Francie then went out to tell Joe to bring in the steaks.

When they were seated, Francie asked if anyone would like to say grace.

Eddie volunteered and recited the traditional blessing he'd learned when he was young and Catholic, then added, "We also thank you, Lord, for the blessing of our new friendships." "Very nice," said Francie. Thank you and 'Amen.' " Everyone responded in unison with an "Amen."

Joe opened two more bottles of cabernet to go with dinner and filled everyone's glass. Marie thought she'd better pass, but then decided she'd be OK because she'd be eating.

He served the steaks from the still-hot pan. Marie thought they were the most tender, juiciest, most flavorful filets she'd ever had, even beating the prime cuts served at the O-Club. She proposed a toast to their hosts. "To Francie and Joe, the best hosts imaginable." All responded with glasses raised.

Eddie captured everyone's attention with a tale told to him by his bunkmate Jerry, a gunner in World War II who'd missed the call to General Quarters when his cruiser was dodging kamikazes in Okinawa Bay.

"He had a good reason. He was sleeping soundly and he jumped out of the top bunk when the alarm sounded. Just as his foot hit the floor, he realized in horror that his private parts were caught in the bedspring. The chief gunner's mate went looking for him and found him in his skivvies, holding on to the bunk with both hands. One foot was on the floor and the other was propped up on the bunk. He didn't dare move, which was no small feat considering the ship's rolling and rocking.

"The chief asked him how in hell he managed to do that and Jerry says, 'It was easy. Even you could do it.'"

"With that, the chief yanked him free. He screamed so loud that his shipmates on deck later said they heard him even above the ship's antiaircraft guns blasting away at the swarming Jap Zeroes and Kates, which was a stretch. Disregarding the blood and the pain and resisting the temptation to take a peek at the damage, he threw on his dungarees, shoes, helmet and life jacket and very carefully walked up the stairway and across the deck to his gun tub. By then, the attack was over so he cleared the weapon, told his assistant gunner to clean it and reload the ammo clips, and reported to sick bay.

Winter Roses

"The doctor whistled when Jerry walked in with his crotch soaked in blood. He had Jerry lie down on the examination table and pulled down his pants. "Jesus Christ," he exclaimed. "What a place to be hit by shrapnel." Jerry was tempted to go along with the doctor's shrapnel guess, but his chief knew what really happened.

"Jerry shared his thoughts with me: *'Worse yet, the sadistic bastard caused the tears in my crotch and scrotum. He actually bragged about it. When I walked off that ship for the last time after the Nips had surrendered and our ship had been decommissioned in Diego, I told him that it had been my fondest hope that the Japs would put a 20mm cannon round right into his crotch."*

He told the doctor the whole story and the doctor replied that he'd seen many strange wounds, but this was a first and one for the medical books because of the accident's unusual cause.

He invited his whole staff to look at the wound, since it was one they wouldn't likely see and treat very often. Jerry didn't appreciate their attention, particularly the whispering, sniggering and snorting after they'd filed by him, trying hard to act like professionals as they bent over and carefully examined the tear. After they left, the doctor prepped for surgery and gave Jerry a local anesthetic. While sewing him up, the doc told him how lucky he was that the tears were repairable, not unlike darning toe-holes in old socks. Jerry told him that the comparison didn't do much for his confidence and asked if he could spare the small talk and instead stick to his knitting.

Eddie warmed up. "The repartee catches the doctor by surprise and he starts to laugh. His laughter turns into a laughing fit. He bends over with tears in his eyes and his screeching starts to hit high C. The ship's chief surgeon walks by, hears the commotion and comes in to see what's going on. He looks at Jerry splayed out on the operating table, all bloody where nobody should be bloody, and then at his up-and-coming understudy laughing his fool head off while standing at attention and saluting. He shakes his head, smiles, returns the salute, bends over Jerry and says, 'Son, we're not all crazy here but it helps. Good luck and I'll look forward to reading about your wounds. Carry on!' He was gone and so was the laughing fit. The doctor hurriedly finishes sewing the tears, sponges off the scabbed blood, stands back to admire his handiwork and invites Jerry to inspect it. Jerry sits up, looks down and says he's impressed. Sort of."

"Good," says the doc. "Now go easy for a few days and give the wounds a chance to heal, OK?"

"Sure," says Jerry. "You tell the Japs that." "Sir."

"The doctor told Jerry that he'd talk to his CO and recommend putting him in for a Purple Heart. Jerry politely refused. He said there was no way he could tell his fiance, family and friends how he earned it."

No one noticed at first that Marie was trying to cough. Jack saw that her eyes were wide open in fear and that her facial color was changing fast, from pink to a pasty gray. He leaped from his chair, raced around the table and whacked her hard between the shoulder blades. *Nothing.* He lifted her up and then sat down on her chair, laying her carefully across his lap. He hit her hard again and this time she was able to cough. *Good. She's got some air in her lungs.* He hit her once more. This time she coughed and an oversized piece of the steak flew out of her mouth and landed on the floor. He took her napkin and picked up the chunk with it. "Here's the culprit," he announced. "A wolf would have a hard time swallowing a piece of meat this size."

Joe and Eddie complimented Jack for his fast action and Francie added that it was a good thing he was there. Jack answered, "Everyone here would have done the same thing. I just happened to be the closest to her." Everyone knew that wasn't true, that he'd been sitting across the table when she started to choke.

Winter Roses

Marie tried to stand up but was too weak. She sat back down on Jack's lap. He put his arms around her and told her to try and relax, and breathe slowly and deeply. He smiled at her and said, "It's time you went upstairs to bed, kiddo. You've had enough excitement for today." He stood up with her in his arms and asked Francie if she could show him where Marie's bedroom was. Francie said, "Of course," and he followed her upstairs and into the bedroom. He gently placed her on the bed. Francie thanked him, gave him a big hug and said she'd get Marie into a pair of her pajamas and tuck her in for the night.

No one could finish the meal after Marie's near-choking accident.

Eddie suggested that it had been a long day and that it was probably time to leave. Joe pushed back his plate and said that he'd go around back, get the car and meet Eddie and Jack at the front door.

Eddie and Jack asked Francie where the bathrooms were. She directed Jack to the downstairs bathroom and Eddie to the upstairs bathroom at the far end of the hallway.

Before going back downstairs, Eddie tiptoed into Marie's bedroom. She was sound asleep. He leaned over, kissed her lightly on her forehead and whispered, "Maybe another day, Marie. Sleep well." She groaned and shifted her weight to her side and he left her.

Eddie met Jack at the foot of the staircase and Jack asked Eddie if he'd brought an overnight bag for his weekend shore leave. He said he'd meant to ask Eddie earlier but forgot it. Eddie slapped himself on the forehead. "Jesus," he said, "I'm glad you reminded me. I sure as hell did bring a bag. It's in an airport rental locker. Thanks to White Russia, I completely forgot about it." They continued down the staircase and Jack told Francie that they'd both be going to the airport since Eddie's suitcase was there in a rental locker.

John Bingham

Francie thought for a moment and said, "Wait a minute. Driving you both to the airport tonight makes no sense, since Joe's taking Marie there early tomorrow morning, anyway. You two plan on spending the night here and Joe can get the three of you there in the morning. There's another guest room upstairs with twin beds; you two can share it. And speaking of suitcases, where's Marie's? Was it checked through on the connecting flight she'd missed or was it still in Houston? Or was it in the lost luggage area from her Cleveland flight, or in a rental locker like yours, Eddie? I'll go upstairs and get her purse and see if there's a locker key in it, or a luggage ticket that says the bag was transferred to the Phoenix flight she'd missed."

That said, Francie marched upstairs and retrieved the purse. While she was upstairs, Jack remarked that she was a woman who took charge and had a lot of common sense. Eddie agreed.

Francie's search through the purse paid off; she found a check-through stub for her suitcase and it should be waiting for Marie in Phoenix if her husband hadn't already retrieved it.

The evening was a quiet one. After Eddie and Jack helped their hosts clean up the dishes, they played team Scrabble against Francie and Joe. They lost three in a row. Eddie said he knew when he was beaten and was ready to call it a night. Francie said she needed a good night's rest after such an emotionally charged day. "Poor Marie," she said. "What a day she's had. Did anything positive happen to her?" "Sure," Eddie replied. "She had the three of us to watch out for her. Think of the trouble she'd be in if we hadn't have been here to help."

Jack nodded in agreement. "From a bartender's point of view, I've seen plenty of nice-looking, well-dressed women like Marie get into real trouble, usually involving some slime-ball looking for an easy score. They're not hookers; I can spot them immediately. I try to tell the classy ones to stay away and most of them appreciate the warning. But some tell me to mind my own business and leave with the creep, anyway. God only knows what trouble they get into. The worst I ever knew of was a woman who was raped, robbed and strangled right in her car, in the airport parking lot. The guy had just been released from prison, where he'd served a 10-year sentence on a robbery-rape conviction. Of course, I didn't know this at the time. He just looked like trouble. Maybe this was my bartender's sixth sense, who knows? But I'd warned her and she told me to buzz off in the most unladylike language."

Francie said that she admired Jack for trying to help the ladies stay out of trouble, but cautioned him that there were plenty who liked to walk on the wild side. "There's not much you can say or do to influence these women. But you can feel better knowing that you at least tried. There aren't many gallant knights left in this world, Jack, and you're one of them." Jack objected, but not too loudly. "I'm no knight. I'm just a bartender trying to keep my customers out of harm's way."

"That's good enough for me," said Francie.

Joe told Eddie and Jack to follow him upstairs, he'd show them their bedroom.

First, he stopped into the master bathroom and found new toothbrushes and toothpaste for them, along with deodorant. Their bedroom had a bathroom with a shower. When Joe said good night, Jack told Eddie he'd like to shower before turning in while Eddie said he'd shower in the morning. He set the alarm clock atop the dresser. "I probably won't need the alarm, since I'm used to waking up at 0500 hours every morning. But it will be good backup."

Jack laughed and said he remembered those "Early bird gets the turd" days well when he was in the service. "The platoon first sergeant's boots crunching across the gravel sidewalk leading up to the barracks was all the noise I needed to wake up. By the time he'd come crashing through the door, I'd be making my bunk while the rest of my buddies would still be in the sack. All hell would break loose if they weren't up and moving when "Reveille" sounded. The sergeant's shouting and throwing their beds around with some of them still between the blankets was all the motivation they needed to get going." Eddie grinned, remembering his own rude and raucous wake-ups as a young recruit at Great Lakes Naval Station.

The two of them agreed on "lights out" and fell promptly asleep.

Daybreak arrived sooner than anyone wanted.

Marie wrapped herself in one of Francie's robes and came downstairs to get a cup of coffee. Francie had just brewed a pot and asked Marie how she slept. Marie replied, "Very well. I must have really needed a good night's sleep. It was hard to sleep last week at dad's house with all of the relatives and friends coming over to offer their condolences and help, and mom's funeral was delayed a day to allow for our out-of-town family members time to get here."

"Your mother's funeral? I didn't realize she had passed away last week. I'm sorry, Marie." They hugged. " Did she have a long illness?"

"She died while lying on the couch and watching TV. Suddenly she sat straight up and cried out, 'No, not yet!' By the time dad raced across the room to see what was wrong, she was on the floor and not breathing. He called an ambulance, which got there in a few moments and the emergency technicians checked her vital signs. There were none, and their attempt at resuscitation failed. One of them stood up and said he'd better call the county coroner. This was no surprise to dad. He knew that she was dead before she hit the floor. At least she didn't suffer.

"I got the word at three a.m. Phoenix time. Frank was on alert but managed to get an emergency pass so he could be with the children while I made my flight arrangements to Cleveland and back. I didn't get there until late that evening and haven't slept well until last night, and I thank you for that."

Francie said that was the least she could do considering just the bad things that had happened yesterday, let alone the sudden and too-recent loss of her mother.

Joe, Eddie and Jack came down the steps, dressed and ready to go. Francie said she'd fry some bacon and make a mess of scrambled eggs with toast and homemade strawberry jam. Joe replied that it would be delicious and that they'd have time for it. "It's 6:00 right now and our drive to the airport will take about a half-hour allowing for rush-hour traffic. Marie, that gives you time to get dressed while we cook breakfast."

Marie took her coffee upstairs and dug into her purse to see if she had a stub for checking her baggage through to Phoenix from Cleveland. She found it and breathed a sigh of relief. At least she wouldn't have to search around the Houston luggage claim area. *This even gives me a chance to get a Bloody Mary before my flight.* Heartened, she brushed her teeth, washed her face, put on a little lipstick and make-up, and got dressed. *This will be a good day.*

She came back downstairs in time to join the others at the breakfast table. She felt as if she should be hungry, but she was shaky and nauseated. She knew that what she needed most to straighten her out was a drink.

Joe read her mind when he saw her hands shaking after she'd taken a strip of bacon along with a small helping of scrambled eggs and a piece of toast. "Does anyone besides me want a Bloody Mary?" he asked? Eddie and Francie raised their hands before Marie realized what he'd asked. "I thought you had to work today, Joe." "Well, yes and no," he answered. "I have a round of client golf to play this morning before we get down to business in the club's small conference room. Most of my colleagues will have a drink or a beer before we have lunch and then get down to business. Frankly, a drink will help me shake off last night's beers, so I'll have one. Just one."

Replied Marie, "Then I'll have one with you. Just one." Everyone smiled while Joe got up from the table and went to the wet bar to make the drinks. Marie waited until her Bloody Mary arrived before trying a bite of her eggs. *I don't dare eat the bacon. It's too greasy.* Joe served her Bloody Mary first and Marie delayed drinking it until the others were served and then she took a healthy swallow, followed by a deep breath of appreciation. *This Bloody Mary is clearing up my head and settling my tummy already. I can even hold my fork steady.*

"Does anyone besides me think that the Bloody Mary was a good idea?"

Everyone agreed and Eddie reminded them that they were also enjoying Francie's delicious homemade strawberry jam with their toast.

"Francie was right," he told Jack. "This jam really would be perfect for your strawberry daiquiris."

Joe couldn't let it pass. "Want me to make a batch?"

"You're kidding, right?"

"Yeah, I'm kidding." He looked at his watch and said, "I hate to rush you, but we'd better get going and finish our breakfast. Marie can't be late and I can't be, either. One thing you never do is hold up your golf partners—especially clients."

Everyone quieted down and finished eating, and Francie said there probably wasn't enough time for seconds. Jack replied that he couldn't speak for the others, but he was full and couldn't eat more even if there was enough time.

Joe stood up and excused himself. "I'll swing the car around to the front of the house and meet you there." Jack noticed that he hadn't finished his Bloody Mary. *Good for him and good for us. I like that guy.*

Eddie walked over to Francie, thanked her for her kindness and hospitality and told her he hoped they'd meet again someday. She stood up and they hugged, and she told him to be sure and call the next time he was in town. He promised he would. Jack followed with a hug of his own and told her that any time she came back to the airport, the drinks were on him. She smiled and said she certainly would come back to see him again and asked him to stay in touch. He told her he would do that and thanked her again for her hospitality.

Francie's biggest and warmest hug was for Marie, whose words of gratitude were choked back in her tears. Francie hushed her and then told her that it was always her pleasure to help when people need help and Marie was no exception.

"Now get on home to your husband and children, they miss you. I'll miss you, too, but maybe we'll meet again one of these days. And if you come back to Houston to testify, you're staying here, hear now?"

Marie nodded, turned around and walked to the front door where Jack and Eddie were already waiting.

Joe came around the corner, driving a yellow, '53 Buick Wildcat convertible with the top down. It looked to be in perfect condition. "Climb into my favorite car," he said.

"While it will be a bit breezy, it's already a sweat lodge out here and we'll be more comfortable with the top down. Besides, I love driving this beauty topless. I mean the car, not me." They all laughed. "Marie, sit up front so we don't mess up your lovely hair. Besides, I need a good-looking woman next to me when I drive this car. Together, we'll turn a lot of heads."

Marie grinned and hopped in. She said that riding in a convertible reminded her of her high school boyfriend's old Ford hot rod. She and her best friend would sit on the boot while they played 'chicken' on a stretch of road near North Platte.

"Whoa," answered Joe. "You really liked living on the edge, didn't you? Obviously, you never lost. I thought that those "chicken" stories were nothing more than high school brag-and-boast BS or fodder for grade 'B' movies."

He started the car and drove down to the gate, opened it with a button on the dash and turned on to a street that he said would get them to the freeway faster than the route his mother prefers.

"The chicken games were for real," Marie replied. "But a classmate alerted our school principal who called the police. They came out one night in an unmarked car, shut us down and slapped our drivers with citations for reckless driving, minors in possession and attempt to cause great bodily harm. That meant going to court and risking a felony conviction. Since my boyfriend already had a record—two convictions for drunken driving and minor in possession plus a juvenile court conviction for petty larceny—we thought he'd be sent to prison. But the judge was lenient. He gave him a choice of a prison sentence or enlisting in the service branch of his choice upon completing high school."

"Graduation day was less than four weeks away, so the day after, he joined the Air Force and we were secretly married by a local JP. This turned out to be a disaster, because I learned the hard way that he was a wife-beater, a drunk and a womanizer.

"Three years and two children later, I finally gave up on him and escaped to a small town in Michigan's Upper Peninsula where the bastard would never find me."

"Was this in the Copper Country where my father taught?"

"No, this was at the far eastern end of the peninsula, a town called Sault Ste. Marie, right on the Canadian border. I went to live there with my parents. My dad was manager of the town's Montgomery Ward store. He rescued me after a local grocer in Omaha called him and alerted him that my husband had been beating me and was literally starving us because most of his pay—which wasn't much anyway—was going for his boozing, partying and womanizing.

"The words 'son of a bitch' are too good for him and I hope the hottest corner of hell is waiting for him. Perhaps living with that man taught me some important lessons. At the very least, it taught me to be very, very careful when choosing a life's partner and that most teenagers don't know anything about the really important things in life despite their know-it-all demeanor."

Eddie and Jack couldn't hear Joe and Marie's conversation because of the wind noise. Eddie dozed off while Jack thought about the previous day's events and Francie's farewell comment about wanting to see him again. *She's a fine-looking woman, but more important, she's really nice. She has a kind heart and a good sense of humor. Maybe I'll give her a call in a week or two.* The thought of getting together with her again warmed him and he fell asleep.

Joe looked in the rear-view mirror and told Marie to turn around and look at the sleeping beauties in the back seat. He smiled. "Maybe they got up extra early for some reason. Sometimes it's hard to sleep in a strange bed, especially if you're staying for only one night." Marie said that certainly wasn't her problem since she had slept hard throughout the entire night, but maybe they had bad dreams that kept them awake.

Joe asked, "Why is it that we can have a vivid dream that often seems real, yet forget what it was the next morning? I'm always doing that."

Marie said she thought that it was because dreams are perhaps too real, too vivid, and so far removed from real life that maybe the brain erases them from our memories as a subconscious defense mechanism that keeps us grounded in reality.

"Look at Jack," she added. "Clearly his psyche was damaged by his war experiences. Maybe he was even shell-shocked. The images of death and destruction that he must still carry in his head probably show up in his dreams with terrifying reality, and forgetting them the next day might help him get through it with less stress and fewer flashbacks."

"Good point. He shuddered when I lit the charcoal with too much lighter fluid and it went up with a loud 'whoomph.' He probably does carry those images with him, maybe every night and day."

"I hope not," said Marie. "He's such a kind and caring man."

"Yeah, Jack's a good guy. I'd like to see him and mom get together again. They'd be good for each other."

"I agree," Marie replied. "Maybe you could play Cupid in the match-up."

"No way. I do my best to butt out of mom's business unless she asks for my help or opinion."

"Smart man."

"I try."

He turned the car into the main access road to the airport just as a huge, propeller-driven aircraft roared overhead on its final landing approach. Eddie and Jack woke up fast, startled by the noise.

"Douglas DC-6B," she said as it set down.

Winter Roses

"How did you know that?"

"When you're married to a pilot, you learn a lot about aviation and aircraft. Frank drives me crazy when he tells me which planes are safe and which are not and I have to tell him that this information is more than I need. No, make that more than I can handle. Nothing like climbing aboard an airplane that you know very well has a poor safety record."

Jack responded. "There are some things in life you're better off not knowing and that's one of them."

Eddie agreed. He said he once flew home from Japan on an aircraft that had a nasty habit of losing a wing in flight. "None of the passengers could sleep after the word got around about the plane's history. My shipmates and I asked for as many drinks as they'd serve us, and one of the stewardesses leaned over as she put my umpteenth beer on my tray and whispered, 'I'd join you if I could.' She knew that I was very much aware of the plane's dismal safety record. I gave her a sickly smile and took a long drink.

"Fortunately, the flight was smooth most of the way home. But even in the mildest turbulence, everyone onboard froze at the thought of the wings snapping off. Boy, were we happy to get off that airplane in Hawaii."

Joe pulled up to the American terminal and got out to say goodbye to his new friends.

After thanking him again for his hospitality and waving to him as he drove away, they walked into the terminal together and exchanged hugs all around. Marie cried and thanked them for all the help they'd given her to get her through the troubles of the previous day. She said she'd never forget them and hoped that they could meet again someday, perhaps if she came back to testify should the robber be caught.

Eddie scribbled his address on a scrap of notepaper she found in her purse and told her to reach him through the base locator. Jack said he'd be waiting for the both of them at the bar, and would remind her again about going easy on the "Sneaky Peteskies." Marie laughed and gave Jack another big hug.

"You saved my life, Jack, and I could never, ever thank you enough for that." Jack, embarrassed, bowed his head and said again, "Everyone in that room would have done the same thing. I just got there faster, that's all." Marie said, "That's not all, you big, lovable lug. You'd make me happy if you asked Francie out because you need a woman's company and you couldn't find a better, more caring woman than Francie. And she cares for you, Jack."

Jack grinned. "I've been thinking already about calling her."

"Well, forget about thinking and just do it, Jack. You'll never regret it."

Now thoroughly embarrassed, Jack mumbled that he'd call her after his shift change that evening.

"Good for you, good for Francie and good for me! Is that a promise?"

"That's a promise."

She laughed through her tears.

They split up, with Eddie heading for the lockers to retrieve his overnight bag. Jack walked to the employees' exit to hop into his car and drive back to his apartment for a quick nap and a change of clothes to get ready for the afternoon shift.

Twelve

THE FOG LIFTS

When Marie regained consciousness, she was standing in the airport's lost luggage area, searching for her suitcase. The attendant asked if she had a routing stub that could tell them whether the suitcase had been checked all the way through to Phoenix the day before. Marie rummaged through her purse and found a crumpled piece of paper that confirmed the luggage was indeed in Phoenix. That settled, she asked the attendant how she could find the American boarding gate for her flight.

The attendant gave her a curious look and told her to go back up the same way she'd taken to get down to the luggage area, turn to her left and the American boarding area would be on her right. Marie then asked for help in finding the boarding gate number, so the attendant walked her over to the departure screen. Marie didn't know her flight number, so the attendant asked to see her ticket. Marie replied she didn't have one. With that, the attendant called the American terminal counter and told the ticket clerk that she was with a woman who was very confused and needed some help in getting on the 8:45 flight back to Phoenix. The clerk asked for her name and said he'd check the flight passenger listings.

"I think it's——it's--Marie. Yes, it's Marie.

"Marie, what's your last name?"

Marie thought hard for a moment and faltered. "I-I don't know." The luggage attendant told the clerk that she didn't know and the clerk said, "Keep her there. We'll send down a nurse to check her out. Maybe she's had a stroke or something."

The attendant took her by the arm and steered her to her office where she could sit down. She asked Marie if she'd like a cup of coffee. "Yes," she said. "That would be nice. Delaney. That's my last name." The attendant called back upstairs. "Delaney," she told the clerk. "Marie's last name is 'Delaney'."

"Good. I'll make sure she's supposed to be on the 8:45 to Phoenix. I'll still send a nurse down to see if she's all right. I'll also have a cart on standby for her near the escalator."

The nurse came down the escalator with a blood-pressure cuff and stethoscope in hand and walked over to the luggage claim office. She introduced herself to Marie and told her that she was going to ask her a few questions to make sure she was well enough to fly. She asked her to recite her social security number, address and home phone number. Marie rattled off all three without faltering. The nurse then asked Marie to extend her arms, close her eyes and touch her nose with her pointer finger—first with the right and then the left. Marie connected on both. Next came Marie's blood-pressure reading, which was a little high but not in the danger zone. Her peripheral vision was also normal and she had full use of her limbs with no facial droop. "Good," said the nurse. "It looks as if you're OK to fly, but you should see a doctor when you get home to see if you suffered a minor stroke, which could explain your temporary loss of memory. If you did, it could be a sign of a larger stroke coming."

Winter Roses

Marie said she would see the doctor, and that she needed a complete physical anyway.

The nurse escorted Marie up the escalator, where they climbed into the cart that was waiting for them. "What terminal do you need?" the driver asked. The nurse told Marie to answer the driver's question.

"The American Airlines counter. I need to get my ticket and boarding pass."

When they reached the counter, the attendant on duty was the same one who'd called for a janitor when she saw Marie vomiting in the ashtray across the aisle. She recognized Marie immediately. "You got sick yesterday afternoon and threw up in an ashtray. There was a sailor who was helping you."

Marie gave her a strange look and said, "I have no idea what you are talking about."

"My God," said the attendant. "You really must have been sick. Are you sure you're OK now?"

"Yes I am," replied Marie. "What's my gate number and how far is it? While I still have almost an hour until takeoff, I'd just as soon not have to rush."

"Well, you're certainly sharp right now. But let's not take any chances. Your gate number is 34 and we'll get you there on the passenger go-cart."

"That's fine with me, and thank you for all of your help."

These memory losses can't be happening. I don't remember anything about yesterday and last night except going to an airport bar while waiting for my flight home and sitting between a sailor and an older woman. And how did I get here? I've heard of alcohol blackouts, but this is ridiculous. Did I have a stroke? Maybe this was just a temporary memory loss and it will all come back to me. But you'd better watch your alcohol intake from now on, Miss Marie.

"Any time, honey. Have a good flight home and thank you for flying American Airlines."

On the way to the boarding gate, the nurse again told Marie that it was very important to see a doctor because she may have had a stroke.

Marie agreed, telling the nurse that she had the same thought when she was listening to the attendant telling her what happened yesterday.

The cart arrived at the gate and the nurse walked with her to the desk. Marie asked for her ticket and boarding pass, and the woman behind the gate counter asked for her ID. She rummaged in her purse, but couldn't find her driver's license. "I must have lost my license," she said. "But I do have a stub showing that my luggage should be in Phoenix since it was checked through Houston from Cleveland yesterday. That, and my ticket for this flight should be sufficient proof of my identity. My name is Marie Delaney. You can call the attendant on duty at the American Airlines ticket counter who gave me the ticket you're holding for me. She will also confirm that I was robbed yesterday in one of your rest rooms and the thief got away with most of my money, my license and other important papers."

The woman asked her to wait a moment while she phoned the attendant, who verified Marie's story and told her that the AA manager in Sky Harbor had approved her ticket to Phoenix. With the story confirmed, the woman handed her the ticket and boarding pass and apologized for the delay, saying that she had to make sure she really was Marie Delaney.

"Apology accepted," Marie said. "I know that you were just doing your job." She walked through the gate and down the entrance ramp, and boarded the aircraft.

Winter Roses

On the trip home, she drank one more Bloody Mary followed by a vodka martini.

Several weeks later, she took a call from the sergeant in charge of Houston Airport Security. He told her that the woman who had stolen her money and ID had been caught but that there was no need for her to come back for the arraignment and subsequent trial.

Marie answered, "I don't know what you're talking about, and please don't call again." She hung up.

When Frank asked who had called, she told him that it was someone from the Houston Airport who said they'd caught the woman who'd stolen her money and ID from her purse, but that there was no need for me to go back to Houston. I told him that I had no idea what he was talking about and asked him not to call again.

Frank didn't say a thing, but he filed it carefully in his memory for future reference. He had the feeling that more of her memory lapses would be forthcoming.

The Lincoln broke down outside of Denver and Marie was beside herself. She and the children were driving from Grand Forks to Phoenix, where they would rent a home until Frank returned from his tour of duty somewhere in Southeastern Asia.

Not knowing with any certainty where he'd be was stressful enough, let alone worrying about his combat tour of duty as a FAC. From his first tour in Vietnam, she knew very well how dangerous his new assignment would be and that the coming year would be the longest she'd ever faced.

John Bingham

Now the damned Lincoln has broken down again—just what we need on top of our other worries. I told him that I'd never drive this luxury lemon again until it was fixed and here we are again, this time stuck in Denver. I hope we can get back in time for our appointment with our realtor.

In the garage's customer lounge, she met a nice young man who was waiting for new tires for his VW Microbus. He told her that he'd always wanted a Lincoln hardtop and asked if she'd like to trade. She hesitated, telling him that the Lincoln was worth much more than a Microbus and he agreed.

He thought for a moment and told her to wait a minute, that he had something for her that should even up the trade. He hopped into the Microbus, pulled out a portfolio of papers and thumbed through it until he found what he was looking for.

He returned and handed her the paper.

"Here," he said. "Get a load of this."

Marie looked it over and then asked Jennifer what she thought it was. Jennifer said that it looked like a certificate of ownership of five acres of property north of Durango in the San Juan Mountains.

The young man said that she was right; it was his deed to the property and he'd transfer ownership of the property to her along with the Microbus for an even-up trade. He said that his uncle owned the property and had given it to him in his will.

"I remember that he once said that he had panned for gold in a stream that ran through the property. When I asked him if he had found any gold, he just smiled and said that he wouldn't divulge that information, not even to me. His secrecy made me believe that he had found gold and that he wanted to keep gold-rush bums off his property."

Winter Roses

"Just think," Jennifer said. "We could all be rich."

Mark and Mike thought it was a good deal, although Frank, Jr., was skeptical. "What if all the gold has already been found?" he asked.

Jennifer replied that finding all of the gold would be impossible for one man, and there must be lots more they could find. "Even if there isn't," she added, "at least we'd have a nice, cool vacation place in the mountains to come to. Maybe we could even build a cabin there."

Marie said that it sounded like a good deal, but asked why would he give up such a valuable piece of property?

"Because," he said, "I'm on my way to San Francisco to live with my cousin and I plan to stay there. I don't have the time or the money to do anything with the property and besides, I have no interest in developing it. If you want it, it's yours, and we can transfer the deed at the county clerk's office yet this afternoon. We can take the VW so you can appreciate its good condition. There's only 34,000 miles on it, so it's hardly broken in. You can see that the body's in top shape. It doesn't have a a speck of rust.

Marie called the rest of the children over to meet her new friend, and was embarrassed because she didn't know his name. He laughed and said, "I'm Jim Johnstone. I just got my Master's degree in Business Administration, and I'm going to work with my cousin in San Francisco who owns a small chain of men's clothing stores. He wants my help in expanding his business, and driving this Lincoln will give me more credibility with my customers than the VW Microbus. It was a lot of fun for school and parties, and I resisted the temptation to hand-paint it like Arlo Guthrie's "Alice's Restaurant" van. I'm not into Hippyville and I have no plans for a change to that lifestyle.

On the way to the county clerk's office, Marie told him that her younger brother Ron was very much into the "Flower Children" lifestyle and had gone to

John Bingham

San Francisco to be at its epicenter. "But he's no ordinary hippy," she explained. "He went to college on the GI Bill and got his Master's degree in Education.

"He also followed his strong sense of social justice and knew the difference between good and evil. He and his wife went down to the Deep South and marched with the blacks to protest against segregation. The savage police dogs, tear gas, water cannons, beatings, and jailings that the blacks and their white supporters endured appalled them and the experience changed his life.

"After he and his wife were divorced, she kept their two children and he moved on to San Francisco where he met and married a true flower child. He also started using marijuana and LSD. When our mother died, he came to Ohio for the funeral service and got into an argument about his long hair with dad. Some things never change."

Jim agreed. "My parents would have small fits and kittens every time they visited me on campus. They couldn't understand why the men wore long hair, including me—and my hair was much shorter than the real hippy wannabes.

The girls' short shorts also blew their minds. I would remind them that they couldn't understand why people liked that filthy, gyrating songster named Elvis who was all the rage in the '50s and is still popular, only now with older people, too."

Marie thought of her own wild childhood and decided against saying anything more.

The deed transfer went smoothly, but the clerk gave her a strange look as if to say, "Be careful, lady," and wished her good luck.

When they returned to the garage, Marie and Jim went into the repair waiting area and the service manager came over to tell them what was wrong.

Winter Roses

"The problem was simple vapor lock. High temperatures in the engine compartment vaporize the gasoline. Since the fuel pump can't draw vapors, the engine stalls. All you can do when that happens is open the hood, wait until the engine cools down and the vapors are gone. You can then go back to burning liquid gasoline. To fix the problem, we recommend installing an electrical cooling fan to supplement the radiator fan. We should also insulate the fuel lines, which are too close to the hot engine manifold. The fixes will get you to Phoenix, where you'll really need them."

"How much?" asked Marie.

"One hundred and thirty-seven dollars will cover the parts and labor."

Marie hesitated. *Paying for this will really stretch my budget for the trip. I might have to cut down the kids' snacks and souvenirs and go to an all fast-food diet—which they wouldn't mind, anyway. I'll also have to ration my vodka but sacrifices must sometimes be made. We're not far from home now and we should be able to make it.*

Jim saw Marie's reaction to the price and said that he'd cover the cost. "I'm the one who will benefit from the repairs. Besides, I'm a long way from 'Frisco and a reliable car is a must."

Marie didn't argue. "That's very fair of you. A quick trip back to the county clerk's office could easily undo the deal."

"You don't understand, Marie. I really want the Lincoln and I'll consider my payment an investment. It's a done deal now." He turned to the service manager and asked, "How long will it take to fix the car?"

The manager said he'd put his best mechanic on it right away and that the work should be done in two hours.

John Bingham

Marie told him to go ahead and she turned to see if Jim would like to join her and the children for lunch. He replied that he'd like that very much, but he had a better idea. "How about you and the children being my guests for lunch to celebrate our swap? There's a nice restaurant right around the corner and the meal will be on me. We'll celebrate our trade and talk about finding gold "in them thar hills."

She turned to the children and said, "What do you think, kids? Are you hungry? Mr. Johnstone has made a generous offer to buy us lunch."

Mike spoke for all of them when he laughed and said, "Are you kidding, mom? We're always hungry!"

"Then it's another done deal. Lead on, Mr. Johnstone.."

The children would split a large pizza, once they agreed on the toppings. The debate made Jim laugh. "You're just like me and my college friends when we decide to split a pizza. Anchovies and green olives were about the only toppings that we could agree we didn't want." Frank, Jr. said he liked green olives, but the other children chimed in…"Yuck!" Marie ended the arguments by telling the waiter to put green olives on two slices. This triggered specific add-on requests by the other three—mushrooms for Jennifer and ground beef for Mark. Jokester Mike's turn came and he told the waiter he wanted anoles.

The waiter replied that, if he would catch them, he would serve them… "live, of course." Mike was surprised and impressed that the waiter knew what they were. He smiled and said that he didn't think he could catch them around mile-high Denver, but maybe he could buy them at the nearest pet shop.

"You'd better start running," replied the waiter. "The nearest one is about two miles from here." Mike turned to Marie and asked if she could drive him to the pet store.

Winter Roses

"Only if you eat them. Live, of course."

The children laughed and Mike gave up. "I'll have chopped onions instead."

"A wise choice," the waiter said. "I'll resist the temptation to tell our chef to stock up on anoles in case they become the newest rage in pizza toppings. He hates lizards of any kind, anyway. But I did enjoy the joke and thank you for brightening my day. Anoles, indeed."

Marie turned to Jim and asked what he was ordering for lunch.

He said he'd like something light, that he'd had a big breakfast. Marie said the same. She'd really felt too sick that morning to eat anything, but didn't mention that. He settled on a chicken salad while she ordered a hot chicken sandwich with gravy, peas and mashed potatoes.

Marie told the children they'd soon be old enough to get part-time jobs. "Then you can order what you want, she said. "But you'll also start dating and pizza wars will be the last thing on your minds." Mark said that, if he had a girl friend, she would be happy to eat whatever he wants on the pizza, and Marie told him that he had some important lessons to learn about girls. Jennifer chimed in. "He sure does have a lot to learn about girls. He embarrassed me every time he asked my friend Judy if she'd like to be on his baseball team."

They all laughed when Mark replied that she had a good fastball.

Jim asked Marie if she'd like a drink to celebrate the car swap. He told her he was having a beer. She said she'd like a vodka martini straight up and he asked the children if they'd like a non-alcoholic drink.

Mike was quick to answer for them. "Sure. How about Shirley Temples?"

Marie corrected him. "Yes, please," next time and not "Sure."

Jokester Mike replied, "Sure. Yes, please, Mr. Cleaver," in his best Eddy Haskell imitation. Jim laughed and went along with the act, asking "Eddy" if he'd please fetch him his slippers and his pipe? Mike answered, "I'd be glad to, Mr. Cleaver, even if they smell pretty bad. I'm always ready to help old people like you any way I can."

Jim laughed hardest of all.

The waiter arrived with the drinks, and Jim raised his glass of Coors with a toast to all of them and their new Microbus and property in the San Juans.

"And a toast to you, Mr. Johnstone," Marie said, " for your business acumen and success in your new job in San Francisco." They all touched glasses and the children continued with the Haskell routines.

Jim asked the children if they knew any real-life characters like Eddy. Frank, Jr. answered. "There are plenty of them around," he said, "and they're easy to spot by their brown-nosing and cheating. There was a guy who sat next to me in math class who was always trying to look at my answers. When I covered my test paper so he couldn't see them, he came over to me during recess and asked why I wouldn't help him. He had a sticky, syrupy, whiney voice that sounded just like Eddy Haskell's."

"What did you tell him?" asked Jim.

"To crawl back under his rock and stop trying to get me into trouble because of his cheating."

"Very good," Jim said. "Did he ever try to start a fight with you?"

"He wouldn't dare. All of us studied judo or tae kwon do when dad was stationed in Puerto Rico, and sometimes we put on exhibitions at school talent shows. Every student in our school knew what we could do and treated us with respect."

Winter Roses

"Wow," exclaimed Jim. "You have quite the family, Marie. "They're bright, athletic and good actors, too. They must keep you on your toes."

"You have no idea," she answered.

They walked back to the garage and were pleased to learn that the repairs had been made and that the Lincoln had been fixed and road-tested.

Marie took the children in the Microbus to the secretary of state's office for the title transfer while Jim drove the Lincoln to check out the repairs and make sure that the vapor lock problem didn't re-surface.

Like the deed transfer, the vehicle swap went smoothly.

They returned and took their suitcases and games out of the Lincoln and put them into the Microbus. Jim saw Marie remove the case of vodka from the trunk. She pre-empted any questions by telling him that she could buy vodka much cheaper at the Air Force Base Exchange than what she would pay in civilian life.

Jim steered the conversation in a different direction. "I admire and respect our troops in Vietnam, but I was declared ineligible for the draft because I have a heart murmur and I can't handle any strenuous exercise. I guess I'm lucky."

Marie told him that she and her husband appreciated any young man or woman who admired and respected our men and women in uniform, particularly in wartime. "Most of the time," she said, "they spit on our returning vets, throw bags of dog shit at them, and call them 'baby killers.'"

"It's a wonder that our returning troops don't chase after them and strangle them with their bare hands."

"It's a credit to them that they've resisted the urge. All they want to do is get back to their lives; they've seen enough violence, death and destruction to last them a lifetime."

Jim's unpacking was simple—one suitcase and suit bag, a tennis racket, skis, boots, poles, briefcase and a case of Coors. When they were finished packing, he wished them good luck with their schooling and prospecting for gold in the summer months.

Marie added her dictum. "Please understand, kids, that the property owner—that's me—keeps one-half of the gold you find and saves it for your college educations. The rest is yours to spend wisely and I will be the judge of what the word "wisely" means when it comes to young teens' spending. Fair enough?"

"Not really," Mike said. "I need a new bike. Marie and Jim cracked up. "First, you find the gold, Mike, " she said. "Then we discuss the new bike, which doesn't sound unreasonable to me providing there's enough to pay for the bike after I take my 50% owner's fee. We can discuss all of this in our new-old Microbus—which we'd better be in and rolling soon if we're to make Grand Junction by nightfall."

"The VW's gas tank is full and you're ready to go." Jim told Marie. "It's been a pleasure doing business with you and I wish you all a safe and pleasant journey."

"Jim, it's been a pleasure doing business with you—and we wish you a smooth trip and good luck with your new business venture.

I have no doubt that you'll do well. We'll think of you fondly, especially if we strike gold."

They hugged, Marie jumped into the Microbus, started it up and they drove away.

Winter Roses

When they reached Highway 70, Jennifer asked her mother why she had traded for another Microbus. "Don't you remember, mom? We got rid of it because it was underpowered and had a hard time getting up hills and mountains. Dad said that it was dangerous in the mountains and we're getting into more mountains right now. He's going to be mad that we traded the Lincoln for another Microbus."

Marie tried to gather her wits. *Is Jennifer right? Did we have another VW Microbus? How could I have forgotten that?* "Of course I remembered the old VW bus, Jennifer. But this one's different. It's a newer model than our old clunker, with a more powerful engine. Your dad will like it for its room and convenience." *I hope to hell it does have a more powerful engine.*

She lucked out. The bus did have a larger engine. While it still struggled on steep or long uphill runs, Marie easily compensated with a heavier foot on the pedal and Jennifer agreed that the engine was more powerful. "I can still hear dad swearing under his breath at the old one when we drove up the Mogollon Rim to the Grand Canyon," she said. "He was afraid that the bus would stall and roll backwards down the hill and crash into the line of cars with beeping horns behind us."

"I remember that trip, too," Marie lied. "That was when we decided to sell it."

The only thing that Marie remembered of this trip was her stops to get another bottle of vodka from the trunk.

Thirteen

Detox And Sobriety

Marie entered two alcoholic recovery centers for detoxification and treatment that year, each lasting 30 days. Neither was successful. When she described her treatments, Ann and I were appalled.

One depended upon electroshock therapy: why, we couldn't understand. Was it to stun the patients as punishment for their transgressions while under the influence of alcohol? Did the caregivers think there was some therapeutic value in shocking that would make them quit drinking? How could any responsible psychiatrist or clinical psychologist believe that this torture was effective?

Was it simply a reminder that there'd be more pain waiting for them if they backslid and came back? There could be no good reason for this Byzantine treatment.

When we visited her, we noticed that her talking had slowed and that she had to choose her words carefully, sometimes stumbling with words that weren't relevant to the conversation at hand. This was a frightening departure from her usual razor-sharp conversations and quick thinking, even when she was under the influence. When Ann asked a therapist why Marie's thinking and speech seemed to be impaired, the stock answer was "Brain damage from too much alcohol." This was patent BS; we would have noticed that long before she entered the recovery center.

When Ann gave her this rebuttal, the woman replied, "Drying out intensifies the brain damage's effect on the patients' thought patterns and speech. It's especially noticeable during detox, but can continue for several weeks after."

Only after Marie had finally quit for good were our suspicions confirmed that electroshock "therapy" was leftover nonsense from a different age; it didn't work back then to treat patients with severe psychoses and it certainly didn't do anything today except risk even more brain damage to alcoholics. By this time, the state had refused to renew the quack recovery center's license and its doors were closed. There was talk about a class-action lawsuit, but the owners had disappeared and no lawsuits were filed.

Marie paid no attention to the center's closing and the possibility of a lawsuit; she was focused instead on her drive with the children to Phoenix. Frank had already left for volunteer FAC duty somewhere in Southeast Asia.

The other center was equally ineffective but at least it was pain-free. There, the patients learned new skills to help divert their thinking away from alcohol and focus instead on learning how to draw and paint, make pottery, knit, crochet, sew, and cook. Local people to teach these skills were recruited by the center and the patients had plenty of hands-on instruction. The premise behind the activities seemed to at least make some sense and there was no doubt that the patients enjoyed their learning sessions. However, it seemed too simple of a solution for an addiction as complex as alcoholism. Our doubts were somewhat eased when we learned that the patients also had individual and group therapy sessions to help them achieve an alcohol-free life.

Of course, the psychologist on staff continually reinforced the need for patients to get completely absorbed in their new skills to chase away any thoughts of drinking's seductive pleasures. Marie chose knitting as her new avocation.

After leaving the center, she said she enjoyed knitting while the children were in school and no wonder.

She drank her straight-up vodka martinis while making scarves and sweaters for the children. Never mind that heavy woolen scarves and sweaters were rarely needed in the Valley of the Sun; knitting was fun. Too much fun. The more she drank, the more she knitted and vice versa.

When Marie was in the recovery centers, Ann took over the household chores for the family. She quickly learned that Marie had no intention of quitting. She found glasses of vodka hidden behind the glassware in the cabinets, and bottles hidden throughout the house. The basement and laundry room had the largest vodka inventory, probably because laundry for six people took time, which meant more drinking time for Marie. Also, she would stash her bottle in the laundry basket should anyone come down the basement and no one would be the wiser.

With Frank gone, she finally got serious about quitting and started attending Alcoholics Anonymous meetings, every day. She had promised herself that she would be alcohol-free to stay before he returned home. Like all alcoholics struggling to give up their favorite pastime, Marie's sobriety came with a big price tag for her and the family. There wasn't a second, a minute, an hour, or a day that went by when she didn't crave alcohol.

Knowing that she'd never be able to handle a day at a time, she instead focused on drink-free seconds. A week later, she stepped up to a minute. Two weeks later, she graduated to a complete hour. Three weeks later, she tried a full day--and made it. Her dry day turned into two, three, and then four dry days and her confidence in her ability to stay dry grew with every passing day. She reveled in her new freedom from hangovers, dry heaves and the shakes: more than anything, the constant fear that she'd run out of vodka.

She knew that she would fulfill the promise she had made and she did. Later, another recovering alcoholic told her that, in her process of recovery, she had also saved her sanity—and her life. He also reminded her how easily she could forfeit all of this with just one drink.

The pain wasn't over. Sobriety also exacerbated Marie's guilt. Jennifer and the children had fended for themselves during the months when she was a stumbling, slurring drunk: doing the laundry, cleaning house, cooking meals and washing the dishes fell on their shoulders. As the new "woman of the house," Jennifer took on the cooking and laundry. She resented this and rebelled; according to Marie, she sneaked out of the house on weekends and weeknights to meet her friends and party and even dated older men. It made no difference to her that Marie had achieved her goal of an alcohol-free life. There was nothing Marie could say or do about the aberrant behavior. Jennifer would simply laugh and say that she wasn't doing anything Marie hadn't done.

Throughout Marie's recovery process, Frank, Jr., retreated into his studies, reading books about war in the air, and building model airplanes. Other than helping Jennifer by washing the dishes while Mark and Mike dried them, he pretty much kept to himself at home and at school. Marie often wondered just how emotionally scarred he and his sister were from witnessing his mother's horrible death. *They went through an experience that no one should have to go through let alone children, and I can't blame them for not accepting me.*

No one could replace their birth mother and I suspected that from the first time Frank and I dated. When I went into the living room of his base home and saw Elizabeth's huge portrait on the wall, I knew I could never compete with her memory and I decided that it would cause nothing but resentment if I tried. Hell, I caused enough resentment by my drinking, let alone piling on more by trying to make myself look good at Elizabeth's expense. Rest in peace, Elizabeth. Only God knows how little of that you must have had during your short life.

Mark and Mike felt badly about the way Jennifer was treating their mother and politely asked her to stop. She told them to mind their own business, which they did. There had been enough turmoil in their lives without adding more. They knew that both Jennifer and Frank, Jr., blamed their mother's drinking for their father's departure. While they disagreed, starting more arguments would achieve nothing. Neither Frank, Jr. nor Jennifer would ever change their minds about Marie's drinking as the root cause of their father's departure.

Marie got an unexpected call from Frank one weekend while he was standing down in Thailand. She let him know that she had fulfilled her promise to stop drinking once and for all, and also told him of Jennifer's behavior. He told Marie to put Jennifer on the line. Since she worshipped her dad, she listened while he convinced her that her behavior was out of line, that what she was doing was dangerous, and that he was very disappointed that she was treating her stepmother so badly. Jennifer tried to blame Marie for her behavior, but Frank didn't buy into that argument. He said that she was a young woman now and responsible for her own decisions, and that he'd be home soon to get Marie part-time help with the household chores so she could focus on reinforcing her AA steps to recovery.

Jennifer settled down after her conversation with her dad, got serious about her schoolwork and cut off her late-night partying as well as dating grown men. She would continue to do the cooking and laundry, but only as a back-up if her stepmother started to drink again and was incapable of housework. Which didn't happen. Jennifer would soon be gone. She had enlisted in the Air Force Reserve and would leave for basic training as soon as she graduated.

When Jennifer's graduation neared, she told Marie she would be leaving. Marie told her she understood why, wished her well and told her she hoped that they could stay in touch. She also apologized for her drunkenness and thanked Jennifer for taking over her housework. Jennifer was taken aback by the apology and told Marie that she'd write as soon as she could. Which she did, and Marie was overjoyed with this turn in their relationship.

When Frank, Jr. graduated, he walked out the door with an overnight bag in his hand. Marie asked him where he was going. He exploded. "None of your damn business. All I'll tell you is that you'll never see me again."

Those were the last words she ever heard from him.

She was devastated. Doubly so, because she assumed responsibility for his decision and her guilt haunted her for years after. On the positive side, his cutting words stayed with her as one more lasting reminder to never drink again.

Fourteen

Ravens At War

A Raven buddy of Frank's told me that, "For a SAC pilot, Frank was very aggressive. He would sort of light his hair on fire and go after the enemy with everything he had. There's a saying among pilots: 'There are old pilots, and there are bold pilots. But there are no old, bold pilots.'"

These words rang true for me when I recalled Frank's age; he was 40 years old when he died. To his young Ravens—most in their 20s—he was indeed an old, bold pilot. And then he was no more.

Frank had written several letters to a Raven FAC buddy who had been severely wounded and was medevac'd to safety after he was shot down and crash-landed his O-1 in a treetop during a major NVA attack on a small town in southern Laos. In one of his letters, he told the downed Raven about the fight: at least three 12.7 mm antiaircraft machine guns had opened up on him. After he'd been picked up by the Air America rescue helicopter and was out of harm's way, Frank looked at the wrecked aircraft and here is how he described it to his wounded buddy.

Winter Roses

"How in hell you got out of it, we can't figure out. Did you know that there are trees coming out of every inch of the cockpit area? They're about 10 to 15 feet tall with branches big enough to ram right through a guy. It looks like a forest growing right through the cockpit."

Frank kept him informed of events that happened in the battle, such as sending him a photo of a NVA tank that he had killed before he'd been hit and went down. Destroying a tank was a real prize for a Raven since the enemy seldom used them; they were easy targets to spot and the enemy troops inside them knew that death usually followed a Raven overfly. On the back of the photo, Frank had written, "Two men chained inside?"

The Raven's rescue was engineered by two of his buddies who were also in the fight. One of them started flying well away from the wounded Raven's crash site in the hope that his diversionary tactic would allow the Air America rescue helicopter—called in by the second Raven--to quickly make the pick-up without getting shot up.

The other Raven had also called in two fighter-bombers whose pilots tried to hit his smoke but couldn't because of poor visibility due to gathering darkness. At his direction, the lead fast mover streaked down in a mock attack to draw enemy fire and then executed a faster climb to get out of harm's way. The ruse worked; the enemy started shooting, revealing the positions of their gun emplacements. The fighter-bombers pounced on them, coming in hot to silence the antiaircraft guns with their 500-pound bombs and strafing the enemy troops that had surrounded the friendly Lao ground troops, enabling them to safely withdraw.

The Air America helicopter nearby on station flew down and rescued the badly wounded pilot. He knew that the bravery of his buddies, the Air America chopper and the fast movers had saved his life, and that their actions and cool heads under fire really meant that the first part of his recovery and eventual journey home were already underway. Never again would he return to the battlefields of Laos.

John Bingham

This battle was unique because much of the fighting was done in the open and the NVA troops were easy targets. They depended upon bad weather to prevent Raven-directed air strikes, but Mother Nature fooled them. Intermittent breaks in the cloud cover—called "Glory Holes" by the fighter jocks—gave the Ravens the opportunity to call in the fighter-bombers. One pilot called the action "A turkey shoot."

In another letter, Frank reported that the NVA had lost over 700 of their finest to Raven-directed air strikes and that the bodies were scattered all over the battlefield. Their comrades weren't able to get to them to administer first aid to the wounded as well as retrieve the bodies for burial. The sight and stench of the carnage was horrific.

The air strikes had stopped the NVA this time but everyone knew this was a reprieve. The bad weather was returning and they would re-group for the next attack. Frank and his fellow Ravens feared that enemy mortar attacks on their airfield would likely start as soon as the enemy opened battle.

The Ravens were not without humor—mostly dark--that probably helped save their sanity and maybe even their lives in such an intense, nonstop combat environment.

Frank's accounts of the battle and the Ravens' never-ending war-fighting reminded me of a "business card" he had sent me that read:

War Is My Business And Business Is Good.
Frank R. Delaney
Major, USAF and FACer Extraordinaire
You call. We deliver. On time. On target.

Another Raven told me of an incident that happened one night when he was flying his T-28 fighter-bomber in northeastern Laos. He spotted aircraft exhaust flares beneath him and checked with Air America and the ABCCC to see if there were any other friendlies flying in his area. There were none, so he figured that the aircraft was a NVA AN-2 Colt, which the NVA often used as a combat aircraft. It was propeller-driven, big and slow, and an easy target for American warplanes.

He dove down to nail the enemy aircraft, but he was so excited about the prospect of an air-to-air kill that he'd forgotten to adjust his gun sight for his .50-calibers. His first burst missed by a wide margin and he realized immediately what the problem was. Now the Raven knew that enemy pilot would be on full alert, but there was nothing he would likely do except bob, weave, and make a dash for the border in futile attempts to evade the next burst of .50 cal and outrun his attacker. The Raven circled around for another pass, this time ready for the kill. Suddenly and fortunately, the enemy pilot came up with a "Mayday" rescue call. The pilot identified himself as a Marine Corps driver of a transport aircraft, headed for a base in Thailand. He was in trouble and didn't know it; he was following the wrong ADF (Automatic Direction Finder) beacon. The Raven told him that he was miles off course because he was following an ADF beacon that led straight to an airport in North Vietnam. The beacons were on the same frequency and the Marine had chosen the wrong one.

The pilot was upset to learn of his navigation error, but relieved to know that he would not be greeted by NVA guards packing AK-47s, followed by torture interrogation and a fast lane to the Hanoi Hilton. The Raven escorted him to the Thai border and pointed him toward Udorn's RTAFB (Royal Thailand Air Force Base). He asked the Raven who he was, and he responded, "The Laotian Forestry Service." "Jesus!," the Marine exclaimed. "Why is the Forestry Service packing .50 cal?"

Quoth the Raven: "Bears. Terrible big bears."

"The Laotian Forestry Service" was one of the Ravens' official responses to questions about why and what they were doing in Laos. No one believed them.

John Bingham

After blowing up a major NVA command post, the legendary Hmong General Vang Pao invited Frank to be his guest of honor. Sensing that an exotic food dish might be served, Frank brought along two bottles of Schlitz beer as wash should the entrée prove to be too exotic. He had heard stories about some of these native delicacies and he wanted to be ready.

After planning for the next day's Raven flights and recon patrol insertions, the general turned to Frank and asked him to stand and be recognized. Everyone then stood and applauded. When they were seated, the general clapped his hands and one of his soldiers came out bearing the dish of honor for the guest of honor. He came right to Frank and bowed, then presented him with a favorite Hmong dish…fresh monkey brains served in the half-skull. Frank took a deep breath, took the skull "bowl" and gulped down the brains with one swallow. He had no desire to chew them and savor the flavor. Instead, he chugged down his two bottles of beer and bowed to the general in thanks, with a huge belch that made everyone laugh. The general beamed while Frank fought to keep the contents of his stomach down.

Fortunately, he was successful.

Rainy season death and destruction from the air: smoke rises from an enemy command post that Raven Frank had spotted and destroyed with 500-pound bombs delivered on target by two "Thud" pilots (F-105 Thunderchief fighter- bombers). The CP was well camouflaged.

Frank Delaney Collection

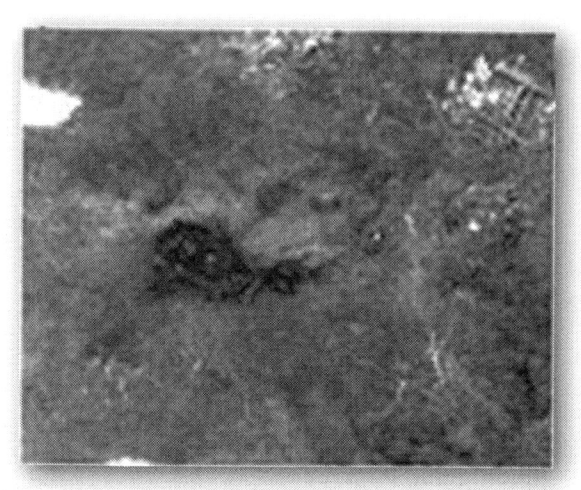

Frank's bomb damage assessment of a tank that one of his fellow Ravens had killed during an enemy's major offensive in southern Laos. On the back of this photo, Frank had written, "Two men chained inside?"

Frank Delaney Collection

John Bingham

Every Raven who flew during the rainy season knew the danger and Frank was no exception; a "rock-filled cloud" was waiting for him when he emerged from this rain squall. He anticipated it and was able to fly around the "rock-filled cloud"--a jagged hilltop rock outcropping.

Frank Delaney Collection

Winter Roses

This debris near the enemy-held town of Paksong is all that remains of American trucks, 105 mm howitzers and ammunition that had to be destroyed by Ravens to keep them out of enemy hands.
Frank Delaney Collection

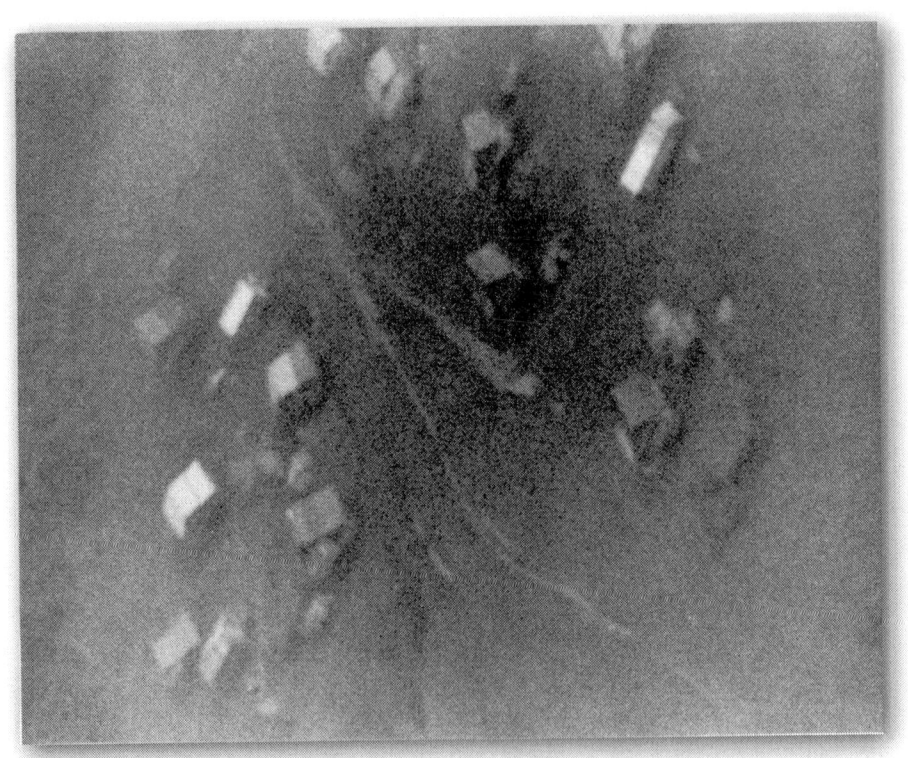

Enemy truck drivers made these roads during the rainy season, which was less dangerous to them because the Ravens often couldn't fly during heavy downpours. This photo enabled Frank to determine the enemy's whereabouts and he called in a strike as soon as the rain let up. The F-105 pilots' 500-pound bombs set off huge secondary explosions.

Frank Delaney Collection

Fifteen

Requiem Revisited

Marie and Mike were at home that afternoon in late October of 1971. He was sick and had stayed home from school.

She happened to glance out the window and saw an Air Force staff car drive slowly by, turn around and then pull up to the curb in front of the house. Terror seized her as she watched a captain and a chaplain get out of the car and walk up the sidewalk. She suddenly felt weak, dizzy and short of breath when the doorbell rang. She cried out to Mike to come over to help steady her, and open the door.

The captain asked if he and the chaplain could come in, and she nodded in response. Mike helped her over to the recliner and motioned the men to sit on the sofa. The captain broke the pained and awkward silence.

"There's no easy way to tell you this and no small talk can make it easy, so I'll just say it. I'm sorry to tell you that we have bad news about your husband. He was hit by enemy antiaircraft artillery fire two days ago and couldn't fly his aircraft. The plane crash-landed and he was killed."

Marie broke into racking sobs, inhaling so hard and so fast that she lost control of her breathing, gulping air in great, heaving gasps. The sudden knowledge that the love of her life was gone forever had taken its first toll on her body and her psyche. The chaplain came over, put his hand on her shoulder to comfort her and began to pray.

In a sudden, cold fury, she regained enough composure to push away his hand and told the captain to get this man out of her house, that he was only making her feel worse. The chaplain said that it would be better if he waited in the car.

Mike didn't say anything throughout the bitter exchange and followed the chaplain outside where he thanked him for coming over to try and help him and his mom. He also apologized for her outburst, but the priest said there was no need, that she was very distraught and that perhaps someday she might at least understand what he'd tried to do. He said that often he's perceived as an angel of death rather than a messenger of faith and hope for eternal life that were once the cornerstones of his calling. He added that sometimes he felt more like the former and that days like this made him wonder why he became a chaplain.

The captain told Marie that Frank's body would arrive the following day from the Philippines, where it had been embalmed and dressed in his Air Force blues with all of his decorations. He said he would call her the next morning to discuss the funeral arrangements. Before he left, he told her that Frank had died gallantly in the service of his country, which set her off again.

"Get this straight, captain. I don't give a damn about your notions of my husband's gallantry or his service to our country. All I care about is sorting out my feelings without your help, the chaplain's help or any fool who thinks he can make me feel better with rehearsed platitudes and canned prayers. Please leave me and my son alone, and now!"

Winter Roses

All the captain could say was "Yes, ma'am." He turned to leave and closed the door too hard on his way out. His departure became an escape and he walked quickly down the sidewalk, jumped into the car, started it and hurriedly slipped the clutch without feeding the engine enough gas. The car lurched forward and stalled.

"God-damn these cars!" he blurted. "When the fuck are they going to spend a few extra bucks and get them with automatic transmissions?" He glanced at the chaplain and apologized for his outbreak. The chaplain forced a smile and told him not to worry, that the Lord understands how difficult their job is and He would forgive him. "Besides," he added. "These cars really are pieces of shit." With that, they both had a needed laugh. The captain re-started the car, gunned it and disappeared around the corner with a screech of the tires.

They had become kindred spirits in wondering how and why they'd ever been tapped for this duty. "I may as well be a fucking mortician," the captain said. The chaplain said, "I may as well be a car salesman. Then I could sell cars with automatic transmissions to the fucking Air Force." More laughter, but this time it bordered on hysteria and they suddenly felt foolish. They stopped their laughing as fast as they started it, and finished their ride back to the base in silence.

Mike came back into the house, now visibly shaken as he began to understand the terrible finality of the visitors' words. He sat down on the floor in front of Marie and laid his head on his crossed arms. She started crying again, triggering his tears and shaking her out of her own sorrow. She reached down and hugged him when he asked, "Mom, what are we going to do without dad?"

We still have our close and loving family," she said, "and that's what we'll need to honor his memory and get through what will be one of the most difficult times in our lives."

There wasn't much more either could say to comfort each other. Instead they cried until they could cry no more.

John Bingham

Marie's solution to ease her pain was an old, familiar friend whom she once believed had helped her get through many bad situations. Her voice hoarse with sorrow, she told Mitch to take the car and go over to the liquor store for three fifths of Stolichnaya. She said that she needed them to get through the days ahead and that she knew he had fake ID. He stared down at the floor and didn't answer until she demanded that he get the vodka, and right away.

"Mom," he said, "You know better than anyone that booze isn't the answer. All it does is give you a temporary lift before throwing you into the pits of despair and self-pity. Then you'll want it even more. You've come too far in AA to give up now and look how much good it's done for you and for all of us. I can't tell you how wonderful it is to have you back as our real mom and not the vodka-soaked witch who couldn't even care for herself, let alone for us."

Gaining confidence with each word, he took a deep breath and slowly rose to his feet. He looked down at her and she looked down at her folded hands on her lap. *Don't blow it,* he thought. *Our family's future now depends upon me.*

"No, I'm not going anywhere right now and I'm taking your car keys. If you want vodka, walk to the store and get it. But if you do, I'm leaving tonight to live with friends. I'll quit school and find a job and you'll never see me again. I'll bet that Mark, Jennifer and Frank will do the same thing."

For a moment Marie couldn't believe that happy-go-lucky Mike was saying those hurtful words, then quickly realized that they weren't hurtful at all. They were helpful. They were words that only someone who loved her could tell her. Maybe, she thought, they were the most important words she'd ever hear.

An image flashed through her mind of staggering and slurring her words at the funeral and she shuddered at the thought.

She apologized and told him that he was right, going back to drinking would be the worst thing she could do. She reaffirmed that the drunk Frank had left behind months ago was no more, and she would neither sully his sacrifice nor dishonor his memory with alcohol.

"No," she said. "I'm going to keep my sobriety streak going one day at a time, just as AA teaches. One hour or one minute or even one second at a time if I have to go back to that."

He reached down and took her hands in his, pulling her up and into his arms. She had never thought that he was that strong. More tears streamed down their cheeks as they hugged, but they were now tears of relief that helped to lighten their guilt loads. All he could stammer was, "Thanks, mom. I'm really proud of you."

She put her finger to his mouth and shushed him. "Mike," she said, "I can't tell you how proud I am of you. You don't know what you just did for me. Did you know that alcohol abuse leads you down only one path; first comes insanity and then comes death? I'll never forget what you've done. You have saved my mind and my life."

When the children returned home from school, she asked them to sit together on the sofa, and then told them the news. They couldn't believe it and sat there in mind-numbing shock. Frank, Jr. couldn't speak. He looked at Marie with glazed-over eyes, shaking his head back and forth as if to deny what he'd just heard and hugging a throw pillow with both arms. Jennifer buried her face in her skirt to hide her sobbing. She looked up and rasped through her tears, "It's not fair! First my mother and now my father! Why, why, WHY?" she screamed.

There was nothing Mike, Mark or Marie could say or do to soften their sorrow; they knew full well how Elizabeth had died and the crushing impact of that terrible afternoon now revisited spread over them like a chilling, choking fog.

They fought back their tears and tried their best to let their agony run its ragged course; they, too, loved Frank and now he was gone.

John Bingham

Finally, Jennifer stopped crying and broke their silence by asking Marie if the Air Force officials were sure it was their dad in the casket and not some other pilot. In their eagerness to deny that he was dead and the thought of a chance he'd be soon coming home alive and well, her brothers chimed in to support her.

The question had not occurred to Marie and she tried her best to answer it.

"Jennifer, I can't be 100-percent sure that the Air Force made a mistake and that your dad is still alive," she replied. "But I know from others' experiences that they don't make mistakes about important matters like this and they're almost always right. But I promise all of you that I will look into that casket tomorrow and make sure that the man in there is my husband and your dad, so we won't have to wonder if the Air Force sent us someone else. You can be sure that I'll tell you if it is your dad. Meanwhile, we have to hope for the best."

They spent the rest of their evening pretending to be lost in small talk and clinging to the hope that their mom would find out that someone else was in the casket. While they wanted to skip their homework, Marie insisted that they get it done. It was a good diversion from their worry, not only for them but for her as she answered their questions and checked their work. After the homework was done, she ordered showers or baths for everyone while she ordered pizza. Instead of their usual rambunctious run up the stairs and jockeying for position to go first, they quietly walked up. They were lost deep in worry and wondering whether what they'd heard was really true. Jennifer took her bath first and the boys alternated their showers according to age…first Frank, Jr., then Mark, who was followed by Mike.

While she didn't hear their usual chatter upstairs, Marie felt for the moment as if their lives were still normal, at least as normal as any family could be with a parent fighting on the other side of the world.

Every serviceman's wife worries about the staff car coming to her house. Only the dreaded car has come to mine, and I believe deep inside that the body in the box really is Frank's. Still, there's always a chance, however thin, that a mistake has been made.

Winter Roses

She also thought about how terrible she'd feel for another wife and family if a mistake had been made. There'd be no good outcome for anyone in either scenario. Regardless, she prayed to her higher power that it was Frank who was still alive.

The pizza arrived, and along with the TV, it helped get their mind off their dad. They couldn't quite grasp that their lives would forever be changed if he was really dead, and they strove to relegate the prospect of his death to the darker compartments of their minds. Sleep did not come for them that night. They spent most of it awake and tossing, wondering if the body inside really was their dad's.

The captain called as promised the next morning and Marie listened politely as he told her the body would be in the base hospital's mortuary late that afternoon. It would be in a casket and readied for the funeral service and burial as soon as she made her final plans. He said that an officer who had flown with Frank in Southeast Asia had accompanied the body to Luke AFB and would be there to help comfort her and the rest of the family. The traditional "missing wingman" formation of F-100 Super Sabres would fly over to honor Frank; the "Huns" were chosen because he qualified on them. The base's senior chaplain would conduct the military service if she so desired. Marie knew this chaplain helped raise a lot of money for the base's Youth Activities Club and she consented.

Her contact to coordinate the funeral arrangements was the captain himself and he asked if she and the children could come over at 1600 hours to meet with him, see the casket and review the details of the memorial service.

She told him that she and the children would be there, but that they would have to stay outside the mortuary while she looked inside the casket to make sure that the body was Frank's.

Her matter-of-fact words jarred him and he replied that opening the casket was out of the question. "That's not military practice," he said. "I have standing orders from the base commander to never allow wives to look inside their husbands' caskets. I'm sorry, Mrs. Delany, but it can't be done."

"I'm sorry, captain, but it will be done. I have the final say on what I will do with my husband's body. Neither you, your base commander, nor Jesus Christ will change that. You must understand that my children and I will not go through the rest of our lives wondering if the right man's body is in that casket. Also, he will not be buried in a casket. His instructions to me were to cremate his remains and bury them in a cemetery close to our home. When I go, my ashes will be placed next to his.

"Meanwhile, I will look in the casket this afternoon. Before doing that, I ask you to think how rotten you'll feel if the wrong man is in there, to say nothing of embarrassing the entire Air Force chain of command. I've been around long enough to know that nothing pisses off top brass like embarrassment because it's always the first gut-busting, learned consequence of a major—you'll pardon the word—fuck-up.

"Now, what's your base commander's name and telephone number? I will call him and tell him what I will do and that you've done your duty in advising me that spouses are forbidden to look in their husband's caskets. If he tells me that I can't, then I'll tell him that I'm retaining a lawyer and there'll be no service until I look in that casket and make sure that the body is my husband's.

"If he still refuses, then I'll raise a stink to the heavens and if I have to, I'll take the matter right up to the Secretary of the Air Force. We'll see how he likes refusing such a simple and logical request by the widow of a highly decorated volunteer combat Forward Air Controller (FAC) in the supposed-to-be secret war in Laos. Along with the press coverage when I leak the story to the *Arizona Republic* and other newspapers. Maybe even to the newswires."

The captain suddenly stood up in anger, puffed out his chest and locked into his parade-rest position, trying his hardest to face her down. *At least I have her here.*

"You don't know that he was in Laos!" He thought that his booming baritone added authority to his words.

Marie rose to her feet and came right back at him.

"In your face, captain. Do you think I'm stupid? I saw an AP newswire item in the *Republic* two days ago that reported an American pilot had been shot down and killed in Laos and that our ambassador in Vientiane was investigating the matter. I wondered when I read it if it was Frank. Widows always think that it must be someone else, don't they? *Don't they?* He couldn't tell me where he was going when he returned to fight in Indochina. From that, I knew he wasn't going back to Vietnam. How many other Southeastern Asian countries are there that the Ho Chi Minh trail runs through? Don't tell me, I'll tell you. Cambodia and Laos, and we already know that Nixon has us in Cambodia."

"OK, ma'am, I give up," replied the captain. "Look, I truly do understand your need to make sure that it's your husband's body in the casket. You've convinced me that it's the right thing to do, but convincing the base CO will be another matter. He is every bit as pig-headed as you are, and he's also equally persuasive. His two stars and a short fuse also help him bring others around to his point of view in a hurry. Let's make a deal. I open the casket for you when you come over this afternoon. You see for yourself whether a mistake has been made. We close the casket and we close our mouths, and no one but the two of us will know I've disobeyed a direct order. Fair enough?"

"Fair enough," Marie answered.

Later that day in the mortuary, he opened the casket and Mary peered inside. He caught her when her eyes rolled back, just before her limp body hit the granite floor.

Sixteen

Post Mortem

Despite our pleas, Marie insisted that Ann and I stay home and not fly out to attend the service because there was nothing we could do but remind her of our good times together with her and Frank, and she didn't need the added stress of worrying about our well-being as her guests. We grudgingly agreed, but this was no time for debate. Instead, we would take the family to Phoenix in the spring.

Her father told us that Marie was terribly distraught at the funeral, crying throughout the entire ceremony. After the jets thundered overhead in the final salute with the traditional missing wingman formation, the young officer, who was highly decorated and walked with a pronounced limp, presented her with the flag with Frank's medals and ribbons displayed on top of it, then held her hand--a simple, comforting gesture that she never forgot. But she could not remember his name. Neither could she remember what he'd said to her.

I tried since to get in touch with the Raven FAC whom I believed was the attending officer, but received no response. Perhaps the memory was a wound that he didn't wish to re-open; if so, I understood and respected that, and took it as a token of his love and respect for his fallen comrade.

With Frank's insurance money and widow's pension, Marie bought a nice condominium on the outskirts of Phoenix and then sought investment advice from a cousin who lived in Tucson who went into real estate development at the start of Tucson's boom years and made a fortune. He introduced her to a mortgage brokerage firm that sold her an office building in a prime downtown location. She wanted the building to give her a steady, monthly stream of rental income that would play a major role in securing her future. This didn't happen.

The brokerage partners turned out to be a cabal of thieves who cooked her books, kept her monthly payments and then bought the building themselves with her money for the back taxes she supposedly owed.

She was stuck without sufficient evidence of her tax payments, couldn't prove her rightful ownership and her lawsuit was tossed out. She thought that the judge was on the brokerage's payroll and she may well have been right. Believing that she'd already felt the heat of at least three corners of hell in her still-young life, she took this theft in stride.

As one of Frank's "good troops"—the highest compliment he ever paid anyone, including her—she learned her lesson and moved on to a long career as office manager and dispatcher for a cross-country trucking company. Even that soured as her retirement date neared. She heard through the grapevine from a customer who was also a close friend of her boss that he was going to stiff her out of her promised retirement pension and use the money to pay for his live-in girl-friend's salary—which would be higher than Marie's because he'd be paying only one salary.

His girlfriend's position as a "truck tracker" would be eliminated. It was a phony job he had created to keep a closer eye on her. She was a head-turner and knew it, smiling and flirting with every man who came within drooling distance of her, which included all the men in his shop. Within two months, every one of the cross-country truckers he hired had tried to get her to go on the road with him.

Their favorite "come-ons" were the promises of seeing the country, partying down after their runs were completed, and a cab that slept two. Marie knew all about their ploys, because over the years, the same sex-minded billygoats had invited her on their long-distance jaunts. She refused every one of them, although she later joked that she would have liked to learn the Texas Two-Step and country-style line dancing. "Besides," she added, "I've always wanted snakeskin boots."

Because her boss was often out of the office, he left much of his paperwork for her to handle and it was only a matter of time until she found evidence; a hand-written note to his live-in girlfriend that promised she'd be Marie's successor, and that she'd start at a salary well above Marie's because he'd pay for it with her pension money.

Marie laughed, not only at the brazenness of his clumsy attempt at fraud and what she also considered to be outright theft, but at the heavy imprint of his girlfriend's garish lipstick on the note with "Good thinking, lover boy!" scribbled underneath.

Three weeks before her scheduled retirement date, Marie showed up at the office to greet her boss with his signature on paperwork that documented both her full pension amount and her monthly payment increments, all based upon her continued good performance.

As evidence, she carried an armful of outstanding performance reviews with his signature on each one, the "lover boy" note, and an attorney who promised not to sue for twice Marie's pension amount if he would sign a witnessed statement that Marie would be paid her promised pension and that he would pay his fees.

After the signing, Marie advised him that she was taking her three-week paid vacation "starting today" and wished him and his girlfriend well--after she'd thoughtfully pushed her vacation check under his nose for his signature.

Winter Roses

On the way out the door, she expressed her thanks and appreciation, and took great satisfaction in leaving him glaring at her and speechless with an untrained office manager-dispatcher. *I doubt if his ditz can handle even one of her new jobs, let alone both. But that's his problem now. I'll have to send him a postcard with my lipstick imprinted on it.*

Marie told Ann and me that it was a good thing that Frank wasn't alive to witness this one. "Otherwise, we'd have a homicide to deal with. Maybe two, if his girlfriend was at her desk or maybe on her boss's lap when he came storming in."

Ann and Marie were as close as two sisters could be, and Ann did her best to help out the family when Marie was incapacitated by alcohol or in detox-rehab centers. Here, they are standing in front of Lake Superior's Whitefish Bay, a safe harbor for huge Great Lakes freighters during Superior's deadly storms.

John Bingham collection

John Bingham

She stayed clean for the rest of her life and it was always a pleasure when she visited us regularly during our Michigan summers while we visited her in the winter months.

Mark divorced his first wife because of her alcoholism and gave up silver-smithing because the smelting's toxic fumes were destroying his lungs. He remarried and raised a second family. Today, he is the supervisor of Peoria's sanitation department. He and his second wife, Rose, live in Litchfield Park.

Mike married a woman who'd had two children from a previous marriage and they had two more of their own. He and Tina live with their daughters in Glendale where they operate a child care center and a medical coding business.

Jennifer is a major in the U.S. Air Force Reserve and a registered flight nurse who has cared for many of our wounded Iraq and Afghanistan war veterans being airlifted back to the U.S. for further treatment. We're as proud of her as we were of her dad and Marie, although she may never know this. How proud both of them and Elizabeth, too, would have been of her.

Jennifer had severed communications with Marie, Ann and I after Marie told her of her father's affair while he served in Vietnam. I had managed to re-open an e-mail dialog with her because we were friends when she was a youngster, but she broke off. I had copied Marie on a note to Jennifer, hoping that this might help bring them together again. This ploy backfired. Marie took Jennifer's address and tried to get back in touch with her. Jennifer responded, telling her how angry she was with me for giving away her e-mail address, and to never try to contact her again. Marie was heartbroken, not only because she had lost contact with her stepdaughter, but also because she couldn't learn anything about her grandchildren.

Winter Roses

The whereabouts of Frank, Jr. remains a mystery. His grandmother visited Marie at her Phoenix home and told her that he was an angry man, who, like his sister, wanted nothing more to do with Marie and the rest of her family. She also said how tormented they likely still were by the remembrance of their mother's terrible death. She felt that their anger and hurt must have spilled over on Marie, whom they perceived as a poor substitute for their real mother.

After the children's grandmother left, Marie carefully thought over what she said. *Seen in that light, if I was Mother Mary herself come back to earth, nothing I could have said or done would have won the trust and love of Frank, Jr. and Jennifer. Of course, that's no excuse for my alcoholism, which added fuel to the fires of their hate and mistrust. Now I can't even reach out to them to tell them how sorry I am, and make amends for hurting them.*

Mark told me that Frank, Jr., had visited him and his wife years ago and asked if his dad really did bring a Vietnamese girl to the United States. Mark replied that he didn't know, that he'd heard the story from his mom but she didn't know for sure, either. Frank, Jr. left and that was the last they ever saw or heard from him.

We believe that Jennifer and Frank, Jr. were convinced that their dad left them for Laos because of her drinking and they may be right—at least partly right. After all, he said as much when I'd asked him why he was returning to fight somewhere in Southeast Asia. However, I never bought into this explanation because it was too simple for such a complex man. I knew the ferocious warrior who lived under his tough skin, a warrior who was likely bored to tears with duty on a SAC base as safety officer.

Not many Ravens earned this patch, simply because they were not in-country as long as others who re-upped for another six months; that, or some like Frank, who had volunteered for a year's tour of duty. He was KIA over Laos soon after he'd passed the 1,000-mission mark and was to rotate home the day after he was killed.

Frank Delaney Collection

While Marie's addiction to alcohol could have been a contributing reason for his decision to return to war, he may also have missed the intense fury of a

Winter Roses

FAC's war. Fighting as a Raven FAC in the covert Laos war would have provided many opportunities for adrenaline highs. But that premise couldn't have been the only reason. The prospect of joining an elite corps of free-minded flyers who detested the endless, stupefying rules of engagement and the hide-bound regulations and standing orders of the regular Air Force was most certainly an enticement. So was winning the respect of all who knew the Ravens for their courage and determination in flying non-stop missions from dawn to darkness, every day, always under fire, until their tour of duty—or their lives—ended. Frank's Laotian 1,000-mission patch bears silent witness to this. The satisfaction of saving the lives of ground troops was also important to him, along with assuaging his deep hatred of communists by annihilating them at every chance he had. His position as a senior Raven FAC in Laos gave him virtually unlimited opportunities to seek out and destroy the enemy.

I believe that he had added up all of these reasons to make his fatal decision. These, and his bulldog "never quit" attitude whether in peacetime or at war.

Seventeen

Death In The Sky

Marie was told that Frank had flown his final mission with an experienced backseater, Wa Ger Cheng—known by the Ravens as "Scar"—and was hit in a hail of enemy small-arms fire. He was too badly wounded to fly the aircraft. In this account, Wa Ger took control of the aircraft from the backseat and landed the aircraft too hard, throwing Frank against the instrument console. The force of the impact killed him instantly. An Air America helicopter arrived at the scene of the crash within minutes and took the body back to Long Tieng along with Wa Ger, who had suffered a bad leg injury in the landing.

I learned another account of his death from Wa Ger's son, Cher, as told to him by his father. Cher presented the story at the funeral of Joua Bee, who was Wa Ger's nephew. Since he spoke no English, a translator interpreted.

Few Hmong backseaters knew the locations of as many enemy positions as Wa Ger. Several Ravens told me—Frank included--that he would say, "Man-y enem-y" while pointing down to the trees below; the Raven would look and see nothing. Wa Ger would point and say again, "Man-y enem-y," until the Raven would fly down and sure enough, the location would be alive with NVA troops and—all too often for the Ravens—antiaircraft guns.

Winter Roses

That fateful day, the mission given to them by the CIA was to investigate a possible enemy encampment in a hilly tree line on the Plain of Jars. Frank reached the location and started a dive for a closer look.

"I do not think we should go down there," Wa Ger spoke on the intercom.

While he didn't speak Hmong, Frank knew that Wa Ger was very concerned about his intended close-in recon. "Don't worry," he replied. "I will fly fast so the enemy will not have time to get us in their sights and start shooting at us."

Now very aggravated as the trees began to rush up at them, Wa Ger shouted, "This is a mistake. We must not go down there!"

Frank tried to reassure him again. "I'll pull out of my dive just above the trees and will fly fast so the enemy will not have time to get us in their sights."

"No!" insisted Wa Ger. "Too many enemy here. Too many guns. Pull out before it is too late."

By then, Frank was already in his final position to make his pass. Wa Ger reinforced his displeasure with rapid, hard kicks on Frank's seat back.

Frank pulled out of the dive, nearly clipped the treetops with his landing gear and flew right through a virtual blizzard of small-arms fire. He was riddled with bullets and died instantly. Wa Ger was not hit.

Knowing that Major Delaney was dead, he knew enough to grab the backseater's control stick and keep pulling up, all the while hearing enemy bullets punching holes through the aircraft.

When he reached a height safe from small-arms fire, he quickly released his safety harness, jumped up and grabbed the radio he knew the pilots used to stay in contact with "Cricket"—the aircraft command post that flew over northern Laos during daylight hours that controlled all U.S. aircraft activity in the area. It was also Air America's frequency, to request a dust-off (medevac helicopter).

After getting back into the rear seat and his safety harness, he practiced with the control pedals and stick, at the same time calling for help in his broken English.

Since he'd been shot down twice before, he remembered the universal call sign for aircraft pilots in trouble and shouted "Mayday! Mayday! Mayday!" into the transmitter. Immediately, an airborne Air America helicopter pilot responded, asking him what the trouble was and his location.

Wa Ger answered that his pilot was killed and that he was now trying to fly the aircraft. As for location, all he knew was that he was near the trees on the Plain of Jars where they had been hit, that they were not far from the town of Muong Sui and the airstrip at Lima Site 108. At this point, the Cricket navigator joined in, giving Frank's mission destination coordinates to the helicopter pilot.

Wa Ger was pleased that his message got through, but his problem required fast action: he didn't know how to land the aircraft. He asked if there was a Raven in the area who could give him instructions. While Cricket's pilot didn't understand Hmong, he picked up on the word "Raven" and understood immediately that Wa Ger needed help from a Raven in flying and landing Frank's Bird Dog. He put out a call for a Raven and within minutes, a Raven answered and said he was on the way.

The Raven checked in and told Wa Ger that he would show him exactly what to do to make a safe landing. He also said that they would fly towards LS-108 and land on the Lima site's airstrip. This comforted Wa Ger because he had been with Ravens who had landed on the strip on previous missions.

Winter Roses

Following the Raven's lead, his instruction began with a banking turn to the left towards LS-108. He recognized the landscape below and knew exactly where he was going.

By then, Wa Ger was beginning to feel more comfortable with the controls. When the aircraft was in line with the landing strip, the Raven told him that they would begin the descent together. Wa Ger dropped the nose of the aircraft and lost sight of the landing strip.

Frank's body had fallen forward, coming to rest on the instrument console with the upper torso leaning against the windscreen and blocking his view. The Raven spotted this immediately and demonstrated to Wa Ger how to raise and lower the front of the aircraft so the body would either fall back into the seat or fall to the side, clearing enough windscreen space so he could finally see for the landing.

Wa Ger managed to put the aircraft through its climb-and-dive paces, but the results stayed the same. Five times he attempted to land, and he was forced to pull up in all five because the body still blocked his line of sight.

The Raven decided to demonstrate a rapid, side-to-side movement, one that he and all of the FACs referred to as "jinking" to throw NVA gunners off their target. He thought that jinking would surely move the body aside so Wa Ger could see well enough to land. Wa Ger caught on to the maneuver immediately, since he'd been with other Raven pilots who had used it to avoid getting hit. On previous missions, he had studied the duplicate stick, pedals and pushrods on the back seat floor as they moved and felt the aircraft respond with a rapid, side-to-side motion. He thought it might throw the body to the side so he could finally see when the nose was down and land the aircraft.

He heard the Raven announce the arrival of an Air America helicopter to fly him and the body back to Long Tieng. He was no stranger to Air America, since

John Bingham

AA had rescued him twice before when he and Raven pilots had crash-landed. The very thought of rescue heartened and refocused him on the task ahead.... jink and hope that the body would fall so he could see and land.

He began the rhythmic movement slowly, getting the feel of the Bird Dog's gentle rocking and then began to pick up speed with faster, more sudden moves. On the last sudden jerk, Frank's body pitched onto the instrument console further to the right and stayed there. Finally, Wa Ger could see through the windscreen well enough to land.

In his anxiety to get down, he began his approach too quickly and with a dangerously steep descent, and he knew that he was running out of time to pull up. He was right: he was already committed in spite of the Raven's calls to pull up and come around again. The Raven watched helplessly as the aircraft landed hard, snapping off the right wheel strut, bouncing once, twice and then a third time on the rough airstrip before coming to rest head-on against a mud-mortar brick wall that guarded a refueling dump. Fortunately, the wing tanks had not been ruptured by the force of the landing, so the risk of fire was minimal.

The Air America helicopter landed right behind the aircraft, and two paramedics ran over with a stretcher. One tried unsuccessfully to get a carotid pulse from Frank while the other reached into the back to get Wa Ger out of the aircraft. He grasped Wa Ger by the arms and pulled him out of the back seat quickly, which made Wa Ger scream with pain; a closer look showed that his leg was bloody and a splinter of bone was poking out. The leg was bleeding profusely, so the paramedic crawled inside, wrapped a tourniquet above the wound and gave him a hefty dose of morphine. Wa Ger was in happy land within moments and lay there slack-jawed with a foolish grin as they carefully lifted him out of the aircraft.

The co-pilot came over to help. The paramedics asked him to pull the body out of the cockpit and lay it on the ground while they carried Wa Ger back to the 'copter and strapped him on his stretcher to keep his leg stable for the flight back to Long Tieng. The co-pilot managed to get the body out and placed on top of a body bag, and leaned against the fuselage, breathing heavily from the exertion. When his breathing returned to normal, he retrieved Frank's CAR-15, his ammo bandoleer and the radios.

They loaded the body on a stretcher and ran it back to the helicopter, strapping the stretcher down right next to Wa Ger but leaving the body without restraint. They didn't put it in a bag since the flight surgeon back at Long Tieng would have to pronounce Frank dead. Wa Ger told one of the medics that he'd counted at least four bullet holes in the body.

During the flight back to Long Tieng, the body suddenly sat straight up, which startled everyone. The pilot called in to say that Frank might not be dead, he'd just sat up. The flight surgeon called back and asked if one of the medics could check to see if Frank had a pulse, was breathing and if his body was rigid. The medic checked all of the vital signs and radioed back to the flight surgeon that Frank was indeed dead; there was neither breathing nor pulse and that the surprise sit-up was rictus, the body's last major-muscle contraction.

Wa Ger survived the crash with a compound, complex fracture. He was taken to the Long Tieng hospital where the doctor anesthetized him and repaired the leg as best he could. As a measure of respect and appreciation, General Vang Pao himself visited Wa Ger the same evening he was wounded and demanded that he be put in a separate room by himself, and that every effort was to be made to ensure his comfort and speed his healing.

In the early 1980s, the Pathet Lao captured Wa Ger in the jungles of Laos and executed him.

Eighteen

Aftermath

"*.... Frank always came down on the side of his Ravens. Whether they needed more ammunition, ordnance, better food, improvements to their living quarters, or better aircraft maintenance, he fought like hell for them...*"

A retired CIA operative shared the above comments with me at a Ravens reunion in San Antonio years ago. He knew Frank well, and added that they often argued over issues that Frank thought were important to the Ravens' well-being. He added that Frank was "fearless" in taking his arguments to officers of any rank.

I immediately remembered him calling out the three-star whom Marie had said propositioned her at the SAC brass's dinner dance. That in turn triggered my memory of his MO during his entire tour in Korea as a supply sergeant, which was going to almost any length to make sure that his unit's enlisted men and officers got what they needed to improve their morale and accomplish the mission.

In short, Frank devoted most of his career to taking good care of his troops, his peers and his superiors--as long as they also took good care of his troops. If they didn't, the tiger in him came out and he'd be all over them, but at least he never forgot to add "sir" when he harangued them. This pissed them off no less and most never forgot him for all the wrong reasons. He probably never would have made colonel, whether lieutenant colonel or full bird, but he would always stand tall knowing that he stood up for his men.

Frank thought the world of his fellow Ravens. Here are a few of his words on this subject; *".... a great bunch of guys who know their business but are always getting fucked over by their superiors with freezing quarters, so-so food, and ridiculous notions of a Raven's duties and performance under fire..."* ..."*I will do everything I can to make their lives more comfortable...they sure as hell deserve it, and more..."*

At a recent Ravens reunion, the Raven who had lifted Frank's body from the rescue helicopter, gave a heartfelt account of Frank's death and what it meant to his fellow Ravens; they attributed their survival to his passing. Their lesson learned was to remember that they were fighting a war, and that they could no longer be the adventure-seeking young men they were when they first became Ravens. They learned due caution without compromising their missions, and lived to return home to their loved ones. After he delivered his brief eulogy, I sought him out to thank him and tell him that Frank had loved him, and if Frank felt that way about him—which he most assuredly did--I sure as hell did, too. I will never forget what he did for Frank, for me and for all of Frank's family.

More insights of Frank emerged in a letter that he'd written to a wounded Raven brother-in-arms about his arguments with a new USAF Air Operations Center commander (AOC) who had compromised the Long Tieng Ravens' mission by transferring half of the experienced Ravens to other military regions. This left Frank—who was also new to Long Tieng–with four other Raven FNGs; the five of them would have to learn the enemy's likely whereabouts in their region without an experienced Long Tieng Raven to share valuable lessons that could mean the difference between life and death.

Frank believed the officer did this because he thought he was breaking up a clique that he somehow viewed as a threat. He also thought that the man had a sick need to demonstrate that he was boss. This same officer also attempted to downgrade an excellent Officer Efficiency Report (OER) that Frank had written for a deserving Raven. Frank, however, was able to end-run the AOC with a call to a NKP (Nhakon Phanom) buddy in Thailand, a bird colonel who pulled strings so Frank could throw out the downgraded OER and restore his version for the Raven's record. This happened without the offending officer's knowledge. Frank's rationale was simple:

"He fucked with me, so I fucked with him. He tried to go behind my back, but I went behind his back. He lost because he's a dumb, conniving son of a bitch who doesn't even know that my OER for the Raven still stands, not his. Lesson learned if he's not too dumb to learn it: don't ever fuck with a smart, conniving son of a bitch."

The last straw for Frank was the officer's attempt to have AOCs write the OERs for the Ravens—men who did not fully understand the Ravens' differing missions and MOs, let alone be able to tell who was good and who was not, the reasons why, and actions that should be taken.

Also, the Ravens' real chain of command was the CIA and the State Department. Senior Ravens like Frank wrote the OERs because they knew their men's performance better than anyone else. If the CIA and embassy attaches caved in to this crap and the proposed change became effective in October 1971 as the AOC had wanted, Frank had lined up another job in Thailand with the NKP colonel. When he wrote this letter, he had fewer than two months to live.

Frank and Marie had planned to spend his October leave together in Hawaii and then decided against it at the last minute. He would leave for home soon after he returned from leave in Thailand and they'd save the expense of a month-long Hawaiian vacation. Instead, they'd put the money in the children's college fund and escape for a week's vacation tour of Arizona soon after he returned.

Winter Roses

After 43 years, I still wonder why Frank flew into that sheet of enemy small-arms fire despite Wa Ger's warnings. He was an aggressive pilot, but not foolhardy. The flight that killed him was to have been his last; he was scheduled to rotate home the following day. Instead, it truly was his last.

Marie told us that she learned from another Raven that Frank was supposed to take up a visiting VIP that afternoon for a safe overview of Raven tactics and results, followed by a fast flight into and out of the PDJ. In short, he could skate. Instead, he and Wa Ger went after the enemy once more. The afternoon's VIP mission was canceled in favor of the CIA's need for intel on a NVA PDJ encampment.

My best guess for his fateful decision to ignore Wa Ger's warnings was his aggressiveness and an exceptionally strong sense of duty that would not allow him to quit; he would get the job done and done right, or die trying.

Frank's Bird Dog after its left wing was very nearly blown off by a NVA 37mm gun crew. He managed to crab the aircraft back to its base and safely land it. The Ravens who saw Frank make his approach and land said it should not have been able to fly…a tribute to his flying skills.

Frank Delaney collection.

John Bingham

A good example of his persistence and determination came from a fellow Raven who had urged him to be very careful when firing his unused marking rockets into enemy AAA gun emplacements that were strung along a ford in southern Laos. He told Frank that those gunners were the best in country. Now, a "best in country enemy" would have been an irresistible challenge to Frank. No enemy could possibly be better at anything than he was. He thanked the Raven for his advice and then continued his standoff fire against the same gun emplacements until his Bird Dog took a hit from one of the NVA 37mm cannons that blew off a major portion of his left wing. Thanks to his superb flying skills, he was able to fly the aircraft—which another Raven said should have been unflyable—back to his base. I have a photo print of the aircraft on the tarmac that clearly shows the extensive damage with his message to Marie scrawled on the reverse side: "Come Fly With Me."

I wrote back after I saw the print and told him that Frank Sinatra—his favorite vocalist--would have been proud.

Other examples of his aggressiveness included his off-limits flight through the Grand Canyon during his fighter pilot qualification training, and constantly seeking out other exceptionally dangerous enemy gun emplacements that defended ammunition, weapons and food caches in both Vietnam and Laos. Heavily guarded and well-camouflaged trucks, tanks, and heavy construction equipment were also prime targets.

A Raven buddy of his may well have got it right. He died because he could not quit. That, and he'd be damned if he'd leave behind anyone who knew he'd skated on his last mission. Skating never was his forte and he would not rotate home with that on his conscience. How ironic it was that this mission truly was his last.

Creating a caring, loving family is not an easy task for any couple with a spouse serving in the military, particularly one who is making a career in the armed forces.

Winter Roses

Marie and Frank were no exception. For them, melding each other's two children from their first marriages into a happy, one-family foursome was not possible.

The children needed time to learn to accept, trust and love their new parents, new siblings and especially, themselves. Unfortunately, their time with their dad was a commodity in short supply during America's long years of war in Southeastern Asia.

Marie and Frank shared only five years together as man and wife, when his year in Vietnam as a FAC, his final 10 months in Laos and his many TDY training assignments away from home are excluded... five years to be together; five years to raise their children from tweeners to teens; five years for their love to blossom and mature; five years of wondering and worrying if Frank will survive his tours of combat duty; five years for Marie to fight and win her own war with alcohol; five years for the children to grow up together; five years to move four times; and five years to try and find ever-elusive lasting happiness and inner peace.

Alone on a school day not long after Frank's funeral service, Marie thought once more of an old friend that she'd always sought for solace--alcohol. There was none in the house except a magnum of Dom Perignon that Frank had bought four years earlier as a surprise for the two of them to celebrate his homecoming from his tour of FAC duty in South Vietnam. They had decided back then to save it for a more momentous occasion; this time for his homecoming from Laos that was not to be.

Marie carefully opened it, walked to the kitchen sink and poured it down the drain. As the last of it disappeared, she whetted her finger in it to at least get a taste.

It had turned to vinegar.

Nineteen

COMRADES-IN-ARMS

No story of a Raven and his family would be complete without reference to the valiant Hmong and Lao soldiers, pilots and their wives and families who fought a hopeless war against a near-endless stream of North Vietnamese soldiers and their equipment coming down the Laotian side of the infamous Ho Chi Minh trail.

The Lao peoples who fought the invaders saved the lives of countless American soldiers; otherwise, those same NVA soldiers would have been fighting our troops in South Vietnam.

The stories I learned from Hmong and Laotian friends are studies in courage of a people who struggled for their freedom for over 14 years against impossible odds, giving up neither hope nor faith that their persistence would eventually prevail. Here are but a few.

The Children's War

In his fine book, "The Ravens," which documents the story of the Ravens' war in Laos during the Vietnam War, the late Christopher Robbins wrote of an entire generation of adult Hmong men lost in the never-ending battle with the North Vietnamese soldiers who invaded their country. The only people left to continue the fight were small children and old men.

Little boys scurried about the Long Tieng (LS20-A) airfield, stockpiling and staging every kind of munition from .50 caliber strafe and small-arms ammo to 500-pound bombs for the T-28 fighter-bombers flown by the Hmong and Lao pilots, along with the white phosphorus marking rockets for the Raven FACs' O-1 Bird Dogs. Often, the older, stronger children would be called upon to help load the 500-pound bombs in the T-28 fighter-bomber wing racks and WP marking rockets in the racks mounted under the Bird Dog's wings. These activities, of course, were supervised by adult specialists and inspected by the pilots in their pre-flight walk-arounds.

I learned from a former Hmong soldier that other, younger and smaller boys were taught to identify the units of enemy soldiers coming down the Ho Chi Minh trail, and count them. They also identified the types of weapons the soldiers carried, including the AK-47 assault rifle, RPG and B-40 hand-held rocket launchers, and 60mm and 82mm mortars, along with heavy weapons, such as large-bore mortars, artillery and anti-aircraft guns trailered by trucks and smaller utility vehicles.

The children had a unique advantage over grown Hmong soldiers when gathering intelligence; they were virtually impossible to find, let alone catch, in the thickets of underbrush, deep jungle foliage and saw grass tangled along the trail's edge. If seen by the enemy, they were small enough to run back to safety underneath the brush and through the exposed roots and trunks, like rabbits scurrying from predators and hunters. Sometimes, infuriated NVA soldiers would try to crash through the underbrush in pursuit of these child reconnaissance teams, but most often, they would get hopelessly entangled and could not make any forward progress—let alone sufficient speed to catch the child warriors.

One of the enemy's solutions was to bulldoze holes through the underbrush and send patrols through them to capture, torture or kill their young tormenters.

This ploy backfired since Ravens observed the brush-busting bulldozers from afar and called in airstrikes. An enemy bulldozer was a fine target. Or, Hmong regulars would ambush enemy patrols coming through their passageways and escape with the young ones on Air America helicopters standing by for extraction. Ravens would then take over the battlefield and smash the enemy with air strikes. Later, the NVA troops tried burning passages through the brush; unfortunately for them, the smoke from the green thickets was also an open invitation for more ambushes and airstrikes.

The "older" boys—those over 10 years old—carried American M-1 semi-automatic and M-2 automatic carbines, M-1 rifles, M-15 automatic carbines, M-16 and AK-47 assault rifles, and M-79 grenade launchers.

They went to war with their older brothers-in-arms and were every bit as brave. They celebrated their victories, grieved at the death and wounding of their peers, and cared for their wounded as best they could as time and the enemy permitted.

Requiem III

Joua, a former major in General Vang Pao's Hmong Army and commander of Hmong Special Guerrilla Unit (SGU) Battalion 201, passed away at his southeastern Michigan home in March of 2014. Revered by his superiors, his peers and the troops who served under him, he earned a posthumous promotion to the rank of lieutenant general. He was Wa Ger's nephew, and I came to know him, his wife Palee and son Cha through an internet search of Wa Ger's family. My initial goal was to try and find Wa Ger to learn more about his missions with Frank and thank him for fighting the NVA and saving American troops' lives in the process. He had long been dead, but I had the pleasure of meeting Joua and his family, and thanking them for their service to our country.

The greatest tribute to the Hmong that I can think of is that America is much the better place for their war with the NVA and the Pathet Lao. Their exemplary courage and determination earned them the right to be here; their fight for their freedom also turned out to be our fight for freedom. Sadly, over 25 percent of their estimated 400,000 population died, a terrible casualty rate that speaks eloquently of their sacrifice.

Several Ravens sent me condolences to Joua's family and their many friends who attended the funeral, which included their comments about fighting with and for the valiant Hmong people. I was honored and humbled to deliver an eulogy that included their comments:

"I did not know Joua, but I did fly with his uncle, Wa Ger. He was very focused and nearly unflappable in what was a very difficult environment. I think it fair to say that the Hmong people were, and are, the most resolute and courageous people that I have ever observed. Those attributes have been tested too many times and one hopes that those days are past. I don't think I can say enough about my admiration for the Hmong, or my sorrow for their sacrifices."

"Wa Ger was the man that Ravens used to say was a very brave and good man. These qualities run in the family tree like water to the sea. We share the loss of another champion of freedom's cause, a member of our family also: the honorable Hmong Special Guerrilla Unit major, Joua Cheng. They orbit in peace and still guide us from on high. They continue to soar in the wind with other great eagles—and angels—for our benefit. Peace at last and God bless."

"Wa Ger was the guy that used to say "many enemy" as his attempt to aid us Ravens in finding the bad guys. He was not able to write as far as I could tell BUT he could tell one hell of a war story if a book could come out of him. I would ask him where the bad guys were and he would say 'Enemy to the north, enemy to the south, enemy to the east, enemy to the west, many, many enemy!' And of course, he was right. He was one of the top backseaters and always a good guy to fly with. All of those guys were brave, but some were more skilled than the others and Wa Ger was one of the best…" "….he was a mighty brave guy and a good man to have with you."

John Bingham

As the covert war in Laos wound down and the Royal Lao government surrendered, the communist Pathet Lao forces intensified their search for Hmong and Lao soldiers who'd fought against the Pathet Lao and NVA; if caught, these men would often be tortured during interrogation, executed on the spot, or both. If their families were captured, they would be taken to "re-education centers" located in remote jungle areas for intense indoctrination and mandatory conversion to Communism. Anyone resisting risked torture and death.

Joua joined Vang Pao's Hmong Army and started his military career with training from the CIA and American Special Forces units at secret bases in Udorn and Phitsanulok, Thailand. He was among the first Hmong soldiers to win his parachutist wings.

Like all newly trained infantrymen in Vang Pao's army, he was thrown right into battle immediately after his training ended.

There was no time to learn new skills with more tactical training experience: the nonstop onslaught of the NVA invaders dictated that any new tactics would have to be learned the hard way. Joua was a fast learner. His comrades-in-arms, along with his unit's NCOs and CO, respected his courage in battle and his leadership skills--so much so that he was quickly promoted to sergeant in charge of a rifle squad and then moved up to the officers' ranks.

As a second lieutenant, he commanded a rifle platoon in one of General Vang Pao's elite Special Guerrilla Units, SGU Battalion 201. He was hit in the leg by shrapnel in late 1962 and was still recovering in early 1963 when he met his wife, Palee. She and her brother, who served with Jou, had visited him in the Long Tieng hospital. The wound was his first and worst ones were yet to come.

The next stepping-stone in his rapid advancement was a battlefield promotion, taking over as captain of his rifle company after his CO was killed during a particularly savage and bloody battle with a NVA battalion that had them surrounded. With only a rudimentary understanding of close air support, he was able to call in a Raven to direct a mission for USAF air strikes against the massed NVA troops. The Raven also radioed for Air America helicopters, whose pilots flew in after the air strikes to extract Joua and his men.

His exceptional leadership from the front and cool head under fire gained the attention of Vang Pao's senior officers and the general himself, and he was promoted to major in command of SGU Battalion 201. His new command helped him hone his ability to plan and successfully execute both guerilla tactics and all-out conventional warfare—sometimes simultaneously--against the best of the NVA's battalions.

Joua was tested in General Vang Pao's "Operation-About Face" in 1969, when he combined both guerrilla ambushes to sever the NVA's overextended supply lines on the Plain of Jars, at the same time directing attacks by the main force of his SGU Battalion 201 that was fighting side-by-side with Vang Pao's other SGU and conventional-warfare battalions.

With the Ravens' help, they knocked the NVA off two strategic mountains in the PDJ, Phou Khean and Phou Than.

After radioing General Vang Pao to report his battalion's position and the enemy's positions, along with a brief summary of progress and an assessment of enemy strength, Joua requested approval for Raven support. The general agreed with the proviso that every bit of ordnance that the USAF could muster be used, in multiple flights if needed. Joua and his interpreter called the Ravens, gave them the enemy position coordinates to help them guide the USAF fighter-bombers to their hilltop targets, and stressed the importance of continuous saturation bombing. Joua then directed his radioman to tell the other battalions to keep their heads down because a huge aerial bombardment was coming.

The Ravens concentrated their first strikes—"Hit my smoke!"—by carpet-bombing the enemy's hilltop positions with every weapon in their arsenal and then bringing in five more waves of fighter-bombers, four aircraft in each wave, that repeated the initial strikes with 500 and 1,000 pound bombs, napalm, cluster bombs and strafe to obliterate--or at the very least, neutralize--the enemy's ability to counterattack when the Hmong Army attacked immediately following the bombardment.

To Joua and his troops watching, listening and feeling the shock of the continuous bomb blasts fluttering in their chests along with the breath-sucking roars of napalm bursting and the thunder of the attacking jet aircraft, it was hard to believe that anyone could survive such an aerial barrage. But he remembered Vang Pao's warning that the NVA troops would be well dug in and that he must be ready for them. Sure enough, they came under enemy fire while advancing uphill. Joua halted the battalion's advance to call the Ravens for close-in air support, as did his fellow battalion COs.

They marked their FEBA (Forward Edge of Battle Area) by throwing smoke grenades that served as targets for the Raven's white-phosphorous marking rockets. This time, the planes dropped napalm, creating jellied-gasoline hell intended to incinerate NVA troops caught in the open and suffocate the hapless troops still underground. The Hmong troops gave the charred trees and underbrush a brief cool-down, then attacked with savage fury. Joua Bee was once more in the van as they charged up the hill with fixed bayonets, shouting as they ran.

Hearing the Hmong voices grow louder, the remaining NVA troops who survived the napalm strikes by huddling in their deep bunkers realized they had two choices; die if they stayed where they were or come out and fight. They chose the latter and Joua Bee's warriors were ready for them. They streamed out like rats in a flood, firing their AKs wildly as their eyes adjusted to the bright sunlight. The waiting Hmong immediately gained fire superiority and slaughtered them with automatic fire from their M-16 assault rifles and M-60 machine guns. They also used their M-79 grenade launchers and WWII-issue 3.5 rocket launchers ("bazookas") to good effect, blasting enemy bunkers from a distance to take out the machine guns and open safe lanes for further advances. As they continued uphill, they tossed a grenade into every foxhole and two satchel charges into every bunker to collapse and bury alive any enemy soldier who might be hiding inside.

Joua sustained life-threatening wounds while leading a flanking movement of a pincer attack on what was the last line of enemy bunkers. A RPG detonated on a nearby tree and laced his neck, face and eyes with sharp, ragged fragments, and blinded him. As soon as he was hit, a platoon medic raced over to help. The hilltop battlefield was still too hot to bring in an Air America rescue helicopter, so the medic rounded up two soldiers who carried him down the hill to a clearing at the base until a helicopter arrived. After taking aboard Joua and six other badly wounded troops, the chopper flew straight to Udorn.

The helicopter's co-pilot radioed ahead and was able to reach a doctor at NKP's hospital to alert him that seven more casualties were coming in.

The doctor triaged the troops and saw that Joua needed immediate attention to avoid the risk of steel splinters penetrating further into his eyes and permanently blinding him. The others were assigned to a visiting doctor, assisted by a nurse and five experienced combat medics who were in NKP to help treat casualties from the fierce battle raging on the PDJ.

He carefully plucked out the splinters from Joua's eyes and face, taking great care to avoid lateral movement of his head that would tear delicate eye tissue. Two sandbags on either side of his head along with two medics holding down his arms and legs kept him still throughout the delicate procedure. A morphine shot followed quickly by three shots of Johnny Walker Black also contributed to a positive outcome. There was no general anesthesia; the doctor had used it all on others who had been wounded in the battle. No resupplies could be flown in until late in the following day. By then, Joua was chafing to return to his beloved SGU Battalion 201, even though his vision was severely impaired.

John Bingham

He had argued with the doctor when he was wheeled into the OR that his troops must be treated before he was. The doctor thanked him for his generous gesture and told him that only a true leader would trade his life for the lives of his men. He told Joua that his risk of dying or suffering permanent and incapacitating wounds was greater than the lives of the wounded troops who'd flown with him, that his men would be terribly demoralized if he did die, and that the wounded men who'd flown in with him were being treated as he spoke by an experienced doctor with a team of combat medics. Satisfied that his men were in good hands, Joua asked the doctor to proceed.

Later, when all of the wounded had been treated and stabilized, the exhausted doctor passed around the Johnny Walker Black to the equally exhausted medics and the visiting doctor. He told them about Joua's order to treat his men before treating him, and made a note to tell this story to Joua's officers so they can tell their troops that their commanding officer puts their well-being before his own.

"Mark my words," he said. "That man is going to be a general someday." Little did he know that his casual prophecy would someday become a reality.

After they had one last pass at the bottle, he asked them to save him a sandwich at the cafeteria, because he was going to skip dinner and take a nap. He fell asleep on a gurney, but only after he'd made one more trip around the ward to check on the wounded and make sure they were stable and as pain-free as they possibly could be.

Joua's wife, Palee, and her sister had hiked from their mountain home to Long Tieng to visit him, thinking that he was still there. A Raven who was ill and had to stay behind while the battle raged on told them he'd heard that Joua had been wounded on the PDJ and was flown to Thailand for treatment. They didn't find out what had happened to him for three weeks, when a wounded and out-of-action troop brought her a letter from Joua, written the night before he returned to his unit.

Winter Roses

Hounded and pounded by Hmong, Lao, and USAF fighter-bombers, the NVA were driven all the way back across the Plain to their original staging positions along the Ho Chi Minh trail. Once again, the Ravens, the Hmong and Lao pilots, along with American aircraft from their secret bases in Thailand and carriers in the South China Sea, had played a critical roll in the Hmong Army's victory.

Like the Hmong and Lao T-28 pilots' mantra--"Fly Until You Die"-- Joua believed that his death in battle was inevitable—not desirable, but one preferable to capture, torture and execution.

He and his fellow SGU fighters had seen too many of their comrades' bodies that were badly mutilated and knew that torture had preceded a bullet in the back of their heads.

The victory with its ensuing peace did not last long. The NVA regrouped, reinforced, and attacked the following year, this time driving the Hmong Army back to Long Tieng. Once again, Joua was wounded, this time by a mortar round fragment that struck him in the hip. The U.S. flight surgeon assigned to LS20-A operated in the Long Tieng hospital to remove the fragment and make sure that he could walk and run well enough to fight once more. Satisfied that Joua Bee could lead his soldiers in battle once again, the surgeon discharged him after three weeks of recovery and rehabilitation.

The next morning, an Air America helicopter delivered him to his unit where he found his troops on full alert, expecting another NVA attack and readying for a counterattack.

Never again would the Hmong Army win a major victory against an enemy that had overwhelming numbers of experienced troops and commensurate firepower. By then, most of the soldiers Vang Pao had left in his Hmong Army were boys, old men and wounded soldiers who could still lift and fire a weapon to defend their homeland.

John Bingham

After the Royal Lao government had capitulated, Joua and Palee recognized that their situation was hopeless and that the complete collapse of a free Laos was inevitable. They decided it was time to execute their planned escape across the Mekong River to safety in Thailand. Palee and their nine children crossed the river in truck tire tubes, which—along with rafts and even tightly woven giant wicker laundry baskets—had become the Hmong people's watercrafts of choice.

The few boats available for hire were outrageously expensive; moreover, some of the people who put their boats out for hire were Communist sympathizers who would deliver their customers into Pathet Lao hands and reap their rewards in blood money for their treachery.

Families floating across the river were always in danger of being fired upon by Pathet Lao soldiers hiding in the brush on the river's banks. This happened often, but still-armed Hmong SGU soldiers who patrolled the banks lessened the threat of these riverine ambushes. The battle-hardened Hmong knew the Pathet Lao soldiers had no stomach for fighting them and the enemy's knowledge of their presence was an effective deterrent. Still, their numbers were few and they could not cover all of the river's access points.

Palee said that the Hmong women quieted their babies to help protect against Pathet Lao capture by giving them small amounts of opium. She also took this precaution with her own little ones.

Joua followed his family across the Mekong on a small raft that carried rice and additional clothing for Palee and the children. He threw his pistol, M-16 assault rifle, a bandoleer of ammunition, and fighting knife into the river as soon as he was safely across.

Lutheran Social Services brought Joua, Palee and their family of nine to America, where they settled in Petoskey, Michigan. Not long after the family had settled in this beautiful small town, they learned that their best friends, Yee and his family, were also nearby. Yee had opened a restaurant in Petoskey after he had been laid off at Saginaw Steering—then a division of General Motors. Joua and Yee had met several times when they were serving in General Vang Pao's Army and they had become very close. When Yee and his family left to go the Detroit area, Joua Bee, Palee and their family went with them.

The family resides today in suburban Pontiac, Michigan.

Joua was one of the Hmong and Laotian veterans who were honored during a 1997 congressional ceremony, where he and his comrades-in-arms were presented with framed certificates that honored their service during the covert war in Laos.

In 1995, he was also awarded a Congressional Defenders of Freedom Citation, followed in 1998 by a Congressional Commendation and Citation for Vietnam War Service. In every one of these presentation ceremonies, their role in saving American soldiers' lives was recognized; they had fought as many as 70,000 North Vietnamese soldiers who otherwise would have been fighting American troops in South Vietnam.

In 1997, the Hmong and Laotian veterans were also honored with a living memorial at Arlington National Cemetery.

Yee Chang, S-2

Yee joined the Hmong Army when he was 16 years old, and like Joua and thousands of other enlistees, he was trained at a secret base in Udorn, Thailand. He recalls that the CIA station chief who commanded the training facility was Pat Landry, one of the legendary CIA officers who demanded much from his trainees. The rugged training paid off with soldiers who could fight face-to-face with any NVA unit in any combat situation, be it all-out war *en masse,* guerrilla warfare, or counter-guerrilla warfare. The latter two were especially effective against the NVA invaders.

John Bingham

Yee had the good fortune to be trained in basic infantry tactics and small-arms weaponry by none other than the legendary Anthony Poshepny, aka Tony Poe, a former Marine who was on Iwo Jima, fought in Korea, and joined the CIA as a station chief in Laos, serving as a trainer and advisor for his region's indigenous forces. He was known as a ferocious warrior, skilled in every form of combat, whether on the ground or in the air.

While Yee appreciated Tony's training, he decided to leave the infantry and join the Army's Signal Corps where he became a radio operator. He was transferred back to Long Tieng where he became a radio operator for an infantry platoon.

While his job was dangerous—along with the platoon leader, the radio operator was often the first targeted during a firefight—he liked the stature and respect his comrades-in-arms gave him. They knew his job was to get them the artillery and air support they'd need in desperate circumstances and they went out of their way to teach him good practices that could save his life, such as proper camouflage techniques and hiding his whip antenna on the march by doubling it up and taping it to the radio pack on his back.

He honed his skills, including map reading and learning how to find and call in accurate coordinates for on-target artillery and air support. This provided the platoon leader and his NCOs with good backup should they be killed or too wounded to call for help. In his first year, he was promoted to sergeant and transferred to company HQ as chief radio operator. During his tenure as RO, he proved his courage, intelligence, quick thinking, and leadership abilities in many firefights, both small and large. In one major battle—when his CO was killed and his unit defending a hilltop position was in danger of being overrun—he won a battlefield commission for his coolness under fire, calling in a Raven's napalm strike with such accuracy that almost all of the hard-charging enemy soldiers were killed. The ones lucky enough to survive ran screaming back down the hill, right through the Hmong's wide-open field of fire. The sharpshooting SGU soldiers and machine gunners easily cut them down.

Winter Roses

At General Vang Pao's nightly dinner meeting to recap the day's unit actions and plan the next day's moves, the Raven who'd directed the F-4's napalm strike told the general he was impressed by the calm way the radio operator had called in his coordinates and advised him of the exact locations of the enemy and his own positions. Yee's cousin, Colonel Hang Sao—who was in charge of Vang Pao's S-2 (Intelligence)--said he knew who this man was. He suggested to VP that he might consider transferring Yee to S-2, where he could put his skills to work in intelligence gathering, liaison with CIA S-2 ops, field reconnaissance and eventually, prisoner interrogation. The general agreed. Yee's new position gave him much exposure with the general and his staff, and they were impressed with how fast he'd learned his new skills.

A promotion to major made him the full-time liaison officer between Hang Sao, the CIA and the line units. With the latter assignment, he went out of his way to personally gather critical information in the field rather than depend wholly on subordinates. The work was dangerous, but he was no stranger to firefights. Common sense, however, told him to be careful since VP and Hang Sao depended heavily on him for accurate and timely information about the enemy units' strength, locations, weapons, supply lines, movements...any information that could be used against them in future attacks. When in the field and carrying his CAR-15 and .45 Colt pistol, he was glad that Tony Poe had taught him how to use them.

Yee was in "Operation: About-Face," the same major offensive that Joua had fought in. Using coordinated guerrilla attacks against the enemy's vulnerable supply lines and all-out, battalion-sized attacks on the main enemy forces, the Hmong—with the help of the Ravens and air support from Hmong, Lao, and American pilots—drove the NVA off the Plain of Jars.

These battles yielded a wealth of information that he and his interrogators gleaned from captured senior and junior officers and NCOs, even enlisted men who were couriers carrying important enemy papers.

During my interview with Yee, he also recalled visiting a Hmong SGU field fortification that was also staffed by four U.S. Special Forces advisors. It was located on a small, wooded hill near the Plain. The fortification had observation towers at each of its four corners and was surrounded by triple-apron razor wire. The machine guns—M-60s and the heavy .50 calibers—were well-placed in their pits to provide sweeps of interlocking fire around the entire perimeter. Riflemen in their foxholes were interspersed with the machine gunners' foxholes and gun pits. The camp's 81mm mortars—along with 4.2 inch heavy mortars and 105mm howitzers from a Special Forces camp four miles away--were also sighted in on the most likely enemy approach and escape routes. Claymores and antipersonnel mines were laid everywhere and observation and listening posts were manned in key locations around the fort's perimeter.

In short, this fortress would not be easy to take.

Yee and three men on his staff had been helicoptered to the fort to interrogate NVA prisoners that Hmong combat patrols had captured. From them, they learned that the NVA were planning an attack at 0300 hours the next morning. Whether it was to be a quick reconnaissance by fire to ferret out the Hmong gun positions or an all-out assault to capture the fort remained to be seen, and the Hmong prepared for the latter.

As a major, Yee was the senior officer in the fort, but he left the Hmong's preparations for the attack to the Hmong officers and their Special Forces advisors. Still, four men came to him and told him that they no longer wanted to man the towers because they would be the first ones to be killed in an attack. They had tried to explain this to their own officers, but were turned down. The towers would have to be manned.

Yee listened to their plea and told them that he had no authority to relieve them of their tower duties, but that he had an idea. He would suggest to their

CO that they make cardboard cutouts of soldiers with their "rifles" at the ready and place them in the towers when darkness fell, then scurry down the tower ladder and run to their foxholes.

He took the idea to the young Hmong captain who was in charge of defensive preparations. The captain laughed at the idea, but Yee argued that it was bound to work. When the enemy fire hit the silhouettes, it would signal that the enemy attack had begun. It would also likely save the lives of four men who could provide additional firepower to repulse the attack. The senior American Special Forces advisor—a captain with a great deal of combat experience—helped seal the deal by commenting, "The idea is just crazy enough to work." The captain agreed and the men gathered cardboard for their cut-outs.

At 0300, automatic weapons fire struck the cardboard and the attack was on. Huge explosions shook the camp. NVA sappers—the equivalent of American combat engineers who often fought as infantry and were experts in explosives--had blown lanes through the minefields and were running towards the wire. They were shot down by machine gun and automatic rifle fire, but a second wave followed right behind them. Many of them fell, and several feigned death. Sappers hugging the hillside behind them pushed up bangalore torpedoes to the "dead" sappers, who snaked them through the razor wire and rolled away as the explosive-packed aluminum tubes blew the wire apart.

NVA regulars—now too close for mortar and artillery fire--swarmed through the wire lanes and attacked the Hmong positions in every direction, leaping over the bodies of their comrades, screaming and dying as the machine gunners and riflemen in their foxholes cut through them. Still more came. The camp's generator was hit with a B-40 rocket, but the Hmong had surrounded it with welded steel plate. The lights blinked, came on again instantly and the generator kept running. Yee wondered after the battle why the NVA soldier who fired the B-40 didn't simply run to the generator and flip the kill switch.

By this time, the perimeter was littered with bodies. Yee thought that the enemy was determined to take this fort regardless of their heavy casualties that were mounting by the minute as the firefight turned from extreme intensity into pure chaos. The heart-rending cries from the wounded, the continuous ear-splitting gunfire and explosions of hand grenades, B-40 rocket grenades and RPGs, and the shouting of officers and NCOs directing fire all combined to form hell's own cacophony.

Yee and his men were also in the fight. Their foxholes were higher up on the hill, which gave them a good overview of the battle. The NVA who spotted them tried to flank or surround their position and paid a high price for their efforts.

With his CAR-15 carbine, Yee concentrated his fire on the officers and NCOs, carefully placing his rounds in their lower extremities so they could neither run nor walk, but writhe on the bloodied earth in agony, hopefully (for Yee) staying alive until after the battle when they could be searched and questioned. His marksmanship was that good. Once again, he was glad for Tony Poe's training.

The firefight's intensity began to taper off at the first dim light of dawn, and the sound of whistles signaled that the enemy was breaking off. Yee noted that the NVA soldiers and sappers were professionals who ensured an orderly retreat as best they could with covering fire for their flanks and rear.

The camp's M-81 mortar squad began a murderous barrage the moment the enemy broke off contact. The pre-planned fire of the 4.2-inch heavy mortars and 105 mm howitzers also joined in to continue the slaughter in the killing fields below the camp. Yee and his men watched the mortar and artillery shells "walk" through the kill zone, blowing the retreating soldiers to pieces all the way to the jungle's edge where the few survivors disappeared from sight. He couldn't believe that anyone could have lived through such a deadly barrage.

The Hmong soldiers were too exhausted to counterattack. The firefight's intensity and the experience of nearly being overrun by what seemed to be an endless stream of sappers and soldiers had robbed them of their strength. Besides, no one knew how many enemy soldiers might be waiting in the jungle to ambush them. They would send out reinforced patrols that night to find out if the enemy was still in the area and had enough men to try once more to take the position. Yee estimated that they'd been attacked by at least three reinforced rifle companies, all at full strength which indicated that the attackers were new in-country and that this attack could have been their first. The new uniforms on the bodies confirmed his observation.

The dead lay everywhere and the groans and cries of the wounded were pitiful reminders of the fight's bloody toll.

Soldiers walked among the dead and wounded, picking up weapons and ammunition. At Yee's direction, they also rummaged through the pockets and rucksacks of the enemy dead, looking for documents that could give away plans for future movements and attacks. Yee also told the combat medics--after they had attended to the downed Hmong soldiers-- to care for the enemy's wounded to ensure that some would still be alive for interrogation.

Rather than wait for the medics to complete their tasks, his top interrogator also walked the perimeter to find wounded NVA who might provide useful information. He was lost in thought about the prospect of a new NVA division or at least a regiment in-country when he jumped in surprise. A M-16 rifle had barked twice close to his ear and he turned to ask his chief interrogator why he had fired.

"Look over there, near the generator."

John Bingham

He looked and saw an NVA soldier frozen in death with blood streaming down his face, leaning against the generator and gripping a B-40 rocket launcher. Even in the throes of death, the soldier had kept the weapon pointed directly at him. *What fire discipline and devotion to duty*, he thought. *If every enemy soldier is as determined as this soldier, we will have a very hard time winning this war.*

"I saw him rise up beside the generator and aim the B-40 at you," the interrogator said. "I was able to get off two quick shots that knocked him down before he could fire. I think he's dead, but to make sure, I'll put two more rounds in him."

When the interrogator returned from his *coup de grace*, Yee thanked him, congratulated him on his marksmanship and then promoted him to master sergeant.

When the Royal Laotian government surrendered to the communists, the Hmong realized that their war was also over. To stay there would risk capture, imprisonment, probable torture, and perhaps even summary execution by the Pathet Lao.

Yee began to plan his family's escape to Thailand's refugee camps along with his own. With his high S-2 position and connections with General Vang Pao and his staff, he was able to commandeer a Jeep and driver to take his wife, their eight children and two fellow officers from Long Tieng to Vientiane, where a helicopter would be waiting to fly them over the Mekong River to Thailand. One can only imagine 12 people with the few belongings they could carry crammed into a vehicle designed to carry four people, five at most. They took primitive back roads for the 100-plus mile journey to avoid contact with Pathet Lao units combing the countryside for Hmong refugees.

The roads were so bad and the jammed-together passengers were so uncomfortable that they had to take frequent stops to make sure mud holes were not mud lakes and also to stretch their aching limbs and try to change positions. If the mud holes were too deep and wide to cross, the men would cut a new path around them, slowing their journey even more. The officers kept their CAR-15s slung on their backs so they'd be ready if the Pathet Lao found them. Everyone knew that a close-in firefight with a family of nine caught in the middle would be disastrous. Fortunately, this did not happen; their decision to take the back roads had paid off.

They arrived in Vientiane covered with mud and happy that they'd soon be free from the risk of the Pathet Lao's atrocities. The driver went directly to the airport where they found an Air America helicopter waiting for them on the tarmac. The officers boarded last and the helicopter rose quickly up, turned and was over the river in minutes. Everyone on board took a long, last look at Laos, knowing they would never again return to live in their homeland.

Yee told of a meeting in early May of 1975 attended by high-ranking Hmong, Laotian, CIA, Embassy, State Department, NVA, Pathet Lao, and Neutralist representatives, to negotiate the number of key Hmong, Laotian, and U.S. personnel that could be evacuated. The U.S. State Department representative told the group that only 25 officers could be taken out. Hearing this ridiculously low figure, Vang Pao stormed out of the room.

Vang Pao's CIA case officer, Jerry Daniels, remained behind to negotiate for the general and was successful in raising the number of evacuees to 2,500. Knowing that Daniels had only one transport aircraft available for the evacuation of personnel to USAF bases in Thailand, USAF Brigadier General Heinie Aderholt arranged for three more transport aircraft. He had them stripped of all American markings, and between May 10 and 14, American pilots evacuated the 2,500 people. At the time, Aderholt was the senior ranking USAF officer in-country.

Yee, along with his cousin, Colonel Hang Sao, departed for Thailand in one of the transports after they had retrieved the S-2 case files that they had accumulated with the help and cooperation of the CIA. The CIA contributed supporting information and insights for future battle planning, and the documents in the enemy's hands would have endangered many lives.

John Bingham

After Yee had crossed the Mekong and found his family, General Vang Pao visited him and asked him to work for him on a secret project, one so secret that Yee would not tell me, or for that matter, anyone in his immediate family, what it was--even after 40 years.

He was glad to help the general because he thought he would be paid for the assignment and finally get some money for his family's food and clothing. After he'd completed it, the general thanked him and drove away in a Jeep leaving Yee with no pay for his work. While he laughs about this today, his laughter carries an edge of disappointment.

Like so many refugees, he and his family needed money in those early days at the camps. Pay from the general would have bought his family needed clothing and extra food to supplement their meager camp rations.

During Yee's stay, a Thai guard went berserk and began shooting refugees whom he thought were traitors—traitors to what or whom, no one knows. Yee took no chances and went into hiding in another, larger camp, taking along his .45 Colt pistol and his small Nikon camera. There, another guard spotted the camera and accused him of being a spy. Yee convinced him that he was not a spy, but a professional combat photographer who took photos of the brave Hmong soldiers in action against the Pathet Lao and NVA forces who invaded Laos. He invited the guard to take the camera and pull out the film to see for himself. The guard took the camera, pulled out the film, glanced at it, threw it away and tossed the camera back to him.

During his temporary exile, he ran across the Thai guard who had helped him cross the Mekong. He had no money to pay for the guard's services, so he gave the guard his Colt .45. The guard accepted it with pleasure and sincere appreciation, and he became a good friend who helped Yee find small jobs around the camps to earn money for his family.

Winter Roses

Yee spoke of the atrocities of the Pathet Lao. Among the worst was the crossing of the Mekong to Thailand by 94 refugees on their bamboo rafts and truck tire tubes. When they reached the halfway point, the Pathet Lao opened up with a machine gun and slaughtered them. Men, women and children were killed at random, which made no difference to these monsters: the muddy Mekong ran red with their blood and not one survived the onslaught.

He and his family were brought to America by Lutheran Social Services and settled in Saginaw.

His father, Nhice Neng, came with them while his cousin Hang Sao stayed behind. Hang Sao was arrested by the Pathet Lao and spent nine years in prison. When he was released, he emigrated to America and moved to the Detroit area.

Yee worked at General Motors' Saginaw Steering plant. He was laid off and moved with his family to Petoskey, Michigan, where he opened a restaurant that served a wide range of Southeastern Asian dishes. There, he met his old friend and comrade-in-arms, Joua. While the restaurant was successful, Yee left it behind and went back to work in the Saginaw steering components plant, which by then had become a part of Delphi Corporation, an independent automotive components company.

Later, Yee and his family would join Hang Sao in the metro Detroit area. He moved to Fenton, a small rural community located north and west of Detroit where he opened another restaurant that was very successful. Its broad menu of authentic Asian foods attracted people from all over the Southeastern Michigan area.

Yee sold the restaurant and retired. He and his wife recently moved to Minneapolis-St. Paul to be near their son and his wife. Another son was the first Hmong to graduate from West Point and is today a full colonel. His family and many friends all hope that he will one day soon win his brigadier general's star.

John Bingham

The Girl of The Nine Glowing Embers

Kha knew that her two cousins had deserted her. They had told her that they would make the treacherous Mekong River crossing first and then one of them would try to come back with the extra truck-tire inner tube for her. She thought at first they were lying, But when she heard a series of automatic-weapon bursts, she knew they'd been shot at by the Pathet Lao and now they would never return. All she could do was hope that they hadn't been killed and prepare for her own survival as best she could.

The year was 1979. She was 20 years old—old for an unmarried Hmong woman in a society where marriages were carefully arranged and girls in their early teens or even younger were married.

Kha saw no shame in her "older" age. Indeed, she thought it gave her an advantage, particularly in surviving the dangerous situation she was now in. She knew her wood lore and felt confident that the skills she had learned from her mother and father in finding wild edibles would now pay off.

She hid along the riverbank, always moving quietly at night, painting herself with mud to keep the mosquitoes at bay and provide good camouflage while hiding under blankets of leaves and in thickets of brush in the daytime. When the jungle quieted during the heat of midday, she dug for tubers, roots and mushrooms that she remembered were safe. She also drank from the river, knowing full well that she was putting herself at risk from severe diarrhea, perhaps even dysentery.

One day, she ran across a real find; a huge colony of crickets that had made their home in a hollow tree deadfall. Not only would they give her much-needed protein, but the log could serve as a temporary shelter. She moved into the log and ate crickets by the handful. All day she feasted until she could eat no more. When dusk arrived, she filled her pockets with the crunchy little creatures and moved out once more.

Winter Roses

On the 13th day of her wandering, she met two young Hmong women who'd been abandoned by their fiancés. They could only afford to purchase two truck tire inner tubes, one for each couple. But the tubes were old and full of cracks from too much exposure to the sun. They didn't believe they were safe enough to hold two of them at once and so the men went first at the urging of their fiances. Assuming that the tubes would not leak air, they would figure out a way to get them back to the women, perhaps by a trustworthy Thai who ferried refugees across in a motorboat. "They promised to get the tubes back to us," one of the women said. "We haven't heard or seen anyone crossing back over the river with tubes, and we wonder now if our fiancés even made it across. It's been four days since they left us and we are very hungry. Do you have any food you can spare?"

Kha was overjoyed to meet the young women. She would have company at last and she knew that, together, they would find a way to cross the river safely. She replied, "Yes, I have some food that we will share. We will eat shortly. Meanwhile, we will need to plan for our survival and a way to cross the river to safety. My name is Kha. What are your names and where do you come from?

The smaller of the girls spoke first. "I'm Yer and this is my friend, Shoua. We come from a small village north of Vientiane. The Pathet Lao came to detain young men and women like us and place us under guard in their "re-education centers." We didn't trust them, so we ran away and hid from them. We don't have any experience living in the jungle, and we're not only hungry, we're frightened."

"Fear is not so bad," Kha said. "When you can manage it, it motivates you to stay alert and avoid danger. Maybe it will also help us find food and a safe way to cross the river."

They sat down and made a plan to follow the river until they reached a village where they might be able to find help. Yer and Shoua had heard that the

Pathet Lao and their Communist sympathizers were everywhere and that they would have to be very careful to avoid capture. Kha would teach her new friends the basics of finding and identifying edible tubers. They also agreed to continue with travel at night and rest during the day.

They started their trek before dusk and hadn't traveled 50 feet when Yer found the remains of a campfire. Kha knelt down, poked her finger into the still-warm coals and burned her finger. Clearly, the campfire had been abandoned a short time before they found it. Whether another refugee or the enemy had built it, they could not tell. They hoped that they would not find its creator. She dug further and pulled out a half-burned stick with a live coal at its end.

"Now we can gather ground wood and make a fire to cook our meal," she said. Within minutes, they had filled their arms with sticks. Shoua even found a small bamboo log. Kha said, "That's too small to use in a raft, but it will help us make a nice fire. Let's get moving before someone--or some thing--decides to stalk us. There are tigers in this area and we've been lucky that they haven't made a meal out of us."

"I think that you're too tough to make a tiger meal, "Yer said. They laughed and then disappeared into the brush. After they'd traveled about an hour, they decided to stop and eat their meal of tubers and berries that Kha had found and wrapped and tied in her shirt. They reached a small clearing. It was difficult to determine if others had used it as a campsite, but by patting their hands over every square inch around it, they found no evidence anyone had been there recently. There were no empty food cans, piles of excrement, matchsticks, or any paraphernalia that someone may have left behind in a hurry to keep moving.

Kha knelt down and began to clear the spot for their fire and asked her new friends to go to the river's edge and bring back handfuls of mud. She used it to fashion a large, round beehive-shaped cone surrounding the fire to help shield it from prying eyes and concentrate the heat. That job completed, she chose a handful of small broken sticks to use as tinder. She inserted the glowing stick into the tinder and blew on it. Within moments, smoke appeared followed by a sudden burst of flame. Kha carefully placed the flaming ball under the pile of larger sticks that Yer had prepared.

As the flames spread rapidly, Shoua asked Kha why she didn't get burned when she placed the burning tinder under the pile.

"That's easy," replied Kha. "Be quick and there won't be time for the fire to burn you."

"You know much about living in the forest and jungle."

"You can never know enough when you're in the situation we're in. But we'll give it our best try.

After days of wandering, we are still unharmed and we can be grateful for that. Beside, I am grateful that I now have you as my companions. It gets very lonely in the jungle and the three of us can now accomplish much more than one can. This alone may save our lives. Now let's make our dinner."

She pulled the tubers and berries out of her shirt and divided them equally. "Now put the tubers into the coals at the base of the fire. Don't burn your fingers; use a stick to push them under the coals and save the stick to retrieve them when they're done."

"How do we now when they're done?" asked Shoua.

"It's easy. Poke at them with your stick. When they feel soft, they're ready to eat."

They froze in fear. The roar of a tiger had interrupted their conversation. Yer whispered that the tiger sounded very close and perhaps it would pounce on them at any moment. "The tiger may not be as close as it sounds," Kha replied. "Sound carries far at night and especially over water. It may be across the river in Thailand. We don't know where it is, so we must be very careful."

Having said that, Kha stood up and roared right back in the direction that the tiger's roar had come from. She shouted as loud as she could: "I heard you, tiger, and I know you are hungry. But we are hungrier. Do not dare to come here, because we will kill you and eat you!"

"Is that being very careful?" Yer asked.

"Even a tiger will back off if it thinks it will have to fight hard for its meal and that it may even be hurt or killed in the fight. If this one is close, let's hope that my threat made it think that we're not worth a fight.

"Just in case it does believe that it can attack us, we'd better look around and see if we can find another bamboo log that we can use as a weapon. I'm glad that we didn't burn the one you found."

"Maybe," said Shoua, "we can find thinner bamboo cuttings, too. The ends might be sharp and we could use them as spears against the tigers—or against the Pathet Lao or robbers and rapists who may also be wandering nearby and looking for trouble."

"See?" exclaimed Kha. "I knew that three heads would be better than one. Now you are thinking of ways we can survive. Let's eat our dinner. This will be our first hot meal...roast ground potatoes and assorted tubers with names I've forgotten, yum! Maybe we can spear a rock rat, a pangolin or even a wild boar if we can find some sharp bamboo sticks. After we eat, we'll destroy the fire mud-cone and move on downriver."

They used sticks to drag the wild potatoes and tubers from the fire's coals.

Winter Roses

"How do we know that eating these won't harm us?" asked Yer.

"We don't, at least not for certain. But I am quite certain that I recognized them from my younger days when I would follow my father into the forest and dig for wild potatoes and other tubers. He said the worst that could happen would be a bad stomachache, but to never, ever eat jungle mushrooms unless you are absolutely certain they are edible. They can make you crazy in the head or kill you. So I never ate the mushrooms."

"I hope your memory of these tubers is good. But a stomach ache is a small price to pay for food of any kind. I am so lucky to be with someone who knows so much about forest foods."

"And we are all lucky that we found each other. Now let's eat before our dinner turns to charcoal."

Shoua tried to stuff a tuber into her mouth as fast as she could, and just as quickly spit it out. "Hot!" she exclaimed.

"I tried to warn you but you already had it in your mouth and it was too late. Let me see your tongue."

She stuck out her tongue, and sure enough, Kha saw a blister forming at the tip. "You will have a sore mouth for a couple of days. Just don't rub your tongue against your teeth. If it's too sore, I can make a cooling mud plaster that will take away the pain."

"Yuck," said Shoua.

"You really are a city girl, aren't you? This stay in the jungle may do you some good yet. Think of it. Already, you are willing to stab and club tigers and bad men with a bamboo spear and club."

John Bingham

"I wonder what use I will ever have again for such skills?"

"Perhaps none. But for now, we're counting on each other to live through this experience. Here, have some of my tubers. Let's eat, destroy our mud fire cover and move on downriver."

Before leaving the campsite, Kha chose one, good flaming stick from the fire bed and held it in the air until the flame subsided and only a glowing coal remained at the tip. "There," she exclaimed. "We now have tomorrow's fire."

For nine days and nights, they moved downriver, stopping to rest in the daytime, dig for their dinners and search for good-sized bamboo logs they could plug, wrap their arms around and float across the Mekong.

They found their spears; two short bamboo cuttings that looked as if someone else had cut them for weapons. Their ends had been cut by a machete and were quite sharp. Kha wished she had thought to bring a machete. With that, she wouldn't have needed a bamboo spear.

All through their hikes downriver, Kha kept a stick with a glowing ember alive for their fires. They also discovered that, when the mud beehive cones began to bake dry, they radiated enough warmth to take the chill out of a sudden early-evening gust of wind from the river.

One late afternoon when they had stopped to eat, Yer said, "I know now that we will escape. We have become tigresses ourselves, scaring away tigers and even daring to fight the Pathet Lao or other criminals who want to hurt us."

Kha was pleasantly surprised at her companion's newly found courage and confidence. "Knowing your belief that we will escape strengthens my confidence. Now I, too, am convinced that we will escape. No man or beast will try to stop us now; we truly are tigresses!"

Yer stood up and tried to imitate a tiger's roar with her high, squeaky voice.

Kha laughed. "You better leave the tiger's roar to me. One might think you're a rat or an injured monkey brought to ground, which tigers will also eat. We need to fool the tigers that we're stronger, faster and hungrier than they are, not invite them over for dinner. Especially since we would be the dinner. And, speaking of dinner, we better eat quickly and get moving again. The night is closing on us fast."

That was their seventh night, which proved to be the most exciting of all. They had just started to pick the ground wood they needed to carry for their fire. Kha was using her spear tip to scratch the sticks up and make a pile when they heard a loud squeal. They jumped back in surprise when a rat burst out of the brush followed closely by a jungle cat.

The cat hesitated for a second when it saw the women. Acting on pure instinct, Kha stabbed it with the spear as hard as she could, driving it deep behind its foreleg. The cat rolled over, yowling in pain. "Quick, Shoua!" she shouted. "Stab the cat in the throat!" Shoua didn't have her spear close by, so Yer took a heavy stick, ran to the writhing animal and clubbed it on the head with all of her strength. Even after the blow, the cat clawed the air, snarling and hissing at its tormenters. Shoua finally retrieved her spear, raised it and then hesitated for a moment.

"What are you waiting for? Stab the cat in the throat and push your spear through all the way into the ground!"

Shoua shook her head, dropped the spear, reached under her shirt and pulled out a knife. She ran to Kha and handed it to her without a word. The cat was now thrashing around and clawing the air even harder while trying to reach and bite off the spear lodged in its side. Kha dropped to her knees, holding the cat down with one hand on her spear while she quickly slit the cat's throat with the other. The moment the blade severed the windpipe, it went limp and they heard a sighing, gurgling sound as the air and blood in its lungs rushed out. It shuddered and lay still. She stood there staring at it and wondered if what they had done really happened. But there was the cat as proof, dead at her feet.

She was angry with Shoua and asked her where she got the knife.

"My brother gave it to me and he said to keep it hidden in case I'd be attacked by bad men and to trust no one, not even my fiancé, for fear he might take it and leave me defenseless."

Kha carefully fingered the blade, felt its sharp edge and then easily scraped a small amount of tissue from her thumbnail. *This is no ordinary knife. It is a soldier's fighting knife. No wonder it slit the cat's throat so easily.*

"So you couldn't trust even me? After all we've been through together? We could have used that knife for many things to help us improve our chances for escape. I am angry with you, Shoua."

"I don't blame you and I am very sorry. I should have told you sooner, but I didn't know how soon. The first day I didn't know you. You could have been a Communist sympathizer. So I waited until I knew you were my trustworthy friend. But you would have been just as angry then. At least I brought it to you at a time when we needed it most. Please keep it as my way of apologizing. It is better that you have it anyway, because you are older, wiser and stronger than I am and would be better able to defend us. Besides, I honor and respect anyone who isn't afraid of tigers."

She dropped her head and aimlessly toed a few leaves, waiting for the tirade to come.

It didn't come.

"You amaze me, Shoua. I now understand your reason for hiding it. These days, it is hard to trust anyone. My own cousins left me here to fend for myself, maybe even die here. I trust you more than ever now. You could have stabbed me or cut my throat at any time to get my food. This is a desperate time for us all. I will keep the knife as your token of apology and you have my thanks for it.

Winter Roses

Now let's skin and clean this cat. I will count on you to throw the entrails into the brush as far as you can, after I've slit the stomach open and pull them out. Fair enough?"

Shoua smiled. "Fair enough. Let's get started. I'll get the mud for the fire cone while you gut the cat. Then I'll start the fire and use the knife to sharpen sticks to roast our meat."

Kha cut small strips of meat from the cat's hindquarter that could easily be impaled on their new and sharp roasting sticks. They were both excited: this would be the first meat they had—for Kha, over 20 days not counting cricket meat.

They tossed a few of their tubers into the fire to help their digestion.

"We must be careful not to fill ourselves up with all this meat," she said. "We will get very sick if we do because our stomachs will reject it instead of digesting it."

Yer replied, "I'm happy you told me that because I was ready to stuff myself. We are all so skinny but at least we are alive and we still have each other, don't we?

Tears welled in Kha's eyes and she stood up. "Yes, thanks to all three of us, we are still alive." She reached down and pulled up Yer's thin body to her own, put her arms around her and began to quietly sob. This in turn triggered Shoua's tears. She went to them and put her arms around them both. Together they stood, swaying gently as their tears fell on one another's shoulders.

They needed no further conversation and sat down holding hands to preserve their needed moment of love and renewal of their collective strength. Shoua then said it all when she leaned over to tell Kha, "We are not just tigresses. Now we are sister tigresses." Kha nodded and looked her in the eye. "Yes," she said. "Sister tigresses. Forever, because we three will remember forever what we have done here."

They forced themselves to eat their jungle cat strips slowly, enjoying the dark meat's flavor.

For a wild creature, the cat meat was surprisingly tender and mild in flavor. Even the tubers tasted better with it. During the meal, Yer wondered aloud if tigers killed and ate jungle cats?

Kha said "No."

"Why not?" asked Shoua.

Kha smiled and said, "Jungle cats are too mean."

They broke into laughter.

After dinner, Kha took off one of her ragged shirts to wrap the meat and volunteered to carry it. The cat was scrawnier than it looked so it would not be heavy to carry, and she still had her free hand to carry her glowing fire stick.

Before they broke camp and moved on, Kha scraped the hide and cut the fascia from the rest of the meat. Shoua wrapped the cleaned hide around her shoulders as she picked up their first good-sized bamboo logs that had been hidden in the brush near the spot where she'd buried the entrails.

Kha laughed when Shoua came out of the bush. "You look like a lady of high fashion wearing her new fur, just like the women you see in those magazines that the American soldiers read. Only you're wearing more clothes and are carrying a bamboo log. Seriously, be careful, that hide isn't cured and won't be for some time. The smell could attract even more biting insects when we bed down tomorrow morning. Worse yet, its scent might attract a tiger looking for an easy kill."

With that good counsel, Shoua quickly removed the hide and rubbed the fabric on her shoulders with hands full of fire-dried mud to try and erase—or at least mask--the odor. Next, she wrapped it around one of the logs with the inside out. That way, the bugs could help speed the curing process. She was determined to bring the hide with her when they would finally cross the river to safety.

At pre-dawn of the 10th day, the women slipped into the Mekong river, wrapped their arms around their bamboo logs and kicked off.

They had decided to stay away from a village because it could harbor exactly the kind of men they had tried so hard to avoid.

As they crossed, they tried to stay together. Shoua was able to reach land first, kicking into a current that slowly swirled her around in a huge circle and planted her in water shallow enough to drop the logs and wade to shore.

The varying speed of the current was not as kind to Kha or Yer. They reached a bend in the river with a large point jutting out into the mainstream. Kha was ahead and realized that the normally-slow current would gain speed as it swept by the point and that she should strive to cross and get into the eddy formed up-river, behind the point. She was a strong swimmer and was able to successfully land where she wanted, standing up only to sink into the eddy's black muck. All she could do was to struggle through it in the hope she wouldn't sink any deeper and get stuck. She made a final lunge at the bank and pulled herself free of the sucking mud. Now she would have to run to the point with one of her logs and try to use it as a brake for Yer to grasp and hang on. The run consumed every ounce of energy she had left; gasping for air, she flopped down on her belly with the log extended.

Yer came floating right at her, gaining speed with the current. She was able to drop off her logs at the last moment, lunging and catching Kha's extended log. Yer's weight and the current, however, weakened Kha and she was terrified that she'd be swept away if she had to let go. Yer sensed that this was about to happen and lunged once more, this time with both hands extended and reaching for Kha's wrists. Kha let go of the log and clamped her hand on Yer's upper arm, then dragged her up the bank as she would beach a big fish or a boat. She then fell down on her hands and knees in total exhaustion.

When their breathing and pounding hearts returned to normal, Yer rolled over, hugged Kha and shouted, "WE ARE FREE!"

"What a wonderful feeling it is to be safe from the Pathet Lao murderers," Kha replied. "Now we must find Shoua."

"I thought I saw her make it to the beach, Yer told her. "She landed well up-river from here. We can start walking in that direction and call her name as we go."

They stood up. Yer lost her balance and fell on her first step. The meager meals, constant walking and the adrenaline rush of the river crossing had robbed her of her strength.

Kha said, "We should sit down now, rest, and chew on meat strips from the jungle cat to make us stronger. We can take turns calling out Shoua's name. She may be walking towards us as we speak, since she already knows we didn't pass her in the current."

Yer agreed. "I think there's a good chance that she saw us headed for that point. If so, she will probably be trying to find us right now."

They sat down and Kha pulled out the meat strips, handed one to Yer and took one for herself. She called first and didn't receive any response. They chewed the meat, which was by then tasteless and tough.

"At least the jungle cat meat—as bad as it is-—gave us strength to get us safely across the river," she said. "Now I'm hoping that these strips give us enough strength to find Shoua and a road that might lead us to our refugee camp."

"To help get this cat meat down, I'll pretend that it is really meat from a fat, pot-bellied pig."

"If you can do that, you have a better imagination than I have."

Kha called again. This time they thought they heard a response and Yer called back. In a few seconds, they heard a voice that seemed closer. Kha tried once more, this time even louder. A voice came back. "I'm Shoua. Keep shouting and I'll find you!"

Five calls later and Shoua appeared. She was standing on the beach, far upriver. Both Kha and Yer stood up and frantically waved their arms. Shoua waved back. Within a short time, they were together again, hugging and laughing and celebrating their good fortune with the traditional Hmong circle dance that was usually reserved for women and their men. The dancing didn't last long. Kha's legs sagged and she had to drop to her knees.

"We need men to dance with us," Shoua said. "At least they'd have the strength to hold us up."

"Kha laughed and asked, "What man would want to even look at us? Our clothes are rags and we are all so skinny that we look like skeletons with stringy mops for hair. Even that scrawny jungle cat looked better than we do."

Yer said that they might well be as scrawny as the jungle cat, but they at least smelled better.

They sat down on the riverbank and finished the last of the cat strips. While they gnawed at the tough meat, Kha said she believed that there might be a road running parallel to the river where they might be able to stop a truck and get a ride to a village where they could get directions to the refugee camp.

She stood up and tested her legs by slowly walking along the bank looking for a path they might follow to find the road. Sure enough, there was one. It was barely visible; probably one used by animals coming to the river to drink.

The sister tigresses stood and joined her, and they all hoped that the path would lead them to the road and a ride to the refugee camp. The prospect of beginning a new life free from Communist tyranny made them forget their weak and shaky legs.

Just as Kha suspected, a few steps up the path took them to a road. Rather than walk the road without direction, they decided to wait for a truck or car that might stop and give them a ride. They sat on the shoulder of the road while the sun came up to warm them and dry their clothing.

The women ran off the road and into the underbrush to hide when they heard the sound of an engine; a Jeep with two men in uniform had come up behind them. They heard the vehicle stop and peeked out to see two men walking towards them. One of the men—speaking in fluent Hmong--told them not to be afraid. He said that he knew they were refugees who had just escaped across the river to Thailand, and that he and his partner were refugee camp guards who would drive them to the camp where they would get a meal, clean clothing and shelter.

Kha whispered that there was no more reason to be afraid. "Let's go out to greet them. We will be a sorry sight to them with our bony bodies and rags for clothes, but we can't help that." They held hands and stepped out into the sunlight together as gracefully as their shaky legs could manage, and marveled at how clean and nice the guards looked in their uniforms.

Winter Roses

The guard who spoke was the one who came over to her first, thinking correctly that she was the leader of the escapees. "Good morning," he said. "I am Senior Guard Chou and this is my partner, Kla. Welcome to Thailand and freedom. Let us walk back to the Jeep where we will be more comfortable and ask you a few questions before we drive you to the camp. We must be certain that you are not the Pathet Lao."

They turned and walked together up the embankment. After Chou asked their names and ages, they asked how they escaped and if they were attacked by the Pathet Lao or other criminals: if so, were they injured and how severely?

They also needed to know if any were pregnant and if so, how far along? Of course, they asked them to surrender any weapons they carried and Kha gave the fighting knife to Chou, who took great interest in it. Shoua told him how and why her brother had given it to her, as well as why she had passed it to Kha, who knew how to use it better than she could. The guard said he would keep it safe for them, but that they would not need it because he would take great care to make sure they were not harmed by anyone.

"Regarding the possibility that you might be Pathet Lao," he added, "Do you have any friends and relatives who are in our camp who can vouch that you are who you say you are? If you are married and your husbands came here first, what are their names?"

Kha told him that she was not married and gave them the names of her cousins while Yer and Shoua told them their fiances' names.

Chou kept admiring Kha's beauty, intelligence and poise and wondered why she was not already married. He made a mental note to make sure the she was very well cared for in his refugee camp. Of course, he would ensure the same for her partners.

Both men wondered about the strange animal skin that was wound around Yer's waist. She pulled it off and held it up so they could see the cat's head still attached to it and staring at them with glazed-over eyes. "This cat has been dinner for us for the past three nights," explained Kha. "First we stabbed it with a bamboo spear and then cut its throat with the knife. As you now know, it is very sharp. After days of eating nothing but tubers, some berries, many crickets and other insects, we needed the meat badly. This cat helped us survive and we honor its spirit."

Now the senior guard was even more impressed with her.

This woman is truly exceptional, he thought. *She and her young friends have done what few men could do. It's hard to believe that Kha spent 22 days in enemy territory and tiger country—13 of them by herself--and survived. Even with her two companions who were with her for the last nine days, her story borders on the unbelievable. Yet I believe her.*

During the drive to the camp, Yer told Kha that she had a new name for her tigress sister. "What might that be?" asked Kha. "All through our nine-day hike through the jungle you kept the sticks with the glowing coals on their ends alive for our next campsite fire. This was a great feat, one worth honoring, and so I will tell all my new friends here that I was fortunate enough to escape with "The Girl Of The Nine Glowing Embers. "

Kha was flattered. "If you think that this new name honors me, then I agree. The biggest problem I had was to keep the stick ends glowing without knocking the coals off and into heavy dew or a mud hole where they would be snuffed out. That, and try to keep it from setting what's left of my clothes on fire."

Chou smiled, turned his head and repeated the name. "The Girl Of The Nine Glowing Embers" is a good name," he said. "I have been here in the camp for years and have never heard of such an accomplishment. I will also tell my friends about your stories of survival."

Shoua quickly responded. "You should also know that Kha chased away a tiger we believed was stalking us by screaming right back at it after it had roared."

The guards' eyes were now opened wide at these tales of three almost defenseless women and how they had protected themselves from starvation and great harm.

Chou said, "We have much to learn about the three of you. We have not even heard such stories from the Hmong men who have come into our camp. You must tell us more when you are settled in your new home. Will you promise to do that? All of my fellow guards would love to hear your stories and so would many of your countrymen. Your adventures will be valuable survival lessons for us all, as well as good entertainment. I believe the whole camp will be proud of you and honor you."

Kha was pleased and replied, "Thank you for the opportunity. We are proud to be Hmong women and want people to know that even we can do good things that helped us. We are also happy to think that what we learned and what we did might be able to help others in desperate situations."

Yer was not so happy at the thought of speaking before large audiences; it frightened her. She came from a traditional family where the women never did such things and she had never learned how to effectively communicate her thoughts and ideas to many people at a time. She would be too nervous to speak at all. "Although I will not speak, " she said, "I am happy to be safe here in Thailand and that is all the reward I need. I also ask your help in finding my fiancé, who may be here in this camp or perhaps in another. In turn I promise you that I will be a good guest while I am here. Shoua's fiancé is also in one of the camps."

The guard replied that he would personally help them find your fiancés, in any way he could.

John Bingham

Kha stayed on in the camp and told her stories many times to small groups and large, and all were pleased with her efforts. The Girl Of The Nine Glowing Embers had found a new home in camp and made many new friends. She especially enjoyed the visits by her new friend, Chou, who came often.

Late one afternoon, he came into her room behaving strangely, acting nervous and agitated. After stumbling through some small talk, he suddenly stopped and took a deep breath. She asked him if she had done something to offend him. "No, no," he replied. "I'm nervous because I want to ask you to be my wife. I have fallen in love with you because you are beautiful and brave and bright.

"Will you marry me? I will buy you a pig that we can roast for our wedding feast and I promise you a nice home with a view of the river and many chickens and you can ride with me in my Jeep to the market and picnic on the riverbank where you and your friends landed." He ran out of breath and had to stop talking.

She laughed and he was afraid that she was not pleased with his offers. When she noticed the quizzical-sad-angry looks appearing on his face, she realized that she had insulted him with her laughter and quickly stood up, took his face in her hands and kissed him. "Future husband," she told him, "I laugh for joy at your proposal. I cannot tell you how pleased I am that you want to be my husband and that I gladly accept your proposal. On our wedding day, let us feast on the pig, dance with each other and our guests, and then go to the house with the view of the river where we can also begin to make babies."

A smile split his face. He returned her kiss and reached into his coat pocket to pull out a small bottle of lau-Lao. "Let us celebrate with a drink," he said. " I am now off duty and will not get in any trouble."

She reached into her floor cabinet-cupboard for two large ceramic cups that a kind, elderly Hmong woman had given her as a thank-you-gift for sharing her escape stories. He filled the cups and she thought that they might either get into great trouble or great fun that late afternoon and couldn't wait to see which one prevailed—or perhaps both. Whatever happened, she was ready and so was he.

Nothing good happened. They both passed out on her camp cot with Chou's arm flopped over her chest. They awoke the next morning with terrible hangovers, so bad that they decided not to serve lau-Lao at their wedding. Kha decided that she would sleep all day, waking only to sip water for her parched throat and cotton-dry mouth.

After throwing up behind the tent, Chou managed to get into his Jeep, pick up Kla to patrol the river road, and hope that there wouldn't be any refugees that day.

They were fortunate; all was quiet and they were able to hide the jeep behind a tangle of underbrush and take a nap. Unfortunately, the jeep's bumper had ripped open a mound of fire ants. They were able to nap for an hour before the revenge-minded ants found them and began to feast on them, first on their exposed ankles and then moving rapidly up their legs. The ants' bites lived up to the insects' name; the men woke up with a swarm of the ants biting their ankles and legs, and gaining reinforcements by the hundreds so they could launch an all-out assault on their buttocks and bellies.

The bites felt like white-hot pins were stabbing them and they dashed for the only cure readily available—the river. The cool water helped to ease the pain of the bites and the current washed away the ants. Now ant-free, the men still had a problem; how to retrieve the Jeep without getting attacked again. Rather than face that risk, they decided to hitch-hike back to the camp, commandeer another Jeep from the motor pool and go back with a can of kerosene to pour into the ants' mound and burn the little bastards to brittle char. First, however, they'd wipe away any ants that were left in the jeep with kerosene-soaked rags.

Kla thought that the biting buggers were mean enough to eat the Jeep's canvas upholstery, tires and then lap up the kerosene. When they came back to the spot where they'd parked and tore open the ants' huge mound, he would test their ferocity.

They were in luck. A farmer in his empty manure cart who was going to the camps for a refill told them to climb in back. The ride back was anything but pleasant for obvious reasons, but the torment of the ant bites helped take their minds off the smell. The pain of the bites had mutated into the worst itching the men had ever experienced. They scratched until the bites began to bleed and even then they itched. The farmer looked back when he heard them swearing and immediately recognized their problem.

"You come with me into camp and I will make a salve for you that will stop the itching."

The men looked at each other and quickly deduced what the main ingredient of the salve would be.

"No thank you, my friend," Chou plied. "My fiancé has a special ointment that comes from China that will stop the itching."

"You will be sorry. Chinese ointment is shit."

Chou almost insulted the old man by asking him what makes Thai shit any better than Chinese shit, but then realized that this might anger him and they'd be out of a ride. "Perhaps so, but we don't want to offend her," he replied. "We had trouble with ants before and her father gave her the ointment the day before he died." Kla grinned at his partner's bullshit.

"Aaaaah," the old man said. "Now I understand why you want Chinese shit. It must have great healing power, coming from her father just before he died. Please tell her for me, a shaman who knows all about shit, that her shit is good shit."

"I'll do that, my friend. And thank you for your kind offer."

The old man smiled and nodded. They shook hands when they parted, and Chou and Kla washed their hands thoroughly in the motor pool's bathroom.

The plan was working. They were able to get another Jeep by telling the Thai sergeant in charge that their own Jeep was stuck in sand and they needed one with a winch to pull it out.

After they'd wiped away the jeep ants, Kla lit a cigarette and pushed it at a stray ant. It reared up on its hind legs in pain and anger, then dropped down to rush at the cigarette and attack the live coal. It kept attacking until it killed itself.

Kla said he'd never go near these ants again. Chou told him that they should be called NVA ants, because they also fight to the death.

Their plan went to hell. Kerosene hell. When Chou poured the kerosene into the labyrinth of tunnels exposed by the bumper, he tossed a lit match into the anthill's soaked, sandy mud. The kerosene ignited, and the fire raced up the stream into the can's spout, exploding the can in his hands. He dropped it in pain and looked in horror at his hands and forearms. The skin had been burned right through the flesh. Kla kicked the still-burning kerosene can out from underneath the fire-ant Jeep to prevent its fuel tank from catching fire and exploding. He checked his friend's face and neck, which were burned to a deep red but didn't appear to be as badly burned as the arms and hands. Chou's eyebrows were also burned off and his hair was singed.

Kla told Chou to get into the Jeep and hang on to the windshield while they drove to the camp's medical dispensary, but Chou's fire-burned and heavily blistered hands were too weak and too painful to grasp anything. Besides, he was in shock. Kla was worried that Chou would fall out of the Jeep without restraints of some kind.

John Bingham

He solved the problem by tying together the unsoaked rags, turning them into a rope that he wrapped around Chou's hips and tied down on the Jeep's side handgrips. He also took the web belt and strapped it around Chou's body, then fastened it to its retaining clip.

Kla told Chou to close his eyes so dust, dirt and insects could not get in them, and away they went. Kla drove as fast as he possibly could without turning the Jeep over. They arrived at the dispensary just as the nurse on duty was leaving. One look at Chou and she turned right around, telling Kla to get his friend inside and on a gurney so she could examine, clean and dress his wounds.

While the nurse was caring for Chou, Kla drove over to bring Kha to the dispensary.

He dropped her off and then headed for the motor pool to see if the sergeant on duty could come with him to pick up the Jeep and drive it back.

Kha was shocked to see her husband-to-be in such terrible condition. For his part, he was relatively pain-free; the deep burns had killed the nerve cells in the tissue and he could feel nothing except the itching of the fire ants' bites in his legs and buttocks. When he told her what happened, she found it hard to believe that ants had been the cause of their problem. "I've learned my lesson," he replied. "I'll never again try to burn out anthills with kerosene. Next time I'll use C-4." *

*A very powerful explosive bound in plastic that can be molded into different shapes.

They were married four weeks later and many of their friends came to celebrate with them. Kha went through the ceremony of the tying of the strings around her wrists. Chou didn't have the strength to hold up his wrists while the guests tied the strings around them, but that didn't matter to him.

He was just happy that his burn wounds were slowly healing and that the ant bites had stopped itching.

Some guests even brought small gifts of money, which was a scarcity among the camp residents. Among the honored guests were her tigress sisters and their fiancés, who were living in the same camp.

Kha and Chou were very happy in their hillside home with a view, which was far more comfortable than the camp's tent partition. She appreciated the privacy and the hand-operated water pump in the kitchen, and feeding the chickens and pigs running around in their yard. More than anything, she treasured the pleasure of looking across the river to her Lao homeland, now knowing that she was safe from harm and living in freedom at last.

Her happiness there would not last because the refugee camps were shutting down. They had served their purpose by providing temporary food and shelter for the refugees. Their residents were now migrating to other countries, including France, Australia, Canada and South America, and most going to the United States.

Chou left for America first, while Kha stayed back until he found a job and could pay for her airfare to America.

While she was still at the camp, her cousins came to listen to her stories. Word had reached them about a brave Hmong woman who had survived in the jungle for 22 days before crossing the Mekong with her arms wrapped around bamboo logs. They thought it might be Kha and were pleased that they had found her. But they were embarrassed because they left her and apologized. She forgave them and said that she was happy that they had also survived. When she heard the Pathet Lao firing at them while they were in the river, she thought that they had been killed.

She stayed for a year in Thailand and then followed Chou, joining him in Akron where he worked for a company that manufactured precision cutting tools for the metalworking industries. She wondered after sharing tearful goodbyes with Yer and Shoua if she would ever see them again.

They promised to find her when they came to America with their fiancés, and she sent them her address and phone number when she had settled in Akron with Chou. She never heard from them again, but took some comfort in the memories of their time in the jungle together, wandering in fear of tigers and the Pathet Lao communists.

They had seven children in the 30 years they lived there and were divorced after 30 years of marriage. A younger woman had come into Chou's life. Kha still lives in Akron and remains single.

To her children and grandchildren, she is their family's treasure. Who else could have a mother or grandmother to rival the Girl Of The Nine Glowing Embers?

Kha's father, Kha Long, led an extremely dangerous life during the war years, as an agent for the CIA headquartered at the American Embassy in Vientiane, Laos.

Prior to that, he had expressed an interest in becoming the leader of the village where the family lived, replacing the man who was retiring. He could not just walk in and tell him that he would replace him; trust must be earned. The incumbent challenged him to do something to prove he was worthy of the job.

Kha Long did just that. He went to a neighboring village, stole six hogs and brought them back as his proof. Combined with his shaman abilities, the hogs carried the day and he won the job.

Then came the war along with the CIA, whose operatives were searching out willing and capable Hmong and Lao men with good visibility of the communist Pathet Lao personnel and their operations. A prospect's hatred of the communists was also a helpful criterion, to minimize the risk of hiring double agents and provide a stronger motivation than money to get their job.

Kha Long was the ideal candidate, one made even stronger by his villagers' dependency on the village's trusted shaman. With very little coaxing and prodding, the villagers—even a few neutralists--would often open up to him, providing invaluable intelligence about Pathet Lao strongholds, their operations and even plans of future attacks or acts of sabotage. Kha Long would then feed the information to his CIA contacts at the U.S. Consulate in the Embassy, whose people would review and disseminate the information to the various military region headquarters for appropriate action. Often, the action would involve the Ravens for troop ground support missions.

Military Region II (Long Tieng, or Lima Site 20-A, also known as "Alternate" to the Ravens) was the most active of the regions with the continuous back-and-forth war that General Vang Pao's Hmong Army fought against the Pathet Lao and NVA invaders.

When the war was over, Kha Long and his wife came to America and settled in California. A measure of the great respect he had earned in his positions as spy and shaman came when Hmong dignitaries from all over the country learned of his presence here in the U.S. and came to visit him. He was honored for the many of his fellow countrymen's lives that his intelligence saved—as well as for the many of his enemy's lives that his intelligence had taken.

John Bingham

He returned to Laos several years later to visit friends and relatives still in country. There, a double agent—or perhaps an old acquaintance turned communist—assassinated him. His wife died three years later.

A year after his death, Kha received an invitation from the American Embassy in Laos to come and get her father's important papers. There was one stipulation; she must arrive in Thailand and then be transferred to an airport where she would board a helicopter and fly over the Mekong to Vientiane. She would land on a helipad near the American Embassy, which was in the old royal palace, and then be escorted inside to receive the papers.

When Kha arrived at Udan Thani Airport, she went inside the small terminal and asked the woman at the lobby desk how they could find the helicopter that was waiting to fly her to Vientiane. The woman asked her to have a seat while she called her supervisor to confirm the request. Within minutes, two young men dressed in black suits and wearing sunglasses appeared and introduced themselves as her official American Embassy escorts who would accompany her into Laos. As proof, one opened his wallet and showed them his identification card, which meant nothing to her.

They walked beside her to a Jeep waiting outside. One helped her into the front seat and climbed in behind her while the driver took his seat. When he started the engine and spun around in a tight turn with the tires throwing gravel and headed for a dirt road flanked on both sides with dark, overgrown jungle and underbrush, she became very nervous. This scene was unfolding like a B-grade spy movie, only it was for real. *Are these men really my escorts or are they my assassins? Are they the ones who killed my father? The escort sitting behind me could shoot me in the back of my head and throw my body into the underbrush and no would know what happened. No one here would even care what happened.*

Kha shivered at the thought and her heart began to race. *Is this how it will end?* She tried hard to breathe slowly and deeply to calm her anxiety. The escort asked if she was nervous about flying, and she replied that flying always frightened her.

Winter Roses

"Don't worry," the escort said. "The flights over and back will only take a short time and the helicopter is very reliable. The pilots are experienced. Both of them flew rescue missions during the war. Does the way we dress and our dark sunglasses also frighten you?"

"Yes," replied Kha. "My father was assassinated in Laos and I am afraid that I will also be killed."

"Don't worry. I am familiar with your father's most unfortunate death. We dress this way to scare away anyone who might want to harm you. We are here to protect you and our black suits and dark sunglasses help us do that."

What a relief! "Thank you," she said. "I feel better now." *Maybe I'll get to Laos, receive the papers and return safely home after all.*

When they arrived at the waiting helicopter on the helipad, the escorts jumped out, ran to the open door and told the people who were waiting inside to get out, they were not flying today because they have an important person who must cross and return alone. The people were not happy; Kha heard them mumbling and swearing and she could not blame them. *I would be angry, too,* she thought.

Next came another surprise. She was given a small cloth imprinted in the Thai, Hmong, Vietnamese, and Lao languages and told she must carry it on her person until she crosses back over Thailand, Laos and Vietnam and is over the Gulf of Tonkin before disposing of it. It was a blood chit similar to ones carried by American pilots who had been downed in enemy territory during the war. It identified her as an American citizen who was protected from harm by the Geneva Accords, and must be treated accordingly. It stated that she must be free to travel to the nearest major airport where she can board an airliner and depart for home, and that the United States government would pay for her food, lodging and air-fare. The government would also pay a reward for anyone who protected her from harm.

John Bingham

At first, she didn't understand why she needed such a cloth until one of her escorts explained that it would be helpful if the helicopter or airplane she was on crashed and she found herself once again on communist soil. It could be especially helpful if she was captured by the Pathet Lao, who might set her free for a reward. American dollars were highly valued in postwar Laos; the communists appreciated the buying power of black-market dollars.

While the chit was no guarantee of safe passage by the rabid Pathet Lao—after all, they had assassinated her own father—she realized that it might at least avoid an otherwise very unhealthy situation.

The flight over the river to Vientiane went quickly as their escort promised. Kha was feeling better and her fears disappeared.

Her escorts took her into the building where the American embassy was housed. The three of them sat down in the lobby to wait while the receptionist called for an embassy representative to take her upstairs where she would meet with the "senior embassy case officer." Two big men dressed in black slacks and white dress shirts came downstairs, welcomed her and introduced themselves as embassy employees. They asked the escorts to stay since the meeting would only take a few moments.

The senior case officer was cordial but brief. After thanking her for making the long journey to Laos, he presented her with a bulging leather portfolio stamped for U.S. CIA "Eyes Only" distribution. Kha had to promise that she would not try to open and read them unless she was given permission by the CIA back home in America.

Her sharp eye picked up a rusty, dark stain on the edge of a sheet of paper that had begun to work its way loose from the portfolio, and she shivered at the thought of what it might be.

Winter Roses

"Is that what I think it is?" she asked, pointing at the stain. The case officer glanced down and realized what she was asking. "All I can tell you is that a very good friend and associate died to protect this portfolio."

Now frightened again, she changed the subject and asked why they couldn't have used other courier services to handle such sensitive documents. The case officer told that no one would suspect a young woman on vacation of carrying them. "Besides, the communists are not as aggressive as they were when your father was killed. They'd rather concentrate their efforts on earning a good living, just like Americans. It is also appropriate and an honor for you to carry your father's documents out of Laos.

"Of great importance," he added with a smile, "we know that these papers will be safe in the hands of 'The Girl of the Nine Glowing Embers.' Your father would be proud of you."

A few days after Kha had returned home, she received a telephone call early one evening from someone who identified himself as a case officer with the Central Intelligence Agency. He told her that a representative from the Agency would visit her at exactly four p.m. the following day, if she could be home at that time.

She confirmed that she would be home. The case officer continued. "He will identify himself to you with his badge and a duplicate copy of the blood chit that you were given, and he will tell you what must be done with your father's important papers by order of the Director of America's Central Intelligence Agency.

"I knew that these papers were important," she said, "but I never thought they were that important."

"The order says it all. Where are the papers now and have they been opened?"

"No. As soon as I got home I went and bought one of those small, fireproof safes and put the papers in there. It's locked and in my bedroom closet and I did not open it."

"Good. To do so would be a breach of national security and people's lives would be endangered if the papers were in the wrong hands. That's all I can tell you, except to say that the director thanks you for your safe handling of the documents and also extends to you his regrets for your father's death. He was a true patriot for his country and for ours."

"Thank you and please tell your director that I appreciate his kind words."

"Yes, I most certainly will tell him. You also have my condolences for your father's untimely death and my thanks for your safe handling of the documents. Goodnight and God bless."

Before she could answer, he was gone. It struck her after he'd hung up that she didn't even know his name.

The agent showed up on time with a companion who stood guard on the steps outside. Both were dressed in ordinary street clothes--khakis, polo shirts and light jackets. Kha brought the agent to her bedroom closet. He lifted the heavy fireproof safe and set it on the bed. She opened it for him and he pulled out the portfolio. After carefully inspecting and testing the lock, he smiled at her, reached inside his jacket pocket, took out a nondescript brown cloth bag and dropped the portfolio inside.

She asked if she would ever be allowed to read the papers.

"Yes, but they won't be declassified for years to come. Certain people will have to die of natural causes before that happens. With luck and longevity, you and I may be able to sit down some night and go over them together.

"I will bring the beer and snacks. Is it a date?"

"It's a date."

"Good. Meanwhile, thank you once more. Your father would be proud of you. We at headquarters certainly are." They shook hands and he walked out the door with the bag in hand. His partner nodded to her and they walked down the steps to a nondescript, blue Chevrolet sedan. Two other men came around from the back of the house and got into the car. As it drove away, she couldn't help but notice the twin exhaust pipes and the deep growl of its engine. A moment later, she saw a big, black SUV with darkened windows pull away from the curb down the block and speed up to catch the Chevy.

Clever, these CIA people, she thought. *What enemy would ever guess that the boss and the important papers were riding in a plain old Chevrolet?*

Master of the White Mountains

"Chao Pha Khao" is Hmong for "Master of the White Mountains." The English pronunciation is "chop a cow."

The contraction, "Chaophakhao," became the Hmong and Lao T-28 fighter-bomber pilots' call sign. Laotian pilot Chaophakhao Red helped me find the surviving relatives of Hmong back-seater Wa Ger, who was with Frank when he was killed by enemy antiaircraft fire over the Plain of Jars.

Chaophakhao Red was one of the very few who flew and fought the Pathet Lao and NVA invaders for nearly 13 years. And survived to tell his story.

Here is his story as written in his own words, reprinted with his permission.

"I flew a T-28 fighter-bomber from 1965-1970 and then transferred to a C/AC-47* from '70 to '77. I also flew a C-123K** from late '72 to '77 when the communist PL (Pathet Lao) captured me and sent me to a "re-education camp"

John Bingham

in the Ban Ban (northern Laos) area. I made daring (sic) escape from that HELL in broad daylight on March 23 around 1980 and then settled down here in the Land of Freedom two weeks before Christmas of 1981.

> *aka "Spooky," a twin-engined gunship carrying three miniguns that deliver extremely rapid rates of concentrated fire
> **a cargo and passenger aircraft that could land and take off on short, unimproved airstrips

"During my fighter career I met and was in actual contact with Ravens via our call signs and radio when we were in the air, but we hardly knew each other. Some times when we remained overnight at LS20-A (Alternate, pilot talk for Long Tieng), we met in person and learned their true names, and many of us became close friends.

"The day he was shot down I was in 20-A and learned that one of our Raven FACs (Frank) was killed but the GIB (guy in back) Wa Ger survived. Every time I learned that somebody downed a Laotian, Hmong or American pilot, I felt the loss of a family member and my brother-in-arms. I'd lost many relatives and close friends, and one of them was a Raven who finished his tour and came back as a F-4 jock out of Ubon (a secret U.S. airbase in Thailand). A couple of years ago I got a surprise e-mail from Karl Polifka who ran into my pictures on the Ravens web site. He thought that I was shot down and KIA in the PDJ (Plaine Des Jarres, i.e., French for Plain of Jars) in mid-1971, just a few months before Frank and Wa Ger were shot down. He had swooped down in his F-4 and was pretty sure the pilot who was down in the T-28 was me, but that was my closest and best friend Lt. Sisay Thiphavong who took over the squadron (and also my call sign, Chaophakhao Red) when I left the T-28s to fly the C/AC-47 "Spooky." But Karl had left the Ravens before I was transferred and he believed I was still flying the T-28.

"I talk to a few Hmong friends from the 20-A era and they believe that Wa Ger was still alive and had settled down in Minnesota. I will find out and let you know.

Winter Roses

"I had my own surprise as well, during the end of '68 I was hit and injured by 14.5 mm AAA (Anti-Aircraft Artillery) at Lima Site 85, the infamous Phou Pha Thi. Somehow I managed to survive and land at 20-A just to find out every doctor and nurse was at lunch, it is noon time, I came back to the airfield and found one American pilot beside a U-10 Helio (a "STOL" Short Take-Off and Landing aircraft that used wing slats to increase wing lift at very slow take-off speeds). I asked him to take me to LS-20 Samthong (Pop Buell's headquarters and hospital*).

"That bold American pilot agreed and scared the hell out of me more than the bloody enemy AAA did when he cranked up his U-10, jammed up the throttle and lifted off in less than 20 meters and banked the aircraft's wingtips, barely avoiding scraping the runway and then skimming above the treetops while climbing above the hill at the end of the runway with the front slats popping back in and out.

> *Pop Buell was a farmer in Indiana who came to Laos after his wife died and ran a hospital and aid mission for the Hmong and Laotian peoples in the village of Sam Thong.*

When I looked at our airspeed, 60 knots, that scared me even more. It's my first ride in the U-10 and I'm used to my T-28's 140 knots when climbing with a full (bomb) load. We got to the hospital and he waited to fly me back and I didn't dare ask what his name was.

"For 30 years I wondered who on earth that bold American pilot was. Then in 1977 my employer, Frank Sigona of Sigtronics, attended a Ravens reunion in San Antonio. When he came back from that reunion he said that, next year, he will arm-wrestle me if he has to, to get me to join him at the reunion. He said that someone wants to meet me badly. This man claimed that he flew me to the hospital when I got hit, and you might guess that I wanted to see the man who scared the hell out of me, so I decide to go and can hardly wait another year.

John Bingham

"When I arrived at the Ravens reunion—and that's 30 years since I saw these great friends—most of them were my parents' age and I felt like I was just barely out of my teens, still I could recognize some of them. It turned out that the one who saved me and scared me more than the AAA was the head of the Ravens at 20-A. I knew back then that he was the Ravens chief but I hadn't yet met him in person and I never expected a Raven to fly the U-10, the O-1, U17 and T-28 airplanes. I met and worked with him later on but none of us brought that incident up because we were too busy fighting the war. Many of us cried when we first met and most of them never thought I would survive the war.

"When I was asked how I survived, I said and will forever say, I was trained by the best in the world, the USAF Air Commandos, and the Ravens were my idols and my heroes.

"I hope you enjoyed my short story and I hope and look forward to meeting you at the next and next reunion."

Best regards,
Chaophakhao Red
NEVERMORE

Author's notes:
Chaophakhao Red was as good as his word. He called one afternoon six years ago and said that he could not locate Wa Ger, but he had learned that Wa Ger's family lives in suburban Pontiac, Michigan--a city that borders Waterford, where Ann and I live. One phone call later, I was in touch with Wa Ger's nephew, Joua and his son, Cha—the beginning of my friendship and my wife's friendship with the Hmong people, whom we greatly respect and admire for their courage during the war and their resourcefulness in starting their new lives in America.

We hope that Americans are now beginning to realize how great a contribution these people have already made to our country. By battling the NVA in Laos, they saved countless numbers of American soldiers' lives. Had the brave Hmong and Laotian warriors not fought the NVA in their homeland, the enemy would have flooded South Vietnam with those

Winter Roses

same soldiers—along with their weapons and supplies--via the Ho Chi Minh trail, all the more to kill Americans, South Vietnamese, Koreans, Australians, New Zealanders, Thai, and Canadian volunteers.

The Chaophakao Lmong pilots had a saying; "We fly until we die."

The late Christopher Robbins estimated the casualty rate of the Raven FACs to be approximately 30 percent. This rate was suffered by men who flew their dangerous missions every day during a typical six-month tour of duty.

The Ravens' dangerous flying experience strongly suggests that the Laotian and Hmong pilots' saying was accurate when you consider that they never stopped flying unless and until they were killed, too wounded to fly, or captured.

From the letter, we know that Chaophakhao Red had flown and fought for over 13 years before he was captured and sent to a Pathet Lao communist "re-education camp." His description of his escape in broad daylight as "daring" is understatement.

As a combat pilot whose duty was to kill and wound as many communists as possible during his career and became very good at it, he was fortunate that his captors did not torture him or summarily execute him when he was first captured. Had the communists captured him after he escaped, he most surely would have been shot. What this man accomplished required unspeakable courage--for his long service spent in the daily dodging of enemy antiaircraft artillery fire while carrying out his many missions, and for his equally daring escape to freedom.

Sadly, many of the Lao and Hmong pilots really did "fly until they die." The odds against them were stacked from the beginning. Fortunately, Chaophakhao Red survived by a rare combination of courage, skill and luck.

The Pathet Lao communists have gone on record with a promise to exterminate the entire Hmong race. To this day, they continue on their bloody, genocidal path to hunt down and execute the Hmong people who chose to stay behind and now fight as guerrilla forces in their mountain homelands.

The world may pass them by, but the Ravens and CIA personnel who fought with them will never forget the pain of leaving their Hmong and Laotian comrades-in-arms behind when America's covert war ended.

The Hmong and Laotian warriors and their families know what they had already done to make America a stronger, better place for their presence here.

We Americans can now understand and appreciate what these brave people already know: that their fight for freedom was also our fight for freedom, and they—along with their Raven brothers-in-arms--fought well indeed. Saving thousands of our troops--and theirs--qualifies them and the Ravens as true American heroes.

And One For Marie

Marie's life was one of despair, hope, love, courage and finally, triumph. Hers is a story of a woman who married an abusive man, yet managed to escape his reach and start a new life with a man who rapidly became the one, true love of her life. This was a man who loved not only her and their new family, but one who was devoted to the dangerous art of delivering death and destruction from the air, followed closely by his love for his brothers-in-arms. In short, he had several loves.

Frank had long been dead when I asked her if she would like to accompany me to an annual Ravens reunion in San Antonio to meet the men who flew and fought with him. Her reply: "John, thank you for asking but I can't go. He belongs to the Ravens now."

She had finally broken out of her compartmentalized rationale for her addiction and found the courage, determination and strength to stop drinking. She did this by sharing those attributes and her down-to-earth, successful experiences with fellow alcoholics as practical and proven means to escape the disease's deadly grip.

Winter Roses

She crossed the whole of Arizona to share her story with hundreds of recovering alcoholics and those who still struggled with their alcohol-soaked demons. Her travels included another trek down to the Grand Canyon floor to meet once more with the Havasupai Native Americans, this time to help their alcoholics learn how to achieve lasting sobriety. They remembered when she, Frank and the children had come to make amends for thundering down the canyon in his Super Sabre. The elders were saddened when they learned of her husband's death, but tried to comfort her by saying that he died as a warrior should die, taking the fight to the enemy.

Word of her success rate spread far and fast, so much so that she was offered the position as the state's AA secretary. She accepted because she believed that the position would give her even more credibility with her followers.

She also sponsored many recovering alcoholics, keeping her phone line open night and day to listen and encourage her charges in their seemingly never-ending quests for alcohol-free lives.

Her most moving moment came after she'd told her story to the Pima Native American's chapter. There she learned the bittersweet story of USMC Corporal Ira Hayes and how he had covered himself and his beloved Pima nation in glory. He had fought through the Pacific in four major campaigns, culminating with his part in history by helping to raise the flag on Iwo Jima. He then stumbled, fell into alcohol's bottomless pit and drowned. The elder who told her about Ira said it was a great shame that he was not there to hear her story and take home the hope and determination she had brought to his Pima brothers and sisters. "Perhaps," he said, "Ira would not have died from alcoholism after all."

On a cold and grey afternoon in Washington, DC, where she was attending a national AA convention, she bought a red rose, went to the Wall, made a gold-leaf rubbing of Frank's name, and then visited Ira's grave in Arlington National Cemetery.

John Bingham

As she stood before the weathering headstone, a light snow began to fall. She thought of the elder's words. *Ira, I wish I could have told you of my higher power. Perhaps the same big medicine that worked for me would have worked for you.*

She looked at her rubbing. *Frank, I wish you could have lived to share my sobriety and my undying love. The rose you sent every month you were away broke my heart--and won my heart.*

She placed the rose on Ira's grave and whispered, "I brought this for you, Ira. From one warrior to another." She stood there for a moment swallowing hard and quietly fighting back her tears, and then walked away.

The snow fell faster, covering her tracks and reminding her of a long-ago October tryst with Frank, who was on the opposite side of a razor-topped cyclone fence when the world was in danger of total death and destruction. Tears ran down her cheeks. She shivered in the cold and walked faster.

———

About the author

John Bingham in his favorite environment, a trout stream: this one is Montana's Bighorn, where he is about to release a nice rainbow trout.

A High Honors graduate of Michigan State University's School of Communications-- majoring in Advertising; member, Kappa Tau Alpha journalism honor society; and MSU Department of Advertising's Honorary Fellow for "outstanding contributions to advertising education"—Bingham's advertising has been recognized for its top readership and sales results during his career as marketing communications manager at Sperry Vickers,

John Bingham

followed by co-ownership and CEO of Brewer Associates, a Southeast Michigan marketing communications company known for its excellence in advertising, public relations, and marketing and marketing communications research. He was twice awarded "Advertising Man of The Year" honors and was inducted into the Tf Club's Advertising Hall of Fame in 1998.

During his 43 years in marketing, public relations, merchandising, event management, marketing and communications research, advertising, trade show marketing, and business presentation training for sales people and executives, he has written uncountable numbers of articles, advertisements, essays, advertising storyboards, white papers, press releases, presentations, newsletters, company newspapers, brochures, research reports, B2B motion picture scripts, and letters for clients, including such companies as Montgomery Ward, Dow Chemical, University of Michigan Business School, ExxonMobil Chemical, Velcro Automotive, Siemens Automotive, Sperry Vickers, and Michigan State University.

Probably his best writing was done at 4:30 a.m. every morning before going to work. It was "The Friday Follies," a two-page weekly satirical essay that focused almost exclusively on our invasion of Iraq and foretold much of its disastrous consequences. The Follies enjoyed readership across the continent. Some readers loved it and some hated it, but all gave feedback. In effect, it went viral before the word itself went viral.

Glossary

AAA Antiaircraft artillery.

ABCCC Airborne Battlefield Command and Control Center: EC-130 aircraft that flew over Laos 24 hours a day, call signs "Cricket" in northern Laos and "Hillsboro" in southern Laos, directing fighter-bombers from secret Thailand bases to the Ravens for their airstrikes. The ABCCC aircraft call signs were changed to "Alley Cat" and "Moonbeam" for night operations.

ACW 56th Air Commando Wing: a clandestine special-operations wing that flew missions out of Nakhon Phanom, a large, secret USAF base in Thailand.

ADF Automatic direction finder: a radio receiver that picks up a steady broadcast signal for pilot homing guidance.

A-7 Corsair II, United States Navy carrier-based fighter-bomber. The aircraft was later used by the USAF.

AK-47 A rugged and reliable Soviet automatic assault rifle that was the primary weapon of North Vietnamese and Pathet Lao communist forces. Captured AK-47s were also used by Hmong and Laotian troops.

AP Air Police

APC Armored Personnel Carrier M113A-1, an armored aluminum troop carrier used extensively throughout the Vietnam War. Typical armament was a pintle-mounted .50 caliber machine gun, often supplemented by the M-60 7.62mm machine gun or .30 caliber machine guns.

APO Acronym for Army and Air Force post office, providing overseas mail service at domestic postage prices.

John Bingham

Arty Troop slang for "artillery."

ARVN Army of the Republic of Vietnam (South Vietnam)

BDA Bomb Damage Assessment, where a Forward Air Controller (FAC) dives down after a fighter-bomber attack to assess damage done and report it to the fighter-bombers for their own mission de-briefings.

BUFF Acronym for the B-52 strategic bomber: "Big Ugly Flying Fucker."

BX USAF Base Exchange: a full-service store for Air Force personnel and their spouses that stocks foodstuffs, alcoholic beverages, and soft and hard goods, all sold at substantial discount prices vs. civilian stores.

B-40 A 40mm rocket-propelled grenade of early Soviet (WWII) design. The rocket is launched from a tube on the shoulder. It is inexpensive, simple and reliable, but limited in accuracy and range.

B-47 The nation's first all-jet, swept-wing strategic bomber that replaced the WWII-vintage B-29. The aircraft's high-altitude ceiling and speed also enabled its three-man crew to fly reconnaissance missions over Soviet territory.

CAR-15 This automatic assault rifle was used by forward air controllers, because it was shorter than its "big brother," the M-16, which was too long and unwieldy to be fired from the FAC's cockpit.

CBU Stands for "Cluster Bomb Unit," a bomb-shaped shell that spins open after release, spreading small bomblets across a wide target area. The bomblets can be timed for aerial detonation or ground/hard-surface target detonation.

Charlie A nickname to identify a communist Viet Cong guerrilla and short for "Victor Charlie." Also see under "VC."

Claymore A command-detonated, fan-shaped mine that stands on four legs and is used primarily as a defensive weapon against attacking enemy infantry. It fires 700 steel balls in a 60-degree arc with an optimum killing range of 50 meters. With a clear field of fire, the weapon's effective range can extend out to 250 meters.

CO Commanding Officer.

C-Rats Soldier's slang for canned wet rations, officially named Meal, Combat, Individual, typically carried in the field and heated by Sterno stove or shavings from C-4, which burn faster and hotter than Sterno. Each meal consisted of meat, crackers, a complementary spread, candy, a dessert, and cigarettes.

ETA Estimated Time of Arrival.

.50 Caliber Heavy machine gun, used by all branches of US military forces.

FEBA Forward Edge of Battle Area, designating the front lines of friendly forces.

F4 F-4 Phantom supersonic attack aircraft and fighter-bomber. A very versatile aircraft that carried heavy loads of ordnance for either air-to-air or air-to-ground missions, and used by the Navy, Air Force and the Marines.

FNG Acronym for "Fucking New Guy," or the nickname for anyone new to a given combat unit. He remained a FNG until he proved himself as a valuable member of his unit.

HC High-explosive projectiles fired by a battleship's 16" guns. Each shell weighs approximately 1.3 tons.

HE High-explosive artillery shells, bombs and demolition charges.

Huey Nickname for the versatile and rugged UH-1 Iroquois helicopter that is used by all branches of the military as troop and supply carriers. It can also be easily converted to a gunship.

Hun Pilots' nickname for the SuperSabre F-100 supersonic jet aircraft, a highly versatile aircraft that was used for "Fast FAC" reconnaissance missions and fighter-bomber missions for close-in support of ground troops.

IP Aircraft/vehicle instrument panel.

Lock and Load The command to ready one's weapon for live-fire practice or combat. A live round is fed into the breech and locked there in firing position by closing the breechblock. Troops maneuvering in combat zones are always "locked and loaded," keeping their weapon's safeties on to protect against accidental discharge.

LP A listening post to alert the main force that the enemy is coming. The post is manned by one or two troops who have dug a foxhole far out in front of the main force. Good camouflage, silence and radio transmission discipline are musts to avoid detection. Often the advancing enemy force is too close for the LP troops to use voice alerts. Instead, they send silent code signals by keying their radio.

M-16 Standard automatic assault rifle for U.S. infantry troops.

M-60 Lightweight and versatile U.S. machine gun that fires 7.62 NATO rounds. It is easily hand-carried and deploys quickly with a two-soldier crew, one to fire and the other to ensure steady linked-cartridge feed and spot targets. The weapon has also been pintle-mounted on military vehicles of all kinds, and wing-mounted in aircraft.

M-79 Shoulder-fired, single-shot 40mm grenade launcher with a grenade kill radius of five yards and a range up to 350 meters.

MOS Military Occupational Specialty alphanumerical identification system that covers every job in the U.S. military. Examples are the fighter pilot's MOS, 11FX, and the infantry's MOS, 11B.

MRE Meals, Ready-to-Eat that replaced C-rations as the soldier's meals in the field. They provide much tastier and more nutritious meals with less grease than their predecessors. A typical MRE package contains a meat entrée, side dish, dessert or candy snack, crackers or bread with spreads such as cheese, jelly or peanut butter, powdered drink mix with mixing bag, a plastic spoon, heater, and convenience items including napkin, towelette, seasonings, and gum.

NAPE Pilots' slang for napalm.

NKP Nhakom Phanom, a secret USAF base in Thailand.

NONCOM Non-commissioned officer.

NVA North Vietnamese Army, or **PNVA**, People's North Vietnamese Army

O-Club Officer's Club.

OCS Officer Candidate School (Army, Navy, Coast Guard). The USAF has Officer Training School.

OER Officer Efficiency Reports: evaluation of officer's performance of duties that become an important part of his or her record, determining eligibility for future promotions.

OIC Officer In Charge.

OJT On-The-Job Training, the last phase of military training that concentrates on duplicating real-world problems and conditions that students are likely to face, including live-fire tactical exercises.

OPS Short for military operations

PDJ Short for Plaine des Jarres in French, Plain of Jars in English. Hundreds of unexplained ancient, huge stone jars lie scattered over the plain's gently rolling hill country. Much of the terrain cannot be safely traveled because UXO (unexploded ordnance) has not yet been cleared. Several sites, however, have been cleared and are now safe for tourists.

Pickle Pilot slang to describe the release of their bombs and napalm canisters, e.g., "I pickled off my two bombs."

PX Post Exchange, the Army's equivalent of the Air Force's Base Exchange.

Recce/recon Pilot's abbreviations for "reconnaissance."

ROK Republic of Korea, pronounced as "rock."

RPG Rocket Propelled Grenade, a shoulder-launched missile with more accuracy, range and a wider kill radius than the B-40.

SAC Acronym for Strategic Air Command.

Sapper Combat engineer soldiers trained in the use of explosives who often attack with infantry to blow up key enemy positions, facilities, heavy weapons, troop concentrations, aircraft, ammunition dumps, and other targets of opportunity.

Snake Eaters Nickname for Army Special Forces troops.

Spooks Nickname for CIA operatives. **"Spooky"** is also the nickname for the C/AC-47 aircraft that carried three rapid-fire miniguns, and was often used for nighttime troop ground support missions.

Strafe Name for low-level aircraft passes at the enemy, firing automatic weapons such as .50 caliber machine guns, mini-guns, and 20mm cannons. The ammunition for these weapons is also called "strafe."

TAC Acronym for "Tactical Air Command." Defines the missions and tactics of short-range fighter and fighter-bombers in support of grand strategy to destroy the enemy's ability and/or will to fight.

TDY Acronym stands for "Temporary Duty," typically training, special combat support missions, or non-combat assignments away from one's home base.

TET Anglicized, the acronym for the Vietnamese Lunar New Year and forever remembered by American veterans as January 31, 1968, the day that the Viet Cong and North Vietnamese Army simultaneously attacked 126 cities in South Vietnam, including 36 of 44 provincial capitals. The battles to retake these cities and fight the enemy in the countryside lasted over a month, with horrendous casualties suffered on both sides. Accurate numbers of casualties (killed and wounded) are difficult to find even now; estimates from sources such as Wikipedia, *NY Times, US News and World Report* and numerous historians differ. The *Times* estimates cover the full month of February 1968, with 58,000 enemy dead and nearly 4,000 Americans KIA. Numbers aside, the enemy won a strategic battle by serving notice on the allies that a long and bloody war still lay in front of them, a war for which the American public was rapidly losing its stomach.

VC Short for Viet Cong, the guerrilla arm of the communist forces fighting in Vietnam. Slang usage by American troops included "Victor Charlie," sometimes shortened to just "Charlie" or "Sir Charles," the latter a backhanded compliment to the VC's formidable hit-and-run tactics. It also served as a reminder to the American forces to never take the VC for granted.

Made in the USA
Charleston, SC
18 February 2016